TWENTIETH CENTURY VIEWS

The aim of this series is to present the best in contemporary critical opinion on major authors, providing a twentieth century perspective on their changing status in an era of profound revaluation.

Maynard Mack, *Series Editor*
Yale University

GENET

GENET

286

A COLLECTION OF CRITICAL ESSAYS

Edited by:

Peter Brooks and Joseph Halpern

Prentice-Hall, Inc.   *Englewood Cliffs, N.J.*

A SPECTRUM BOOK

Library of Congress Cataloging in Publication Data

Main entry under title:

Genet, a collection of critical essays.

 (Twentieth century views) (A Spectrum Book)
 Bibliography: p.
  1. Genet, Jean, 1910- —Criticism and interpre-
tation—Addresses, essays, lectures. I. Brooks, Peter.
II. Halpern, Joseph.
PQ2613.E53Z68 848'.9'1209 79-14081
ISBN 0-13-351148-0
ISBN 0-13-351130-8 pbk.

848.909

G 286

Editorial/production supervision by Betty Neville
Cover design by Stanley Wyatt
Manufacturing buyer: Cathie Lenard

PO.10 - 773

Library
Highland Comm. College
Highland, KS 66035

© 1979 by Prentice-Hall, Inc., Englewood Cliffs, New Jersey. A SPECTRUM BOOK. All rights reserved. No part of this book may be reproduced in any form or by any means without permission in writing from the publisher. Printed in the United States of America.

10 9 8 7 6 5 4 3 2 1

PRENTICE-HALL INTERNATIONAL, INC. *(London)*
PRENTICE-HALL OF AUSTRALIA PTY. LIMITED *(Sydney)*
PRENTICE-HALL OF CANADA, LTD. *(Toronto)*
PRENTICE-HALL OF INDIA PRIVATE LIMITED *(New Delhi)*
PRENTICE-HALL OF JAPAN, INC. *(Tokyo)*
PRENTICE-HALL OF SOUTHEAST ASIA PTE. LTD. *(Singapore)*
WHITEHALL BOOKS LIMITED *(Wellington, New Zealand)*

Contents

Acknowledgments   ix

Introduction
by Peter Brooks and Joseph Halpern   1

On the Fine Arts Considered as Murder
by Jean-Paul Sartre   7

Genet: The Refusal to Communicate
by Georges Bataille   24

The Theater of Genet: A Sociological Study
by Lucien Goldmann   31

Jean Genet, or, The Inclement Thief
by Françoise d'Eaubonne   47

Our Lady of the Flowers
by Brigid Brophy   68

Traps and Allegories: *Miracle of the Rose*
by Richard N. Coe   76

The Thief's Journal
by Philip Thody   86

The Glory of Annihilation: Jean Genet
by Jacques Guicharnaud (in collaboration with June Guicharnaud)   98

Genet: The Struggle with Theater
by Bernard Dort   114

Jean Genet: The Theater of Hate
by Raymond Federman   129

Genet, His Actors and Directors
by Odette Aslan   146

Scenic Space and Dramatic Illusion
in *The Balcony*
　　by Michèle Piemme   156

Profane and Sacred Reality in Jean Genet's Theatre
　　by Jean Gitenet   172

I Allow Myself to Revolt: Interview with Jean Genet
　　by Hubert Fichte   178

Chronology of Important Dates   *191*
Notes on the Editor and Contributors   *193*
Selected Bibliography   *195*

Acknowledgments

Quotations from *Saint Genet: Actor and Martyr* by Jean-Paul Sartre, translated by Bernard Frechtman, are reprinted with the permission of the publisher, George Braziller, Inc. Copyright © 1963 by George Braziller, Inc.

Quotations from *The Imagination of Jean Genet* by Joseph McMahon are used by kind permission of Yale University Press.

Quotations from "Comment jouer les Bonnes" and "Comment jouer le Balcon" from *Oeuvres Completes,* vol. IV, by Jean Genet are used by kind permission of Editions Gallimard. © Editions Gallimard 1968.

Quotations from *La Folie en tête* by Violette Leduc are used by kind permission of Editions Gallimard, Granada Publishing Ltd., and Farrar Straus & Giroux, Inc. © Editions Gallimard 1970.

Quotations from the following works by Jean Genet are used by kind permission of Grove Press, Inc. and Rosica Colin Limited:

Deathwatch. © 1954, 1961 by Bernard Frechtman.

The Maids. © 1954, 1961 by Bernard Frechtman.

The Balcony. © 1958, 1960 by Bernard Frechtman. Revised version. © 1966 by Bernard Frechtman and Jean Genet.

The Blacks. © 1960 by Bernard Frechtman.

The Thief's Journal. © 1954, 1964 by Bernard Frechtman.

Letters to R. Blin. © 1969 by Grove Press, Inc.

The Screens. © 1962 by Bernard Frechtman.

Funeral Rites. © 1969 by Grove Press, Inc.

Querelle. © 1974 by Grove Press, Inc.

Our Lady of the Flowers. © 1963 by Bernard Frechtman.

Miracle of the Rose. © 1965 by Bernard Frechtman.

The excerpt from *Genet: The Struggle with Theatre* by Bernard Dort originally appeared in *Playboy Magazine.* It is used by kind permission of Rosica Colin Limited. Copyright © 1964 by *Playboy.*

GENET

Introduction

by Peter Brooks and Joseph Halpern

For more than thirty years, the name of Jean Genet has been synonymous with scandal. The reaction to his writing and to his life has always been vehemently polemical. His earliest works, written in prison, were his most autobiographical and shockingly pornographic, and if Cocteau presented him to the world in these first moments of his career as "the greatest poet of our time," Sartre refused to allow us to forget who Genet was: abandoned child, beggar, rag-picker, deserter, homosexual, pornographer, male prostitute, thief and convict, society's cast-off, society's nemesis. According to Sartre, Genet was not one to be recuperated by society, neither by critical appreciation nor bourgeois acceptance, and in his works form could not be separated from content, aesthetic achievement from ideology, vocabulary and metaphorical flourish from moral statement: "Do not take refuge in aestheticism; he will drive you from under cover. I know people who can read the coarsest passages without turning a hair: 'These two gentlemen sleep together? And then they eat their excrement? And after that, one goes off to denounce the other? As if that mattered! It's *so* well written.'...So long as you play at amoralism you will remain at the threshold of the work" *(Saint Genet)*.

Sartre taught us to understand Genet's works as acts of revenge on a world that had rejected him. But what happens to Genet in a world he no longer shocks? Genet's explicit descriptions of homosexual activity, his celebration of the criminal and the traitor, are no longer unique in contemporary literature; his plays will probably never again cause riots. He himself has turned outward from a narrow obsessional universe to broader political commitments: over the last decade, he has become a champion of the militant Third World. But as sources of scandal, his novels and plays seem outdated, either because Genet's "verbal victory" is complete, and he has indeed participated in changing the world, or because an essentially unchanged world has simply assimilated him.

In an early book on Genet, one American critic predicted that Genet's works "will be appreciated and enjoyed to the extent that they do not accomplish what Genet wants them to accomplish. Genet's instinctive imagination—the apparatus which forms the terms of his vision of reality—will be rejected, and with it will be rejected his most cherished ideas. But his presentational imagination—the force which allows him to organize the insights of his instinctive imagination and to impose them aesthetically—may very well give his works endurance; it already gives them power as it gives the theatre refreshed vitality" (Joseph MacMahon, *The Imagination of Jean Genet*). Whether one aspect of Genet's writing can be isolated from another, in spite of Sartre; whether Genet's ideas have been or will be rejected (by whom? by what authority?); whether he speaks primarily as a member of an oppressed class or as a poet and universal ritualist are still open questions. But what the critic captures, in the terms he uses to evaluate Genet's work, is the impression left with everyone who has seen or read Genet: power, force, vision, energy, intensity, vitality, passion. Genet's subject is power and his works are incarnations of that power. He defines poetry as a force. His world exists as a theological universe turned upside down, in which hierarchy and the flow of power and energy are reversed. His writings perform apparent acts of adoration and submission, incantation, liturgical dramas that reveal only on a more fundamental level the demiurgic force that shaped them.

In the very first novels that Genet wrote the measure of that power was already evident. There are aspects of Genet's technical accomplishment in the novel—the autonomy conferred on time and space, the framing of illusion within illusion, the breakdown of plot and the contempt for the concept of character, the insistence on the status of the text as fiction—that make of him an intuitive precursor of contemporary experimentation in the form. The impact of his first novels, however, came not only from this kind of originality and from their subject matter but also from a debt to the past. Genet's debt to Proust is unmistakable: a good part of his language, theme and narrative sense seems only to extend aspects of Proust along a single, narrow line—at whose origin stands Proust's character, Baron Charlus. But a surrealist background, too, plays a part in the make-up of Genet's novels. Genet's flexibility in narrative technique, the dismantling of structures and the refusal to let things freeze, the use of metaphor as a violent yoking, the generalized explosive shock of his work, if not a heritage from the Surrealists, at least fell on terrain prepared by them, in a milieu open to the force of his writing. Still, Sartre claims that the explosive surrealist influence was only a foreign element grafted onto Genet's deeper need for strict form. The looseness of the early novels works both for and against Genet; despite the desperate strength of his fiction, Genet does not prove himself to be basically a storyteller, and it can be claimed that he never manages to create a narrative form strong enough to hold the reader. As Georges Bataille says, *"ses récits intéressent mais ne passionnent pas."*

One can nonetheless speak metaphorically of two primary, inseparable sources of form present in all of Genet's work: sexuality and language. In the existentialist interpretation of Genet's life, it is language, the act of naming perceived as an act of violence, that turns Genet into a homosexual and a thief. For Genet as a young man, language seems to have miraculous powers; certain sacred words transform the world and invest him with their power. Through affinities of sound and rhythm without logical signification, he can reify feelings and capture the world. Genet's linguistic imagination extends onto social reality primarily through a sexual construct. We have been told that the episodic nature of his first novels reflects their masturbatory nature, but, beyond that, sexuality organizes the hierarchy of being and sequence of images in his world; it gives structure to his vision of reality. The power relationships so dominant in his work are actualizations of sexual and linguistic potential; out of those fluid energies emerges a patterned world of oppressions and violent acts in ritualized literary forms. Out of the picaresque chaos of *The Thief's Journal* emerges the classic theatre of *The Maids*.

"Try," Genet wrote to Roger Blin when Blin was directing *The Screens,* "try to lead [the actors] toward a more hieratical theatre." Everything in Genet's often weird theatrical practice relates to this central concern with a hieratical theatre: theatre as the place of ritual and sacred mystery. "If we maintain that life and the stage are opposites," he writes again to Blin, "it is because we strongly suspect that the stage is a site closely akin to death, a place where all liberties are possible." This suggests why all the details of Genet's theatrical art are conceived to irrealize, to create a magical world of costume and artifice where characters, often masked, mounted on high platform shoes, ceremoniously enact the relationships and dramas of life, all the while insisting that they are actors, and that the rituals in which they are engaged belong to a special space of play unaccommodated to the demands of the reality principle. Genet is in this manner the inheritor of Pirandello, a playwright ever attuned to the special nature of the theatre as play, as gratuitous performance: as, by its very nature, "celebration of nothing." Yet the celebration is far from innocent or anodine. Genet also displays affinities with Antonin Artaud's view of the theatre as an assault upon the audience. Rather than seeking the illusionistic realism of traditional middle-class theatre, and without escaping into fantasy, Genet stages dramas of unnerving social and psychological implication by seizing the central issues of life on the borderline of death or. sleep, at the moment where our most thoroughly repressed wishes and fears glimmer into consciousness.

So it is that each detail of action, gesture, costume, and language must for Genet be essentially artificial. He urges Blin to avoid having the actors make any natural noises in their stage movements, he complains that the striking of a match onstage will always appear a real rather than an imitated action; he even seeks to denaturalize actors' voices; and of course he gives to his characters language of a rich and decadent sumptuousness which breaks with any representative function. As Susan Sontag has written, Genet's language is always "in drag": dressed up, travestied, artificialized. It is thus that the characters can imagine, shape, and express the essence of the being of their roles, rather than their mere function. In *The Blacks,* for instance, the characters are first of all concerned with what it means to play at being blacks—or to play at blacks playing at being whites. In *The Balcony,* Madame Irma exhorts Carmen to "exalt" her role as whore, to work on it so that it may "illumine" her being.

It may be worth dwelling for a moment on *The Balcony,* possibly Genet's most perfectly successful achievement, and the play that makes clearest the central tendencies of his theatre. The bordello in which the play takes place is referred to as a "House of Illusions," and each client who comes there is playing out an erotic fantasy which engages the whole of his being. For each of the "scenarios" that unfolds in the multiple specialized rooms—stage sets—of the bordello, there must, as Irma explains to Carmen, be an authentic detail and a false detail: a seeming paradox which enables the clients both to enter into their fantasies and to conceive their realization as essentially theatrical, a moment of self-conscious play and artifice. One "false" detail is maintained throughout the play: the elaborate chandelier that hangs above the stage, as if to remind us that we cannot leave the role of spectatorship. The very name of the bordello, "The Grand Balcony," suggests spectatorship and voyeurism, and insists that the imitation of life going forward on the stage is an imitation of life as theatre, life as the place of enactment of roles, behind which there is no stable "reality." Not only are Irma and Carmen stage managers and spectators of their clients' enactments of censored desires, the clients themselves are witnesses to their own stageplay. Everyone is double, reflected in the bordello's ubiquitous mirrors. As Genet states, it is a play of "Image and Reflection."

When revolution breaks out in the streets of the town beyond the bordello's walls—offstage—it threatens to disrupt the paradise of illusion. There is the risk, for instance, that Chantal, one of the prostitutes, will become "virginized" by her revolutionary ardor (a romantic revolutionary cliché) and that the victory of the revolutionaries will bring a puritanical regime that allows no place to the House of Illusion. But all will return to the theatrical order: Chantal dies from a stray bullet, and Roger, the revolutionary leader, enters the bordello with the request to play the role of his archenemy, the Chief of Police. The self chooses to enact the Other, revealing the profound instability—and essential theatricality—of the notion of self. Political action as dis-illusion, the path to firm self-definition, has met defeat—or so we may want to interpret Roger's act of self-castration at the end. At the same time, the Chief of Police by Roger's choice to play him as a role himself becomes a Personage: a mythic figure whose being, like that of the Bishop, the Judge, and the General, will be replayed again and again in the House of Illusion. Everything in the world exists to become theatre, and when Irma at the end, extinguishing the lights of the stage, bids the audience to exit and return home, she assures them that back in "reality" everything will appear still more false than it has here, in the House of Illusion, onstage.

Genet has understood an authentic mission of the theatre: to induce a suspicion of the real through theatrical acting out, to blur the sharp boundaries that we like to maintain between fantasy and reality, art and life, sleeping and waking. As the Envoy suggests, in Scene 9 of *The Balcony*, "This is a true image, born of a false spectacle." All Genet's plays (and most of all *The Balcony*) are filled with a kind of theatrical metaphysics, reflections of what it means to play a role, to act a personage, to "be" someone. Through theatricality, we reach an unsettling reversal of perspectives, and a challenging reflection on the stuff of our social relations. Whether it be imprisonment *(Deathwatch)*, servitude *(The Maids)*, blackness *(The Blacks)*, colonial exploitation *(The Screens)*, each of Genet's plays explores an existential condition through a full dramatization of the roles which its victims—be they slaves or masters—are forced to play out. In each instance, the stage contains both actors and spectators— those watching from "the balcony"—and there is always a moment of reversal, where such an opposition is called into question, and where the larger body of spectators—the audience in the theatre— must ask about its own role. If Genet's plays through their artificiality and ritualism refuse the status of direct social realism and *théâtre engagé*, they do not fall into frivolous fantasy. Through their thorough and vertiginous exploration of the experience of theatricality itself, Genet's plays make central probes into man's condition.

For all that has been written about Genet the man, he remains a figure of mystery: his truth—including the facts of his biography— seems inextricably interwoven with his fictionalized self-images. He clearly wishes to remain protean, ungraspable. And it is difficult to know what surprises he may yet produce as an artist— if any. His recent creative activity seems to have principally taken the form of political articles and the production of a film. It has been more than a decade since his last major work—*The Screens*—and it may be that his *opus* is substantially complete, ready for overall critical estimate. But it will be a long time before we arrive at a cool, "objective" verdict on Genet. He continues to be an unsettling force in culture, difficult to assimilate and to make peace with.

On the Fine Arts Considered as Murder

by Jean-Paul Sartre

Allow a poet who is also an enemy to speak to you as a poet
and as an enemy.   —THE CHILD CRIMINAL

It is within the framework of Evil that Genet makes his major
decision. Moreover, he has not at all given up stealing: why should
he? It is hard to imagine him renouncing burglary for belles-lettres
the way a repentant embezzler gives up swindling and opens a shop.
"The idea of a literary career would make me shrug." When he
writes these words, he has already had two plays performed and has
published a volume of poems and four of his great books; he is com-
pleting the fifth and is preparing a film scenario; in short, it is the
moment when people are beginning to talk about his work. All the
more reason for affirming his loathing of the idea of having a literary career. Each of his works, like each of his thefts, is an isolated
offense which may be followed by other offenses but which does
not require them and which is self-sufficient. In each of them he bids
farewell to literature: "If I finish this book, I finish with what can be
related," he says in *Miracle of the Rose*. "The rest is beyond words.
I must say no more. I say no more and walk barefoot." And in *Funeral Rites:* "If I submit to the gestures [of thieves], to their precision
of language, I shall write nothing more. I shall lose the grace that
enabled me to report news of heaven. I must choose or alternate. Or
be silent." And in *The Thief's Journal:* "This book is the last...for

"On the Fine Arts Considered as Murder." From Jean-Paul Sartre, *Saint Genet:
Actor and Martyr,* translated by Bernard Frechtman (New York: George Braziller,
Inc., 1963). Reprinted with the permission of the publisher. Copyright © 1963 by
George Braziller, Inc.

five years I have been writing books. I can say that I have done so
with pleasure, but I have finished." This mania for taking leave may
make us smile: one would think he were Mayol bidding farewell to
the stage. But it is true that Genet's creative act is a summing-up. *All*
the basic themes of his thought and life are to be found in each of
his works; one recognizes the same motifs from book to book: would
anyone dream of reproaching him for this? If so, one would have to
condemn Dostoievsky for having written the same novel over and
over and Kafka for having written the same story a hundred times.
Nothing is more foreign to Genet than the prudence of men of
letters who are careful to reveal themselves gradually — a little bit of
oneself in each work — so as to remain new for a longer time.

And, in another respect, he is even further removed from Zola
and the famous *nulla dies sine linea*. He would find it intolerable
to force himself, day after day, to work away patiently, like a crafts-
man: literature would become an honest trade, a livelihood. When,
after long months of idleness, he is seized by a desire to write a
book, he sets to work immediately and keeps going day and night
until the job is done. Or rather he considers it to be done when the
desire ceases. Often he slackens before the end and quickly knocks
off the last few pages. In *Our Lady of the Flowers,* he suddenly declares that "Divine is beginning to bore him"; in *Querelle of Brest,*
he writes: "A sudden weariness made us drop *Querelle,* which was
already beginning to peter out." He scamps the conclusion of *The
Thief's Journal.* He has no particular desire to produce a "well-
made work"; he is unconcerned with *finish,* with formal perfection:
for him, beauty lies elsewhere, in the ceremonious splendor of
sacrilege and murder. When the criminal impulse is satisfied, he
lets go, finishes off as quickly as possible, shuts up shop and returns
to everyday life. The creative tension, like the orgasm, is followed
by a period of relaxation and dejection in which the very thought
of writing is repulsive to him. And it is not the least strange or least
charming . feature of these severe and classical structures, these
ceremonious and complicated works of architecture, that suddenly
they soften, "peter out" and come to a stop, as if the artist, who is so
contemptuous, so haughty, were finally turning his contempt upon
himself, as if the "wily hoodlum" were saying to the poet: "I'm sick
and tired of your nonsense."

But what chiefly repels Genet in the man of letters is that he remains, regardless of what he does, on the right side of the barricade.

The literary man is, to be sure, a liar: literature is a tissue of lies and hoaxes, it hides everything, it hushes up scandals, and if a writer does speak out, his work is expurgated or burned; but that is precisely why the window dressing of the man of letters gets an official stamp; he is honest, he does not misrepresent his merchandise: he writes to meet the demand and sells his products at the official price; often he specializes and builds up a clientele which he does his best to please. Genet does not deign to be a shopkeeper, particularly an honest shopkeeper: he is unconcerned about the demand, he offers nothing; above all, he does not want to please his readers. He wants to make money from his writings, but on condition that the money be obtained by fraud: the purchaser will derive no advantage from his acquisition, it is unusable; Genet lies no more than does an academician, but he lies otherwise and his lies are not edifying. The fact is that if he prefers the work of art to theft, it is because theft is a criminal act which is derealized into a dream, whereas a work of art is a dream of murder which is realized by an act.

"I remained forever haunted by the idea of a murder that would detach me from your world irremediably." What tempts him in crime is not blood, and even less the suffering and cries of the victim or the soft sound of the knife entering the flesh, but rather the glory it procures. In this "irremediable detachment" we recognize "the infamous glory" of the condemned man. As we have seen, a "beautiful" murder breaks through the police barrier, installs itself in the consciousness of honest folk, violates it, fills it with horror and giddiness; the great criminals are more famous than honorable writers who are their contemporaries; there are people who remember the name of Landru but who never knew or have forgotten that of M. René Doumic. No doubt, Genet knows perfectly well that he will not kill anyone. But since murderers achieve glory by forcing good citizens to dream about Crime, why should he not enjoy similar glory by forcing them to dream about it without becoming a criminal? The criminal kills; he *is* a poem; the poet *writes* the crime; he constructs a wild object that infects all minds with criminality; since it is the specter of the murder, even more than the murder itself, that horrifies people and unlooses base instincts, Genet will call forth this specter within society. Crime is the major theme of his works;* all the other motifs twine round this black

---

*Except *The Thief's Journal,* which closes a period of his agitated life and which is more a commentary by the poet on his writings than a poem.

marble, like the queens round the pimps. Genet's work resembles the symbolic sacrifices that replace human sacrifice in religions which become humanized. Everything is present: the officiant, a corpse in effigy, everything but the blood. A fake murderer who has really been sentenced to death haughtily confesses, from the top of the scaffold, to his crime. All of Genet's books ought to be called *"Exécution capitale"*—in every sense of the term.†

The fact that society considers these imaginary confessions to be felonious is sufficient proof that they are mitigated crimes. The poem of the evil action is itself an evil action. Moreover, it is fitting that the fate of the work reflect that of its author. The book, which is a corpus delicti, must be hounded, forbidden, like Genet himself; our author writes so that they will prevent him from writing; if they do not succeed, so that they will prevent him from publishing; if they fail again, so that they seize his writing and try to suppress it. Unlike our "great minds" who proclaim the non-responsibility of the writer, he means to pay for his work, and the greatest tribute one could pay him would be to imprison him for inciting to murder. It would thus be manifest to everyone that his literary creation is indeed an act and that it undermines the foundations of our society. The wild object, which is an apology for evil, a felonious work of a delinquent, must exercise, by a return shock, a magical action on Genet's life and provide him with the blackest of destinies. Creation will then really be a *Passion:* a passion because the author suffers, in the realm of the imaginary, with the sufferings of his heroes and because his characters' crimes will entail further persecutions in real life. He writes proudly: "If I am worthy of it, [my book] will reserve for me the infamous glory of which it is the grand master, for to what can I refer if not to it?...Is it not logical that this book draw my body along and lure me to prison?"

Before writing, what is he? An insignificant little worm, a bug that scurries, unnoticed, between the slats of the floor. He has a feeling that he is horrifying all of Society, but he also knows that this horror is purely virtual and that, moreover, it relates to the thief *in general,* to *any* delinquent and not to Jean Genet. Society condemns theft: but it does so without thinking about it, by means of a specialized organ whose function is precisely to substitute systematic and general repression for diffuse repression, in short *to hush up scandal.*

† The term *exécution capitale* means "capital punishment." But the author is suggesting that it can mean "major work" as well.—Translator's note.

The culprit's crimes *never* come to the knowledge of the just man; the just man *never* thinks about the culprit; as a citizen of a democracy, he alone is qualified to punish, and the judiciary power emanates from him, as do all powers: but he has delegated his functions to the police, magistrates and prison guards and no longer thinks about the matter. The contempt which these civil servants display for Genet in the name of the just man is not true contempt: it is impersonal, professional, like the smile of a salesclerk; they are paid to display it. As an anonymous object of an impersonal and, in general, virtual loathing, Genet is, in point of fact, ignored, forgotten: he squirms about in a shaft of light, blinded by the gaze that Society has been fixing upon him since his childhood; this gaze penetrates him to the soul and sears all his thoughts; he is public, never alone with himself. But *at the same time* he knows that *nobody* is looking at him, that nobody, except a few cops, is aware of his existence. He would like to cry out to them: "Look at me, I'm a criminal, it's you who have condemned me." No one hears him, people come and go, he calls out to them. Wasted effort. He will end by believing that he is invisible. If he has been dreaming since childhood of horrifying them *for good,* it is in order to be able to feel that he exists for someone and to transform these phantom witnesses into a real audience. He wants the dead gaze which enveloped him to sparkle, and, since the relationship which constitutes him in his very core is a relationship to all, he wants to actualize his dimension-for-the-Others. Whoever sees him despises him, but nobody sees him: how restful it must be to be seen: "The newspaper photo shows Nadine and her husband leaving the church where the priest has just married them. She is stepping across the swastika. The people of Charleville are looking at her hostilely. 'Give me your arm and close your eyes,' her husband must have murmured to her. She walks smilingly toward the French flags which are bedecked with crepe. I envy this young woman's bitter and haughty happiness." Genet steals so that people will think about him, so that he, too, can become a taboo object: *an object of loathing.* Loathing is closer to love than indifference. The perfidious solicitude that an examining magistrate shows for him in order to trip him up is, as we know, enough to make him confess to his crime: "a trifle would suffice" for that solicitude to become tenderness. When he was a child, other children spat in his face: "Yet, a trifle would have sufficed for that ghastly game to be transformed

into a courtly game and for me to be covered with roses instead of
spit. For as the gestures were the same, it would not have been hard
for destiny to change everything: the game is being organized...the
youngsters make the gesture of tossing...it would cost no more for
it to be happiness...I awaited the roses. I prayed God to alter his
intention ever so little, to make a wrong movement so that the
children, ceasing to hate me, would love me. ...I was then invested
with a higher gravity. I was no longer the adulterous woman being
stoned. I was an object in the service of an amorous rite." When love
is absent, blame and sanction are sacralizing rites. No sooner has
Querelle killed than he belongs to all; he thus becomes a sacred
object. What Genet wants is to become an accessory of the cult, a
ritual object. But the more he steals, the less they are concerned with
him. And furthermore, although he feels, in the scene related
above, that he is being metamorphosed into an object, he has no
perspective that would enable him to enjoy his objectivity: the latter
is only a flight of all his being into the fathomless freedom of his
tormentors. A later experience suggests another ruse to him: instead
of becoming an object for the others, why not identify himself with a
particular, material object that would be the butt of their hatred?
He would then be able to see himself: he would see *the object that
he is,* shining with their gobs of spit, shimmering in the light of
their gazes. That is what happened once in Barcelona: the police
arrest him; before jailing him, they search him and confiscate a
tube of vaseline that he used when making love. The ignominious
accessory is taken from him and put on a table; it becomes Genet
himself: firstly because it is his property, and secondly because it
reveals and symbolizes his homosexuality. "I was in a cell. I knew
that all night long my tube of vaseline would be exposed to the
scorn—the contrary of a Perpetual Adoration—of a group of strong,
handsome, husky policemen. So strong that if the weakest of them
barely squeezed two fingers together, there would shoot forth, first
with a slight fart, brief and dirty, a ribbon of gum which would continue to emerge in a ridiculous silence. Nevertheless, I was sure that
this puny and most humble object would hold its own against them;
by its mere presence it would be able to exasperate all the police in
the world; it would draw upon itself contempt, hatred, white and
dumb rages. It would be slightly bantering—like a tragic hero
amused at stirring up the wrath of the gods—indestructible, like
him, faithful to my happiness, and proud." The tube of vaseline,

which is an effigy of Genet, flouts the cops *by its inertia*. Genet "in person" would be less able to resist them: he is sensitive, he can suffer. The inertia of the matter represents an invincible haughtiness, and yet this matter is haunted by a soul. Sheltered from blows and insults, Genet can peacefully dream in his cell about that obstinate little brute which he has delegated to receive them, in short he can take pleasure in himself.* Although he remained passive during the operation, it was purely by chance that the policemen found the tube in his pocket.

But what if he gave himself, *by an act,* the power of existing elsewhere, in all his virulence, for horrified minds? What if he conferred ubiquity upon himself with his own hands? What if he deliberately invented a way of embodying himself in strange substances and forced the others to discover him there? Then the contempt of "all the police in the world" would no longer be undergone but demanded, and the bantering pride of the inanimate object would rightly express Genet's irony. Hidden behind a wall, this crafty hoodlum could enjoy at will the astonishment of decent people. He would *see* them *seeing* his image, and they would become objects for him precisely insofar as his reflection was an object for them. We have just defined the work of art according to Genet: it is an object of horror, or rather *it is Genet himself engendering himself by a criminal act as an object of universal horror and turning this horror into his glory because he has created himself in order to provoke it.* In *Our Lady of the Flowers* he says of a poem: "I have shat it out." Such is his aesthetic purpose: to shit *himself* so as to appear as excrement on the table of the just. "Without disappointing the enthusiasm of the peasants" Sarah Bernhardt could have appeared in the shape of a little box of matches. Box of matches, tube of

*The sticky tube of vaseline reminds Genet of a beggar woman over whom he had wanted to "slobber." It is apparent that we are dealing here with a "constellation" of images: the child who was dripping with spit compared himself to a penis wet with sperm; and the tube which he uses to smear his penis with vaseline makes him think of a face sticky with slaver. Finally he dreams of smearing the entire body of his lovers with vaseline, and "their muscles bathe in that delicate transparence." We turn to a new theme: that of the transparent veil, of the gauze that puts objects into a kind of aesthetic perspective. One can see the gradual transition from one term to the other. Spit, sperm, vaseline: vitreous transparency which protects bodies and makes them shimmer. The basic image is sperm. Furthermore: the insult appears as a protection of pride. Lastly, tulle: "voracious" beauty derealizes, inserts itself between the gaze and things, like a transparent veil.

vaseline, poem, they are all one. There are wild objects which embody persons. When one produces one of these objects, one is an artist, and when this object arouses horror, one is a criminal to boot. Haunted by the problem of the Other, which is *his* problem, Genet has spent his life meditating on the phenomenon of embodiment. He had to *make himself become* the Other that he already was for the Others. He had tried everything, he had attempted to make himself be reflected by a mirror, by the eyes of a lover, by those of the beloved, to have himself be possessed by the Other, by himself as Other: each undertaking ended in failure. Recourse to art is his final attempt: thus far he has been unable to be his own cause except in imagination, since it was the Others who had first, and spontaneously, affected him with this otherness. He now *realizes* this imagination in an object-trap which forces the Others to see him as he wants to be seen. He will be his own creature since his book is himself creating himself as Another and making the Others breathe life into his creation. They made a thief of him; he now turns their formidable objectifying power against them and forces them to make him a fish, a flower, a shepherd, whatever he wishes. At last he sees himself, he touches himself: this big banned book that is harried by the police* is he; if you open it, you are suddenly surrounded by characters, who are also he. He is everywhere, he is everything, men and things, society and nature, the living and the dead. Imagine his joy: he lives alone, secretly; he hides from the police; he signs hotel registers with a false name; he effaces his footprints, all traces of his presence; he barely exists: yet he is everywhere; he occupies all minds, he is an object of veritable horror. About his books one could say, without changing a word, what he said about his tube of vaseline: "I was sure that this puny and most humble object would hold its own against them; by its mere presence it would be able to exasperate all the police in the world; it would draw upon itself contempt, hatred, white and dumb rages. It would be slightly bantering...indestructible...faithful to my happiness and ...exposed to scorn—the contrary of a Perpetual Adoration."

Will he succeed? Will his clandestine works be able to shock, whereas his thefts, which were more serious offenses, and more severely punished, went unnoticed?

---

*All of Genet's books (that is, his nondramatic works) were at first privately printed in limited deluxe editions and sold by subscription. It was not until several years later that they were issued in trade editions.—Translator's note.

Yes, because Society puts up more easily with an evil action than with an evil word. For specialists, magistrates, criminologists, sociologists, there are no *evil* acts: there are only punishable acts. For the man in the street, there *are* evil acts, but it is always the Others who commit them. Genet wants to reveal to the former that Evil exists and to the latter that its roots are to be found in themselves.

Genet, who has been a victim and instrument of the good citizen since childhood, is now able to avenge himself at last: he is going to apply to him the *lex talionis*. He will make that innocent discover the Other in himself; he will make him recognize the Other's most improper thoughts as his own; in short, he will make him experience with loathing his own wickedness. Poetic traps will captivate his freedom and will reflect it to him as being half his own and half alien. He will be forced to see himself and will be able neither to *recognize* himself nor reject himself. It is with words that Genet will lay his traps. Words are the matter and weight of the soul; if they assemble within it to form evil thoughts, the soul is lost. It served as a refuge against threats and suffering: what will be its refuge against itself? The trap is a book, an object as stubborn and inert as a tube of vaseline: black strokes on sheets of paper sewn together. Nothing more. And the object will remain that dead thing which is waiting for nothing, which fears nothing, which continues to grow until its owner himself decides to attend to it, to link up the signs, to project their meanings through the words, to organize the meanings among themselves. No sooner is it opened than an idea emerges, or a feeling, or a vague figure, and the reader knows that these furtive beings were already there in some way, but he also knows that they would not have appeared in that place and on that day without the complicity of his mind. He had only *not* to read, and moreover he can always stop. If he settles down and tries to understand, he constructs a complicated object which exists only through him and which will be dispersed in a multitude of black pothooks as soon as he diverts his attention from it: it is he who draws these phantasms from nothingness and maintains them in being; to read is to perform an act of directed invention. No doubt he does not adhere completely to what he reads; no doubt he waits until he has understood before giving or refusing his assent. But he has already circumvented himself: to understand is to accept; if later he wants to reject this foreign sensibility, he will have to take himself in hand, will have to make a sharp break, will have to tear himself away from the increasing giddiness.

His freedom, which keeps the phrase suspended in its light, seeks thoughts everywhere, seeks memories which will facilitate an understanding of the text. If he reads that "beauty is Evil," the sentence has no meaning for him at first: if he wants to understand it, to breathe life into it, to adapt it for his personal use, he must recall the most beautiful faces, most beautiful paintings, that he has seen, those which he has been particularly fond of. No doubt he evokes them only as examples, but that is sufficient: he sees the Other's voracious thinking with his own most inward being, with his beautiful regrets, with his beautiful cares. The words are already hemming him in, giving him, despite himself, a past, a future which he does not recognize: if he wants to understand what he is reading, he must refer to what he has just read; thus, all the paradoxes which he condemns form, despite himself, his immediate past; he senses the existence of others which are on the horizon and which are making a new future for him. Invisible walls surround him; he is in a world which he would not have wanted to create and which would not have been if not for him. He spontaneously shapes his present thoughts and feels himself shaping them: they are indeed his own; and yet, despite their transparency, they have the disquieting depth of the thoughts of others since he does not hear them at first and has to decipher them. You may point out that that is what happens whenever we read a scholarly or philosophical work. But that is not so, for Genet demonstrates nothing. He is far too clever to attack the good citizen head-on, to arouse suspicion by offering theories. No, he relates as simply as can be things that have happened to him. He has a simple way of referring to his own principles as if they were accepted by everyone or of deriving some unacceptable consequence from those of the just man: the bamboozled reader starts by following Genet and then finds himself in the process of affirming the opposite of what he thinks, of denying what he has always affirmed.

Genet is careful not to propose: he *demands*—therein lies his diabolical cleverness. In order for him to fight against the restive attention of his readers, in order to force them to have thoughts which are distasteful to them, there must be a categorical imperative —constantly lurking behind the words—that requires unconditional adherence. In short, the work must be beautiful. I have shown elsewhere that beauty presents itself as an absolute end: it is the free appeal that creative freedom addresses to all other freedoms. And as nothing can be created once and for all, except bridges and dams, since, as Mallarmé says, being has taken place, artistic creation is imaginary: through the work of art it presents the entire world as if it were produced and assumed for human freedom. Formerly the beautiful was an integral part of theodicy: the artist "showed" God his work as the enfeoffed vassal showed his lord the fief which the latter had just given him; he used his freedom to create appearances in order to reflect the supreme freedom which had devoted itself to creating being. Today God is dead, even in the heart of the believer, and art becomes an anthropodicy: it makes man believe that man created the world; it presents his work to him and justifies his having made it. There is an ethic of Beauty; it requires of us a kind of demiurgic stoicism: optimism without hope, acceptance of Evil as a condition of total unity, affirmation of human, creative reality over and above its failures, of a universe that crushes it, assumption by freedom of suffering, faults and death; we must will being as if we had made it.

Genet is quite aware of all this, and there is a certain amount of trickery involved, for, after all, we have not made the world, and, besides, when we yield to the artist's demands, it is *his* universe that we are approving. Genet prepares to make diabolical use of this inconsequential mystification. By the beauty of his style, of his images, by the aesthetic depth of his inventions, by the rigorous, classical unity of his works, he will make us reperform spontaneously the free act that makes it possible to reassume the world: but the world which is assumed will be that of crime. It has been said that beauty in itself is a proof. Precisely: it will prove itself. Now, as we have seen, for Genet the other face of the Beautiful is Evil. Thus, Beauty will be a proof of Evil. Genet tempts us by the best of ourselves; he addresses our generosity, our free will; he demands, as does any artist, that we be a party to his undertaking, at least sufficiently to discover its beauty. We obey this order, as we do whenever we approach a new work: and we find ourselves in the process of accepting for its formal beauty a universe whose moral ugliness repels us. As I have said, there is a stoical and foul optimism of beauty: it asks us to accept pain and death for love of order, of harmony, of unity. Genet plays on this optimism: but it is not *a* particular suffering, *a* fault that he makes us accept in the name of general order, but rather Evil in its entirety. Isn't that the best trick one can play on decent folk? There would be no point in remaining on guard and taking the Beautiful while leaving Evil, for the Beautiful and Evil are one and the same thing. Indeed, one is entitled to think that the Beauty of the works will be the verbal representation of the terrible Beauty of the aesthetic gesture, of that devouring Ogress who changed Being into appearance. As a woman reader of Genet has written to me: "When you shake off his prose, it's too late: you've been hooked by Evil." Too late, yes, for to read is to reperform the writer's operation of synthetic unification; it is to will each sentence and to organize it with the others. We must affirm if we want to understand and must give if we want to feel. Is the author guilty? If so, the reader too will be guilty. In short, in openly and frankly asking us to will with him that the Beautiful be, he has forced us to make Evil exist. We catch ourselves willing what we do not want, affirming what we have always denied. Since to read is to re-create, we re-create, for the sake of its beauty, the homosexual intercourse that is sumptuously bedecked with the rarest of words. But the words vanish, leaving us face to face with the residue, a mixture of sweat, dirt, cheap perfumes, blood and excrement. Is *that* what we willed? Behind us Genet snickers: "Poetry is the art of using shit and making you eat it." Genet's art is a mirage, a confidence trick, a pitfall. In order to make us eat shit, he has to show it to us, from afar, as rose jam. That is the purpose of the "magnifying judgments" of which we have spoken. In any case, the purpose is achieved: Genet has got even with us; he makes us experience the original divorce which transformed the religious child that he was into a hoodlum. Without ceasing to be himself, the Just man is already the Other.

But Genet does not yet feel satisfied: the good citizens had endowed him with a fictive and monstrous Ego which he was unable either to assume or reject; he wants to return it to them and install it within them. In order to make sure that he is substituting his own self for that of the reader, he talks about himself in the first person. Now, regardless of who the writer is, when the sentence starts with "I," a confusion arises in my mind between this "I" and my own. No doubt if I saw the other person, if I saw the words come out of his mouth, I would relate his speech to his person. But I am alone in my room, and if a voice somewhere utters the words that I read, it is mine; in reading, I speak in the bottom of my throat and I feel myself speaking. At the present moment, in this room, there is only one man who says "I," to wit, myself. Caught in the trap: since, in order to understand the sentence, I must relate the "I" to a subjec-

tivity, it is to my own that I refer. That is the way in which a reader
of novels spontaneously identifies himself with the character who is
telling the story. "I was afraid; I ran down the stairs": that is all that
is needed to endow us with an imaginary past; we have the feeling
of gradually recalling the events of a bad dream; little by little
someone familiar yet unexpected emerges from the mist: a person
suffering from amnesia starts remembering things, the members of
his family relate to him his past actions, and, as they begin each
story, he wonders anxiously: "What else did I do?"

Note how artfully Genet introduces himself in *Miracle of the Rose:*
he is a disenchanted thief who is being carried off to prison. We let
ourselves be caught up immediately: we are used to that kind of
beginning, we do not disdain to read the books in the *Série Noire**
and to identify ourselves with the delinquents. This man can't be
really guilty. Besides, what has he done? Stolen. He must have been
driven to it by poverty or perhaps a bad environment. Furthermore,
he will repent toward the end; that is a law of this type of book; he
will find Wisdom in prison, like so many others. The decent man
very gingerly sticks his toe into this still water, then makes up his
mind and dives in: there he is, filled with pity, in the office of the
court clerk; he has become a petty crook who is going to serve his
sentence. He has only to turn ten pages to discover himself: *I* am
bad, repentant, a homosexual, *I* am a monster. Meanwhile, the story
goes on, innocently, as if Genet were sure of our agreement in advance. At times he even apologizes for not having been bad enough:
"I could have put his eyes out, torn out his tongue, but after all, one
has one's weaknesses." Or else: "I had to rely on a little physical
beauty in order to attain Evil." And it is *in us, to us,* that he makes
these surprising apologies. It is we who are sorry that we were not
bad enough. But there is even more trouble in store for us, for Genet
now tells us about his loves. If Restif de la Bretonne informs us of
his sexual exploits, we are delighted; we are eager to be that Hercu-
les who is so flattering to our sex; our arms will gallantly carry
swooning beauties to a sofa and we shall not refuse to prove our
ardor a dozen times an hour. Now, the "I" of *Miracle of the Rose*
starts by bewitching us in the same way: it draws us into itself and
endows us with its desires. When Genet tells us of his love for Bulkaen, of his vain efforts not to betray his excitement in the presence
of the beloved, of the latter's coyness, we cannot refrain from slip-

*A widely read French series of detective stories and thrillers.—Translator's note.

ping our personal memories into his account: have we not tried to conceal our feeling for a coquette who would have shamelessly taken advantage of them? Have we not had the feeling of being detected and played upon? It is we who are being talked about; or rather *it is we who are talking*. It is we who say: "Two beds away from me is his little face, which is contorted by some mysterious drama...his perfect set of imperfect teeth, his mean, shifty, look, his stubborn, never satisfied expression and, under the white, starched shirt, that splendid body which neither fasting nor blows have been able to impair, as noble and imperious as I saw it when we went swimming in the summer—with its heavy torso, the chest like that tool which is called a maul, at the end of a flexible handle. His waist; his chest which I also dare compare to a rose whose head is too heavy, on a stem that bends." Through Genet's eyes I see this young creature, a new and eternal object of my love; in comparing the person's chest to a heavy rose, *I* occasion the swelling of two rich and delicate breasts. But at the same time I know that Bulkaen is a man; and this knowledge arouses strange feelings in me. Yves Mirande relates in his memoirs how he met a charming woman at the Opera Ball, took her home in a carriage, and how, when caressing her, suddenly realized that his conquest was a man in disguise. What he felt at the moment of this discovery gives a good idea of the state of mind of the reader of Genet: the horror-stricken desire which nevertheless remains, unable to fade away, and which persists in seeking the woman in the unmasked male. That anguished desire is *our* imaginary desire in the presence of Bulkaen, who is a little woman, Divers' kid, and at the same time a formidable hoodlum. Captive of this *I* which I have animated with my own consciousness, I struggle in vain; *it is I* who desire the boy. If I have the slightest inclination for men, even if it is repressed to my very depths, I am caught, constrained, in the shame of avowing my tastes to myself. If I really have no partiality for boys, then *I* become, in myself, the Other. Another uses me to desire what I cannot desire; my freedom lends itself, I am possessed by a homosexual zar and, what is more, voluntarily possessed. If I want to free myself, to return to myself, then the young hoodlum takes on—without ceasing to be a male—all the secondary characteristics of womanhood: his skin becomes smoother, his curves rounder, he molts and becomes the most boyish girl I can desire or, more accurately, the matter grows, as it were, lighter; I find myself in the presence of a half-abstract, asexual but living and desirable flesh, or, better still, confronted with the anonymous desirability of all flesh, as an ultimate signification of the words. The very next moment the face of the androgynous creature has hardened; an adjective has covered that soft blond skin with a fuzzy fleece; I again become that Other who is an enemy to myself. The right-thinking man, caught up in a whirlwind, oscillates continually from one extreme to the other: either he desires the flesh of a boy who is secretly a girl or he desires the boy insofar as his *I* is a secretly homosexual Other. In *Our Lady of the Flowers*, the web is even better woven, since Genet calls his hero "Divine" and speaks of him in the feminine. Let us listen to him: "Divine was limpid water...and just as the wind turns leaves, so she turns heads. ... From a tiny black satin purse she took a few coins which she laid noiselessly on the marble table top." Who would not desire this charming adventuress? The trouble is that this woman is a man. Homosexual because of the power of words, we taste for a moment, in the realm of the imaginary, the forbidden pleasure of taking a man and being taken, and we cannot taste it without horrifying ourself. "But," you may object, "what if I *really am* homosexual?" Wait! Genet reserves his hardest blows for homosexuals: women do not particularly like each other. He will lead them a little further than us, perhaps to the point of embrace and then, all of a sudden, he will show his cards: filth, shit, organic smells, farts; all of a sudden, that is what you must like if you want to follow him. Will you, like his Hitler, lick your befouled mustache? As you can see, you *must* abandon him sooner or later: but he holds you, and you will follow him with horror to the very end, and the longer you are his accomplice, the more horrified you will be: Genet's worst enemies are to be found among homosexuals.

What does he care about homosexuals? He has played his best trick on decent folk. Fair revenge: formerly it was they who thought inside him; now it is he who thinks inside them. The word *thief* was a bottomless abyss: if they open his books, it is now they who topple over the precipice. His procedure has not varied since the time when he was a young hoodlum who let himself be taken by the Pimps in order to steal their ego. He lets himself be taken by readers: there he is on the shelf of a bookcase, someone takes him down, carries him away, opens him. "I'm going to see," says the right-thinking man, "what this chap is all about." But the one who thought he was taking is suddenly taken. How could Genet dream of a fuller restoration of civil rights, since the Just man who reads him, with veritable and singular passion, loses himself so that Genet may be.

I know: there is a defense. One can pull oneself together, can stop reading, can thrust the book aside with disgust. But, in the first place, Genet expects this disgust, he hopes for it: is it not the inverse of a Perpetual Adoration? He is delighted that, more or less everywhere in the world, his books are the impassive objects of impotent fury. And besides, what is disgust? Quite simply an incipient vomiting. And what you vomit must in some way have been inside you. How Genet laughed at M. Mauriac's painful efforts to vomit him out: he would have liked, I think, to speak to him somewhat as follows: "The disgust which you manifest when confronted with my books is a magical effort to reject that Other who is no other than yourself. But when, in desperation, you make such a fuss, it is already too late. One does not vomit up one's soul, and it is your soul that is rotten. Is there any way of my knowing, when confronted with your wild frenzy, what loathsome instincts have awakened in it? After all, you were considered a specialist in Evil before I appeared on the scene. We are confrères. You, however, had got into the habit of stopping in time, out of respect for your public, or else, after describing lost, ignoble souls, you wrote a preface to praise the divine creation and to recommend that we practice Christian charity. I, on the other hand, do not write a preface. I have led you further than you wanted to go. In unmasking myself, I unmask you. You are an evildoer, like me, but a shamefaced evildoer. Your fury sheds a very singular light on your own works. Wasn't Thérèse Desqueyroux a poisoner? How glad I am to write openly and how the wickedness that dares not speak its name must suffer." He would be greatly disappointed if it occurred to anyone to say to him that M. Mauriac's clownish indignation simply expressed a mediocre author's hatred of a great writer.*

There remains the simple possibility of *not reading* him. That is the only risk he runs, and it is a big one. But, in the last analysis, whether he is read depends *on him,* on him alone. Let his works be beautiful: that is the necessary and sufficient condition for his hav-

---

*The preceding passage refers to a violent attack on Genet by François Mauriac, who, though recognizing Genet's genius, denounced him as an instrument of the devil. — Translator's note.

ing readers. And if his reputation is established, the Just man who wants to object to him will force himself to ignore a social and cultural fact. It is this restive gentleman who will make himself conspicuous, who, on at least one score, will dissociate himself from the society in which he lives. If Genet's fictions have sufficient power, they will compel recognition; the community will socialize them in spite of itself, as it has done with Julien Sorel, that murderer, and Baron de Charlus, that homosexual.

Genet: The Refusal to Communicate

by Georges Bataille

Impossible Communication

Sartre himself noted a curious difficulty at the basis of Genet's work. Genet, the writer, has neither the power to communicate with his readers nor the intention of doing so. His work almost denies the reader. Sartre saw, though he drew no conclusions, that in these conditions the work was incomplete. It was a replacement, half way from the *major* communication at which literature aims. Literature is communication: a sovereign author addresses sovereign humanity, beyond the servitude of the isolated reader. If this is the case, the author denies himself. He denies his own peculiarities in favour of the work, at the same time as he denies the peculiarity of the reader in favour of reading. *Literary* communication—which is such in so far as it is poetic—is this *sovereign process* which allows *communication* to exist, like a solidified instant, or a series of instants, detached both from the work and from the reading of the work. Sartre knows this: he seems, though I cannot think why, to credit only Mallarmé, who certainly expressed it clearly, with a universal supremacy of communication over beings who communicate: "In Mallarmé," says Sartre, "reader and writer are cancelled out simultaneously: they extinguish each other mutually, until the Word alone remains" [*Saint Genet*].

Instead of saying "in Mallarmé," I would say "whenever literature really appears." However this may be, even if an apparent absurdity

"Genet: The Refusal to Communicate" by Georges Bataille, excerpted from *Literature and Evil*, translated by Alastair Hamilton (London: Calder & Boyars, 1973), pp. 106-67. Reprinted by permission of Georges Borchardt, Inc., and John Calder (Publishers) Ltd.

results from this process, the author was there to suppress himself in his work, and he addressed the reader, who read in order to suppress himself — or, if we prefer, to render himself sovereign through the suppression of his isolated being. Sartre speaks somewhat arbitrarily of a form of sacred or poetic communication in which the spectator or the reader feels himself "changed into the thing." If there is to be communication, the person to whom the process is addressed momentarily changes himself into communication (the change is neither complete nor lasting, but it does, strictly speaking, *take place:* otherwise there is no communication). In all events communication is the opposite of *the thing* which is defined by the isolation into which it can be relegated.

In fact there is no communication between Genet and the reader — and yet Sartre assumes that his work is valid. He suggests that it is based on conversation, then on poetic creation. According to Sartre, Genet had himself "consecrated by the reader." "To tell the truth," he adds immediately, "the reader has no knowledge of this consecration." This leads him to maintain that "the poet...demands to be recognised by an audience whom he does not recognise." But this is unacceptable: I can assert that the consecrational operation, or poetry, is communication or nothing. Genet's work, whatever a commentator may say about it, is neither sacred nor poetic because the author refuses to communicate.

The idea of communication is difficult to understand in all its potentiality. I shall later try to convey a richness of which we are rarely conscious, but I would now like to insist on the fact that the idea of communication, which implies the duality rather than the plurality of those who communicate, appeals, within the limits of the communication in question, to their equality. Not only has Genet no intention of communicating when he writes, but, whatever his intention may be, in that a caricature or replacement of communication is established, the author refutes this fundamental analogy which the vigour of his work might reveal to the reader. "His audience," writes Sartre, "bow before him, willing to acknowledge a liberty which they know full well does not acknowledge their own liberty." Genet places himself if not above, at least outside, those who are called upon to read him. By putting out his hands, he forestalls any possible contempt, although his readers are rarely tempted to despise him: "I acknowledge," he says, "that thieves, traitors, murderers, cheats have a profound beauty — a sunken beauty — which you lack" [*The Thief's Journal*].

Genet knows no rule of honesty: though he never actually says that he wants to laugh at his reader, this is what he does. This does not bother me, but I can just perceive that vague area where Genet's qualities are squandered. Part of Sartre's mistake is to take him literally. Only rarely — in the case of certain heart-rending themes — can we rely on what he says. Even then we must recall his indifference, his readiness to abuse us. In him, we arrive at that complete infringement of the laws of honesty which not even the Dadaists could achieve. For the Dadaists were honest in that they wanted nothing to have so much as a meaning. They wanted any proposition that appeared coherent to lose this deceptive appearance. Genet mentions "an adolescent honest enough to remember that Mettray was a paradise" [*Miracle of the Rose*]. There is obviously something pathetic in the use of the word *honest* in his context: the reformatory of Mettray was a hell. To the severity of the warders was added the brutality of the prisoners. Genet himself has the "honesty" to show that the children's gaol was the place where he discovered that infernal pleasure which made it a paradise for him. Yet the Mettray reformatory was not very different from the prison of Fontevrault (where Genet again met the "adolescent" from Mettray). In most respects the population of the two gaols was the same. Now Genet, who frequently exalted prisons and their inmates, ended by writing:

> Stripped of its sacred ornaments, I see the prison naked, and its nakedness is pitiless. The prisoners are mere wretches, their teeth rotting with scurvy, bent by illness, spitting, hawking and coughing. They go from the dormitory to the workroom in huge, heavy, noisy clogs, they drag themselves about on cloth slippers full of holes and stiff with dust and sweat. They stink. They cringe before the warders who are just as cowardly as they. They are nothing but an outrageous caricature of the handsome animals whom I saw when I was twenty, and I will never be able to reveal how hideous they have become sufficiently to avenge the harm they have done me, the boredom their unparalleled stupidity has caused me [*Miracle of the Rose*].

The point is not whether Genet's testimony is accurate, but whether he has written a work of literature, in the sense in which literature is poetry and profoundly, not just formally, sacred. I think I must insist, therefore, on the shapelessness of the aims of an author who is sustained solely by an uncertain instinct—a dissociated, tumultuous, but basically indifferent instinct, unable to reach the intensity of passion imposed by true honesty.

Genet himself never doubts his weakness. To create a work of literature can only be, I believe, a sovereign process. This is true in the sense in which the work requires its author to go beyond the wretch within himself who is not on the level of these sovereign moments. In other words the author must look, through and in his work, for that which denies his own limitations and weaknesses, and is not part of his profound *servitude*. He can then deny, safely and reciprocally, those readers without whose thought his work could not even have existed. He can deny them to the extent in which he has denied himself. That means that the idea of these indecisive beings, burdened with servility whom *he knows,* can make him despair of the work he has written. But each time these real beings bring him back to the humanity which never tires of being human, which never succumbs, and which always triumphs over the *means* of which it is the *end*. To produce a work of literature is to turn one's back on servility as on every conceivable form of diminution. It is to talk the sovereign tongue which, coming from that sovereign part of man, is addressed to sovereign humanity. Obscurely (often in an almost oblique manner, hindered by pretensions), the lover of literature feels this truth. Genet himself senses it, and he says: "The idea of a work of literature would make me shrug my shoulders" [*The Thief's Journal*].

Genet's attitude is poles apart from any ingenuous representation of literature which may be considered pedantic but which, despite its inaccessible quality, is universally valid. Not that we should stop when we read "I wrote to earn money." Genet's work as a writer is worthy of attention. Genet himself is eager to be sovereign. But he has not seen that sovereignty involves the heart; it requires loyalty and, above all, communication. Genet's life is a failure and, though it has every appearance of success, so is his work. It is not servile; it is infinitely superior to most writings which are considered "literary"; but it is not sovereign. It does not satisfy the elementary requirements of sovereignty—that ultimate loyalty without which the edifice of sovereignty would collapse. Genet's work is the fretting of a crotchety individual of whom Sartre said "If he is pushed too far he will burst out laughing, he will immediately admit that he is laughing at our expense, that he has only tried to shock us further by calling that demoniacal and sophisticated perversion of a sacred notion 'sanctity'. ..."

Genet's Failure

Genet's indifference to communication means that his tales are interesting, but not *enthralling*. There is nothing colder, less moving, under the glittering parade of words, than the famous passage in which Genet recounts Harcamone's death [at the end of *Miracle of the Rose*]. It has the beauty of a piece of jewellery: it is too rich and in somewhat cold bad taste. Its splendour is reminiscent of Aragon's feats in the early days of surrealism — the same verbal facility, the same recourse to devices which shock. I do not believe that this type of provocation will ever lose its powers of seduction, but the effect of seduction is subordinated to the interest in a purely external success, to preference for a deception which can be immediately appreciated. The servility of the quest for this type of success is the same in the author and the reader. Each one, author and reader, avoids the pangs, the annihilation of sovereign communication. They both limit themselves to the prestige of success.

This is not the only aspect. It would be pointless to reduce Genet to what he managed to extract from his brilliant gifts. He has a basic desire for insubordination, but this desire, however profound, has not always corresponded to his work as a writer.

The most remarkable thing is that the moral solitude — and irony — into which he sinks have kept him outside that lost sovereignty, the desire for which brought him into the paradoxical situation I have mentioned. Indeed, the quest for sovereignty by the man alienated by civilisation is a fundamental cause of historical agitation (whether it be religious or political, undertaken according to Marx, because of man's "alienation)". Sovereignty, on the other hand, is the object which eludes us all, which nobody has seized and which nobody can seize for this reason: we cannot possess it, like an object, but we are doomed to seek it. A certain utility always alienates the proposed sovereignty — even the celestial sovereigns, whom imagination should have freed from all servitude, subordinate themselves to useful ends. In *The Phenomenology of the Mind*, Hegel pursues the dialectic of the *master* (the law, the sovereign) and the *slave* (the man enslaved by work) which is at the basis of the

Communist theory of the class struggle. The slave triumphs, but his apparent sovereignty is nothing but the autonomous will for slavery: sovereignty must inhabit the realm of failure.

So we cannot talk of Jean Genet's failed sovereignty as if such a thing as the accomplished form of a real sovereignty existed. The sovereignty to which man constantly aspires has never been accessible and we have no reason to think it ever will be. All we can hope for is a momentary grace which allows us to reach for this sovereignty, although the kind of rational effort we make to survive will get us nowhere. Never can we *be* sovereign. But we distinguish between the moments when fortune lets us glimpse the furtive lights of communication and those moments of disgrace when the mere thought of sovereignty commits us to seizing for it like a positive benefit. Genet's attitude, eager for royal dignity, nobility and sovereignty in the traditional sense of the word, is the sign of a calculation doomed to failure.

Let us take those many individuals who still study genealogy. Genet has a capricious and pathetic advantage over them. But the scholar who imposes titles on people demonstrates the same stupidity as Genet, who wrote these lines about the time when he travelled through Spain.

> Neither the guards nor the local policemen arrested me. The figure they saw was no longer a man, but the curious product of misery to whom laws cannot be applied. I had exceeded the limits of indecency. No one would have been surprised had I entertained a prince of the blood, a Spanish grandee, had I called him my cousin and talked to him in the finest words.
>
> Entertain a Spanish grandee. But in what palace?
>
> If I use this rhetorical procedure in order to show you the extent of the solitude which conferred sovereignty on me, it is because a situation, a success to be expressed by the words which should express the triumph of the century, impose it on me. A verbal relationship translates the relationship of my glory in terms of military glory. I was related to princes and kings by a sort of secret relationship, ignored by the world—that relationship which allows a shepherdess to be familiar with a king of France. The palace I talk of (for it has no other name) is the architectural combination of the increasingly tenuous refinements which pride imposed on my solitude [*The Thief's Journal*].

If this passage is added to those already quoted it not only confirms Genet's predominant preoccupation with acceding to the sovereign part of humanity: it also emphasises the humble and calculating nature of this preoccupation, subordinated to a sovereignty whose appearance formerly constituted a historical reality. It emphasises the distance between the pretender characterised by his poverty, and the superficial successes of the royalty and aristocracy.

The Theater of Genet:
A Sociological Study

by Lucien Goldmann

Until a few years ago, aestheticians, critics, and literary historians accorded sociology only marginal status. However, the availability of Georg Lukács' early work, the psychological and epistemological researches of Jean Piaget, and the acceptance of the dialectic as genetic structuralism has changed all that.

Traditional sociology—which still dominates university teaching —tried to relate the *content* of a literary work to the *content* of the collective unconscious: how men think and act in daily life. Such criticism becomes more effective the more mundane is the writer being studied, content merely to relate his experiences without imaginatively transposing them. Structural sociology begins from premises that exclude those of traditional sociology. The five most important of these are:

1. The essential relation between social life and art does not lie in content but only in the *mental structures*—the "categories"—which organize both the day-to-day consciousness of a social group and the artist's imagination.

2. Individual experience is too brief and limited to create such structures. They can be produced only within a social group. Individuals within groups experience together a set of problems for which they seek solutions. In other words, mental structures—or, abstractly, meaningful categorical structures—are not individual but social phenomena.

"The Theater of Genet: A Sociological Study" by Lucien Goldmann. Translated from the French by Pat Dreyfus. First published in *The Drama Review*, 12, no. 2 (T38). © 1968 by *The Drama Review*. Reprinted by permission. All rights reserved.

3. The relation between the structure of day-to-day consciousness and the organization of the artist's imagination—in works that can be most easily studied—is more or less rigorously homologous. Often, however, it is a simple significative relation. Frequently, heterogeneous or contradictory contents are structurally homologous: they are related on the level of categorical structures. For example, a fairy tale can be rigorously homologous *in its structure* to the experience of a particular social group; or, at the very least, it can be related meaningfully to that experience. No longer is there anything contradictory in asserting that a literary work is closely linked to social and historical reality as well as to the most powerful creative imagination.

4. The finest literary works are especially suited for such examination. In fact, the categorical structures—which are the object of this type of literary sociology—are what give the work its unity: its specific aesthetic character.

5. The categorical structures are neither conscious nor unconscious in the Freudian sense (which implied repression). Rather, they are nonconscious processes—similar in certain ways to those mechanisms which regulate muscular and nervous activity. These are neither conscious nor repressed.

That is why discovering these structures (and thereby understanding the art work) is beyond the range of both purely literary studies and those oriented toward the writer's conscious intentions or hidden motives. Categorical structures can be found only through sociological investigation.

II

Genet's theater offers a very interesting object for sociological study. He is the product of the French underclass of petty thieves and homosexuals; he describes and transposes his underclass experiences in his early works. But what makes Genet truly interesting (as an example of the relation between modern industrial society and literary creation) is the encounter in his work between an implicit but radical rejection of society and the problems of a still active European intelligentsia which is hostile to today's corporate capitalism. The underclass has been expelled from respectable society. But Genet has interiorized this expulsion and raised it to the level of world vision.

This encounter is complicated. The rejection of industrial society is coupled with the knowledge that this society provides a high standard of living for most of those living in it. A previously un-heard-of number of consumer possibilities (cars, apartments, vaca-tions, etc.) create an apparent unity among individuals. However, this same consumer orientation stifles the deep need for authentic-ity, for communication with one's fellow men, for the development of one's own intellectual and emotional life. This conflict produces a relatively broad sector of the lower middle class which, while seemingly integrated into the existing social order, feels oppressed and frustrated, particularly in its emotional life.

It would seem that the first task of a sociological analysis of mod-ern French theater would be to relate this lower middle class to characters like Ionesco's Bérenger who, although unsatisfied and out of place, is unable to resist; indeed, he cannot even conceive of the possibility of resistance. However, alongside this widespread "Bérenger phenomenon," there are—particularly in France and Italy—strong socialist and anarchist unionist traditions. These comprise a small number of workers and creative intellectuals and a fairly large number of educated people who refuse to accede to modern capitalism. They are concerned with the problem of estab-lishing a human order that will effectively guarantee individual liberties. The frustrated hope for a socialist revolution in the West and the development of Stalinism in the East constituted a set of difficult problems for this group. It now finds itself maintaining a genuinely negative attitude toward capitalism (which it rejects more firmly than does the lower middle class), while knowing that this rejection brings with it intellectual and practical difficulties which are incomparably serious and decisive.

The early novels of Malraux, Robbe-Grillet's fiction, films like *Last Year at Marienbad,* some of Beckett's writings, and, primarily, Genet's theater should be studied as the literary transposition of this latter group's world vision.

Genet's plays result from an encounter between the radical nega-tive of the underclass poet who, as he says, is in no way rebelling against existing society (making no claims on it) and the conscious-ness which exists among progressive workers and the most radical intellectuals, who see the difficulty—increasingly evident as the years go by—of finding satisfaction through revolution. Another characteristic of Genet's theater (and one which is most interesting to the cultural sociologist) is the way in which it unintentionally incorporates certain decisive experiences of the European Left. A play like *The Balcony* cannot be understood without taking these experiences into account. The sociologist must ask, of course, how this incorporation takes place; it is important to know because one finds analogous phenomena in other authors: Gombrowicz's *The Marriage*, for example. But whatever the answer, the fact remains that Genet, the nonconformist subproletarian whose work is essentially moral and lyrical, is the only modern French dramatist who assigns a central place to the problems of history as a whole, thereby making them the key to understanding his work's unity.

III

So far, Genet has written five plays: *Deathwatch, The Maids, The Balcony, The Blacks,* and *The Screens.* These plays show an ever richer and more complex—but also more unified—expression of one and the same problem.

Deathwatch belongs to the poetic universe of the nonconformist underclass. Lefranc strangles Maurice to win Green Eyes' acceptance and become Snowball's equal. But his act is gratuitous, for, as Green Eyes says:

> Don't talk to me. Don't touch me. Do you know what misfortune is? Don't you know I kept hoping to avoid it? And you thought you could become, all by yourself, without the help of heaven, as great as me! Maybe overshadow me? You fool, don't you realize it's impossible to overshadow me? [...] I didn't want what happened to me to happen. It was all given to me. A gift from God or the devil, but something I didn't want.

Later, again Green Eyes:

> You don't know the first thing about misfortune if you think you can choose it. I didn't want mine. It chose me. It fell on my shoulders and clung to me. I tried everything to shake it off. I struggled, I boxed, I

danced, I even sang, and, odd as it may seem, I refused it at first. It was only when I saw that everything was irremediable that I quieted down. I've only just accepted it. It had to be total.

Deathwatch is already a strictly coherent work, although it is Genet's first play. It describes the individual's struggle for moral recognition where the only things of moral value are those which ordinary society condemns. This divides the world into two kinds of men: the weak, the petty thieves and crooks; and the strong, the natural murderers whose criminal character is part of the natural order.

The Maids is more complex and, in certain crucial ways, different. Although the play is as radical and nonconformist as *Deathwatch*, ,it is no longer set entirely within the marginal world of the underclass. In *The Maids* the opposition between the maids and Madame is central: we cannot understand Claire and Solange without knowing of their hatred for Madame. *The Maids* shows the basic structure of Genet's world, the setting for *The Balcony, The Blacks,* and, to a degree, *The Screens.* This world pivots on the relation between the ruled and the rulers: the maids and Madame, the rebels and the balcony, the blacks and the whites, the colonials and the colonists. It is a dialectical relationship, one of hatred and fascination. Hatred is fundamental to all these plays. It becomes love-hate only through the fascination which the ruled have for the rulers, a fascination based on the utter incapacity of revolution to succeed. It is not until *The Screens* that the rulers can be defeated. Madame cannot be killed; the revolt is put down; the whites are routed only in fantasy.

The action of these plays unfolds in a static, insufficient universe; but this insufficiency is compensated by a fantasy ritual which permits the ruled to identify either with the rulers or with subjects who end domination through revolution. In this way, the ruled—but only in their imagination—cause values to exist that are not found in the real world. In *The Maids* Claire plays Madame and Solange plays Claire. In *The Balcony* minor employees play a bishop, a judge, a general (and also, it is true, a slave). In *The Blacks* Negroes on the balcony play whites and below, on the stage, enact the purely imaginary murder of a white woman. In *The Screens,* before the revolt breaks out, Saïd plays a fiancé laden with costly gifts; later his wife and his mother play the owners of a farmyard full of poultry. On one side of the stage Warda—who, through tremendous effort, has become the perfect whore—enables the oppressed to ritualize the poetic and intensely felt communion between man and woman.

In short, in a world where the power of the rulers cannot be shaken, where the ruled are motivated by love-hate for the rulers, an inadequate reality offers the possibility of a poetic-religious ritual through which the ruled identify with the rulers and succeed in fantasy in overcoming them.

IV

Let us return to our structural comparison of *Deathwatch* and *The Maids*. The world of the first play is structurally homologous to middle-class society—not as it is but as it wishes itself to be. Only here it is presented inversely. Love is at the center, but it is homosexual love. Value and recognition are a function of the dangerous nature of the characters' lives. But danger does not consist in choosing a perilous profession or in socially recognized heroism. Rather, danger comes from crime and murder, which lead to imprisonment and death. *Deathwatch* also presents an elitist view which is confirmed by contemporary society. Green Eyes and Snowball are creatures of misfortune; their nature dooms them willy-nilly to be murderers. This is why Lefranc, who kills by intention, can never be admitted to their community. The special power of *Deathwatch* comes from the implicit criticism of the purely verbal and often deceitful values of accepted morality and the intensity which marks human experiences when they are forbidden and acted out by the outcast and condemned.

Just how different is *The Maids?* First, the world here is divided. On one side are the strong, whose lives consist of lies and prating but who are invincible: Madame and Monsieur. On the other side are the maids, authentic, intense, simultaneously hating and loving their masters. A world, therefore, where everything is positive and negative at once and where the one authentic value is the imaginary realization of love-hate in the ritual which the maids resume each evening (and which they now act out for spectators, on the stage).

The maids are authentic, while Madame—powerful and insuperable—is nothing but a puppet. Solange and Claire have a vivid fantasy of following their condemned lover into exile. Later, Madame appears and touches the same theme in almost the exact words. But her verbs are conditional, she is self-satisfied; and, anyway, Monsieur will not be convicted: her words lack all sincerity. "Of course, none of this is serious, but if it were, Solange, it would be a joy for me to bear his cross. I'd follow him from place to place, from prison to prison, on foot if need be, as far as the penal colony, Solange!"[1] The little word "Solange" at the end of the speech betrays how utterly superficial Madame's emotions are: play-acting for the benefit of the maids. But, pushing the farce to its extreme, Genet also has her say that this situation makes her "almost happier, monstrously happy!" until the moment when, exhausted, she ends her speech: "I'll simply die if I don't have a cigarette!"

The telephone call from Monsieur interrupts the maids in the middle of their ritual. He has been released from prison. Solange exclaims: "The judges have their damned nerve letting him go. It's a mockery of justice. It's an insult to us!" They will be discovered, arrested, and sentenced for libel. In *Deathwatch* Solange and Claire would have proudly accepted this as the confirmation of their existence. But the world of *The Maids* is radically different. Here the sentencing will be a shameful defeat. Thus they try to poison Madame, fail, and follow their fantasy ritual into reality. The sentence for libel is transformed into one for murder. In becoming a murderer, Solange has become "Mademoiselle Solange Lemercier. [...] I'm Madame's equal and I hold my head high." She has become an autonomous creature for all eternity.

Before dying, Claire says:

> It will be your task, yours alone, to keep us both alive. You must be very strong. In prison no one will know that I'm with you, secretly. On the sly.

In both human and spiritual terms the maids have won over the powerful puppet, Madame. They really live in appearances while Madame — lying and ridiculous — only appears to live in reality. But this has been so since the play began. Madame cannot be defeated and the maids are forced to destroy themselves in order to preserve the seriousness and authenticity of their existence. *The Maids* is an embodiment of the static dialectic of despair. By interiorizing the conflict between ruled and rulers, Genet becomes a radical pessi-

---

[1]Translation by Pat Dreyfus from the text as printed in L'Arbalete (1963) edition. The Evergreen edition contains a variant text at this point. [Ed.]

mist for whom art and appearance are the only possible compensations for a deceitful and inadequate reality.

V

With *The Balcony*, Genet introduces a new element: he incorporates social and political reality not merely as a framework but as a possible future. Even if this future comes to nothing, its presence brings into his work the principle of motion. *The Balcony* begins as the other Genet plays do: little people acting out their dreams inside a house of illusions. But right from the start, and particularly in Scene Five, two new tensions are present: there is a revolt which threatens the established order, and this house of illusions belongs to the chief of police and his girlfriend, Irma (who are both disappointed that no client has ever asked to play the chief's role). The play shows how the image of the chief of police penetrates the ritual of the house of illusions and how this is related to the revolt's defeat.

Scene Five takes place in the rear of the house—in the rooms of the administration. Here we meet the Chief of Police, the pimp Arthur, Irma, and Carmen, a whore whom Irma has hired to help run the house. A few words about Carmen: she epitomizes the general predicament expressed in the play (a technique repeated in *The Screens)*. The rebels' struggle against the balcony is one between death and life, between an order in which values exist only in fantasy and ritual and the attempt to create a new order in which these values penetrate life itself, making it unnecessary to escape into fantasy because living at last will be authentic. Carmen, like the world, is forced to choose between her genuine love for her daughter, whom she has sent to the country, and her activities as a whore in the brothel—where she used to play the role of the Virgin. Irma tells Carmen that she will have to give up her daughter and because Carmen no longer wishes to help administer the house, she is given the role of Saint Theresa.

> *Irma.* Whether dead or alive, your daughter is dead. Think of the charming grave, adorned with daisies and artificial wreaths, at the far end of the garden...and that garden in your heart, where you'll be able to look after it. ....

Carmen. I'd have loved to see her again. ...

Irma. You'll keep her image in the image of the garden and the garden in your heart under the flaming robe of Saint Theresa. And you hesitate? I offer you the very finest of deaths, and you hesitate? Are you a coward?

Carmen renounces life in favor of illusion, just as the revolt will be quelled and the house of illusions rebuilt.

The revolt is doomed because it has split into two factions—one oriented toward liberty and fantasy and the other, led by Roger, organized in a disciplined, repressive way. Chantal, the girl from the house of illusions who has become the rebels' muse, is killed and her name and image glorified, inscribed on the banners of the repressive forces. In the rebuilt house there is friction between the Bishop, General, and Judge (who are now real dignitaries and therefore puppets) and the Chief of Police, who has the power. The long-awaited event happens at last: Roger presents himself and asks to play the chief of police. But Roger recognizes that this is nothing but play-acting, a ritual. His revolutionary essence consisted precisely in his efforts to create a reality which had no need of fantasy or ritual. Despairing, he castrates himself: thus fantasy accords with the reality of suppressed revolt. Roger's gesture soils the carpet. He is thrown out and the real chief of police takes his place. Outside, machine guns are heard. The Queen (Irma) asks: "Who is it?...Our side?...Or rebels?...Or?..." The answer: "Someone dreaming, Madame."

The Balcony poses a very important problem to the sociologist. The play represents a transposition of the decisive historical events of the first half of the twentieth century in a manner that is very likely nonconscious and involuntary. The theme of *The Balcony* is how awareness of the importance of the executive function develops in a society which has long been dominated by property-owners but in which people still imagine power to be in the hands of long outdated fixtures: the Bishop, the Judge, and the General. And Genet is telling us that this awareness is created by the threat of revolution and its subsequent defeat: a fairly accurate reflection of Western European history between 1917 and 1923. Although we cannot describe the mechanism by which these events were incorporated into *The Balcony,* we do know that the Polish aristocrat Gombrowicz incorporated into *The Marriage* the contrary but complementary experience of Eastern Europe. In neither case is the incorporation conscious or voluntary.

The Blacks represents another step. Here hope and the prospect of victory make their way into the world of the play, if only in a peripheral way. Outside, distantly, the blacks are engaged in a real struggle. One leader has been executed, but another has already replaced him. And this revolutionary struggle is linked to what happens on stage. "Thanks to us, they've sensed nothing of what's going on elsewhere." On stage, however, in the present world, the situation is homologous to *The Maids* and *The Balcony*. Like Solange and Claire, like the humble clients of Irma's house, like the dreamy revolutionaries in the Andromeda network, the blacks enact a nightly ritual: the murder of a white woman. Like the maids and Roger, the only way the blacks can overcome the white on *stage* is in fantasy. As in *The Maids* and *The Balcony,* this fantasy is comprised of revolt, hatred, and fascination.

So much for similarities. What are the differences? Everything points to the lengthening shadow of the real struggle going on outside the theater; and the revolution outside is in the interest of the blacks who charade for their white audience (both real in the theater and make believe on the balcony). But victory off-stage is only a hope, as distant in time as it is in space.

But the nature of the onstage ritual has changed, and this is particularly evident in the way it affects the real world. Claire and Solange commit suicide. Roger mutilates himself, the blacks kill one of their own. This killing, however, is performed within the framework of a real struggle which strengthens the hope of victory. On stage *The Blacks* ends with an apotheosis, as does *The Maids.* In that play the apotheosis is a real suicide; in *The Blacks* it is an imaginary murder of an imaginary white woman but the real hope of future victory over the whites—the self-awareness of the blacks— is authentic. The play ends with Village and Virtue on stage. He wants to express his love for her but can do so only with words and images borrowed from the whites. She is disappointed, but offers her assistance. "I'll help you. At least, there's one sure thing: you won't be able to wind your fingers in my long golden hair." The destruction of the caricatured whites, even if only imaginary, will oblige the blacks to discover authentic words of love, original gestures, a truly black culture rooted in their own essence, which they have just discovered.

Nor is the relation between ruled and rulers the same in *The Blacks* as in *The Maids*. It still involves a synthesis of hatred and fascination; but in *The Maids* fascination was dominant. In *The Blacks* hatred is the authentic fact of black existence. We may now ask: what social group's point of view is represented by *The Maids, The Balcony,* and *The Blacks?* It seems at least possible that the basic structure of these three plays corresponds to the mental and spiritual structure of the French radical Left; this structure includes—among other things—these five elements:

1. Affirmation of the existence of a radical opposition between classes, and the need to strengthen that opposition.

2. Recognition of the fact that the rulers of Western society cannot be overcome by violence: this society is without revolutionary perspective.

3. Fascination with the political and technological success of corporate capitalism.

4. Condemnation in moral and human terms of the social reality created by corporate capitalism.

5. Justification, in the name of moral, aesthetic, and human values, of the radical struggle against corporate capitalism. These values— once compromise and acceptance of oppression have both been rejected—can alone give value to a society found on minority rule, lies, and the decline of culture.

VI

We may now begin to analyze *The Screens*, which, beyond its unquestioned artistic value, has the added significance of being one of the first works of contemporary French drama to be animated by a belief in man's ability to resist regimentation and constraint. The action is divided into four stages, representing both society's development and Saïd's increasingly radical attitudes.

At first we find the ruled-ruler situation already familiar to us from Genet's earlier plays. This social order, however, is extremely provisional—the revolution will succeed—and this means that hatred is tempered and that the ritual, brothel, trunkful of gifts, farmyard, is of only peripheral importance. In the second stage, Saïd, surrounded by his wife and mother, clashes with the social

order and is rejected as a thief and outsider. From that moment, the
ritual loses its importance for all three of them. Saïd no longer goes
to the brothel, because his struggle for an authentic life has begun.
The Arab village, which still accepts the rule and morality of the
colonists, at first rejects Saïd and his family. Kadidja and the village
women prevent Saïd's mother from taking part in the funeral. The
Mother resorts to magic and appeals to the dead man's mouth. But
he too rejects her, in a scene which summarizes the entire play (the
dead man was a member of the revolution and therefore incarnates
the three social orders of *The Screens:* the Arab village, the revolt,
and the kingdom of the dead). In prison Saïd and Leila grow closer
to each other: they go together toward radical politics, monstrosity,
evil, and negation.

The third stage begins with the outbreak of the revolt. Kadidja,
who is the incarnation of the village, is killed. But before yielding to
death she exhorts the village to revolt and thereby embraces the
position she condemned in Saïd and Leila.

> I'm dead? So I am. Well, not yet! I haven't finished my job. So, Death,
> I'll fight it out with you! Saïd, Leila, my loved ones! You, too, in the
> evening related the day's evil to each other. You realized that in evil
> lay the only hope. Evil, wonderful evil, you who remain when all
> goes to pot, miraculous evil, you're going to help us. I beg of you, evil,
> and I beg you standing upright, impregnate my people. And let them
> not be idle!

But Saïd, Leila, and the Mother—who started the resistance as
thieves and arsonists—will withdraw from it now that it is organized
and taken over by the entire community. Their action was personal.
They will pursue their course of negativity and evil to its absolute
limit. Saïd poisons watering troughs, an act which harms the rebels
more than the colonists. The Mother kills a soldier, apparently by
accident. Later, in the kingdom of the dead, she admits that it was
intentional. She denies taking part in the resistance, even when her
deed objectively defines her as a participant.

Stage four: the revolt is successful and a new order has been
created, one which has neither oppressed nor oppressors and which
Genet describes in a manner that is no longer caricature but serious
and dignified. Still, it is an order and it will necessarily reappropri-
ate many elements of the order it has replaced.

As the revolutionary social order adopts the patterns of the order it has replaced, the third and last social order appears: the kingdom of the dead. It is beyond contradictions and all those who previously were enemies exist in harmony before entering the true realm of the dead: Nothingness. The Mother arrives here to wait for her two children. Like Kadidja she is replaced on earth by a mythic figure, Ommu, who declares: "Kadidja! Kadidja! They say you're dead, since you're in the earth, but enter my body and inspire me! And as for Saïd, may he be blessed!" Later, in the kingdom of the dead, Kadidja will say to the Mother: "Ommu has taken over from us, from you and me...."

Saïd returns to the village and meets the representatives of the new order. Ommu, who incarnates the expectations of the village, notes that Saïd did everything he could to betray them but that he "didn't achieve much." She says that she will be able to disappear if —in the new revolutionary order—there is a place for Saïd, whose truth is not of those which must be realized in action, but which alone can become song and give meaning to the new society. "...There are truths that must never be applied, those that must be made to live through the song they've become." The revolutionary leaders offer to pardon Saïd. Saïd is ready for one last act of treachery. "I'm very much in demand. I can set my price...." But the Mother cries out from the realm of death:

> Saïd!...Saïd!...you're not going to give in? She-dog that I am, she-dog big with a mongrel pup, I kept you in my guts not to become one more one less! A dog's life, kicks in the ribs and maybe rabies! Less than a patch of nettles, less than what you're worth, until noon today— it's noon sharp—I thought it was hatred that was leading me, Saïd!

Saïd reconsiders. He is about to leave when he is killed by one of the Arabs. There is still no place for him in the new order, as there was none in the old. Ommu—representing the hopes of the village —must remain on earth. "Burying this one, screaming at that one: I'll live to a hundred." The Mother waits for Leila (who died earlier) and Saïd. But they do not come to the kingdom of the dead. All that gets there of Leila is her veil. As for Saïd, he has bypassed the king-dom of the dead and entered Nothingness direct.

So as not to be guilty of omitting a particularly important element from this schematic picture, I would like to add that the develop-ment of the brothel—the house of illusions—runs parallel to the

other events in the play. With the revolt and the resistance the prostitutes—who were essential and autonomous in the society of oppressed and oppressors—become the same as all the other members
of the community: respected citizens who fight and whose function
is recognized and respected. But after victory there is no place for
them in the new order. Warda is killed by the village women: she
carries Leila's veil to the Mother in the kingdom of the dead.

How does *The Screens* fit into Genet's development? It would be
both easy and inadequate to say that Genet here returns to his point
of departure: anarchy. Saïd does, to be sure, share many features
with the narrator of *The Thief's Journal* and the attitudes which
shaped *Deathwatch*. But there are fundamental differences, too. The
problem of the meaning and the quality of social orders which is so
important in *The Screens* is not even mentioned in the early works.
The characters in *Deathwatch* are nonconformists, outcasts. Saïd is a
universal figure, moral to be sure, but through his negativity, also
political. As Ommu says to the soldiers of the victorious revolution:
"You and your pals are proof that we need Saïd."

Some of the decisive experiences of the European Left have been
incorporated into the play. First of all: the possibility of a successful
revolt in Algeria, and in other countries throughout the world as
well. Then: victory alone will not guarantee men happiness and
freedom, nor secure a place within the new order for those values
which, as Ommu says, are not to be realized in action but are to
become song. The play's three social orders correspond to three
basic concepts of European socialist thought: the class society based
on oppression; the society born of the successful revolt which does
away with oppression but is still rooted in constraint; and the vision
of a classless society with no restraints. This last serves the same need
for socialist thought as the Kingdom of Heaven does in Christian
eschatology.

Saïd and through him Genet refuse to participate in these three
orders. There is another path which must be followed if we wish to
remain men. *The Screens* is the first French theater work to describe
the possibilities that men still have intact and—paradoxical as this
may sound—to put on stage a hero who, in and through his negativity, is ultimately positive. For whatever one may think of Saïd's
values (and needless to say they are not ours) they are authentic and
undisputed within the world of the play. And, unlike Solange and
Claire, unlike the rebels of *The Balcony*, unlike the blacks, Saïd

fulfills his ideals outside of ritual, in his life: he remains unbowed and intact to the very end. Having freed himself of all fascination and all hatred for both the old and new rulers, he follows his own path and enters Nothingness naturally and undefeated.

Is it coincidence that *The Screens* was written recently? Is it just a result of Genet's intellectual evolution, or is something much more at stake: the first symptom of a historical turning point? Difficult as it is to answer this question, let us note that a current has developed in Western European Marxist thought whose objectives will dominate any discussion of socialism's prospects in today's world. This current affirms the inadequacy of the old revolutionary schema and, in particular, the impossibility of revolution within contemporary Western society. This current also sees the dangers to liberty inherent in old revolutionary ideas and the need to replace these ideas with something better adapted to the evolution of modern industrial society. Of course, those who support the new ideas sense that estrangement from the traditional position constitutes a grave and painful predicament. Transposed to politics, this feeling corresponds to a "betrayal" of the old point of view (it is not really, however: Saïd "did not achieve much" in the way of treason) and the stock it put in revolution. Also, insofar as these thinkers are really socialists, they know that the new point of view runs a considerable risk of being compromised and integrated into the existing capitalist order. They know that any reform action, whatever its nature, involves the danger of corruption and that the only defense against this is a radical rejection of any compromise with the technocratic society.

Until now this predicament has been purely theoretical and conceptual. Things, however, are changing; and the cultural sociologist will find the following facts to be of particular significance:

1. That a writer whose last plays were focused on the problem of history can now put a character on stage who, although no longer involved with the traditional path of revolt, rejects the three orders of socialist thought without, however, putting them all on the same level. Indeed, it is not possible to put the caricatured order of the oppressors and colonists on the same level as the successful revolt or death—which are also rejected but treated in a dignified and serious way.

2. That this character, whom nothing has been able to break, maintains his negativity to the very end.

3. That without making the slightest compromise, he is still unbowed when he leaves the world where Ommu (and, with her, the
entire village) must wait for a future in which another Saïd will at last
have a place.

Is *The Screens* an isolated, accidental occurrence? Or is it the sign
of a turning point in our intellectual and social life?

Jean Genet, or, The Inclement Thief

by Françoise d'Eaubonne

And let some candid gentleman say one day
Of you "Vile!" Ah! splendid!
Or let him say nothing, for that is shorter.

TRISTAN CORBIÈRE

To François Mauriac's first cry of alarm twenty years ago, Morvan Lebesque responded with this allegory of Jean Genet: an evening, a hotel, a voyager. The traveller cannot sleep. In the morning he complains indignantly: all night long his disgusting neighbors have kept him awake with their pornographic gasping and muttering. The hotelkeeper sets him straight: the next room was occupied not by lovers but by a woman on her deathbed. François Mauriac reminded Morvan Lebesque of this traveller, and Genet of this dying woman.

Let me suggest another allegory that has appealed to me for some time. Jean Genet is an ordinary damned man. There are many people in hell; those howling in the lower circles keep trying to move up and are constantly being pushed back. But those in the uppermost circle are even unhappier; they are equally powerless but are tortured by the more immediate hope of getting out. The Thief arrives and takes in the scene with a cold eye; of his own will he descends into the lowermost circle and there, declaring that he isn't

"Jean Genet, or, The Inclement Thief" by Françoise d'Eaubonne. From *Les Ecrivains en cage* (Paris: Andre Balland, 1970), pp. 193-219. Translated from the French by Ellen Burt. Reprinted by permission of the publisher.

47

damned enough yet, he starts digging a hole into the very bottom. Although he frightens the damned themselves by this defiance, he still goes through with it. And once the hole is dug, they discover that it opens into paradise.

"The moment people begin interpreting the poet's death over dinner," says Dominique de Roux, "it falls into disrepute." My allegory may possess the modest advantage over the black humor of Morvan Lebesque of going back to the prehistoric Genet, evoking Sartre's young peasant, accursed yet believer still: "The terrible, angry God that he saw shining for an instant in the eyes of the villagers who condemned him." Long after formulating this allegory I discovered in a chance reading the following which the Kabbala reveals: the seventh infernal circle (or the "castle of shadows" according to the myth inspiring Victorien Sardou's drawings) reaches to the limits of Hell with "windows opening into the realm of holy light." No doubt the Thief leans on his elbow at one of those balconies.

Genet, like Christ, has a "hidden life." By no means is it only a "legend," as his detractors claim; rather, for those readers who have the general impression of witnessing something prodigious, his biography seems simply incomplete: this abandoned child, war orphan, little farm-boy, seems to have lived only between a reformatory and a prison given over to prostitution and misery, up until his astonishing discovery by the masters of existentialism, his success, and his fortune—which he treats with as much disdain as all that preceded it. The appearance of *Our Lady of the Flowers,* however, raised a question: where did he learn how to write? In *Force of Circumstance,* Simone de Beauvoir notes this surprise, one little shared by those of her epoch—for most of the time writers repress, albeit badly, a warmed-over mysticism that allows them to accept as literal truth such nonsense as: "The spirit inspires where it will." One writer went so far as to tell me that it is possible, after all, to find reading material in any prison library. It is a shame to have to admit it, but it seems that those devoted to literature need a professor's education in order to grasp the foolishness of such explanations. Doubtless, it is more the professor than the writer in Simone de Beauvoir who asked herself the question that interests me; or perhaps it was enough, in her case, to have an extraordinary intelligence. In my case, it is only the pedagogical side speaking and I was indignant to see that this problem seemed a petty detail to so many — and by no means the least — among us.

To take an example at random, when we read a sentence like this one: "I would make her (Divine) with hips of stone; with cheeks polished and flat, with heavy eyelids, with pagan knees so lovely that they would reflect the desperate intelligence of mystics," how are we to believe that it was written by a self-taught man? Where do they come from, those knees? Are such knees the work of a student of Cocteau? Whether he had encountered the poet in liberty or only read him in prison, Cocteau and his Dargelos could not have instilled in a little peasant locked up in Mettray, in a transvestite of Pigalle or of Las Ramblas growing up without culture and surrounded by stupidity, a knowledge of subtle relationships between notions inaccessible to his kind: mysticism and its despair, the paganism of naked knees, and what they might reflect of another, spiritual realm. A museum-goer apt to have strolled a thousand times through a forest of statues sneaks his way through this piece of literature. An avid reader of the greatest titles in philosophy and poetry is revealed, then makes his getaway. At the time of his appearance in print, the unknown Genet kept, in his relationship to the written word, a thief's cunning. He stole and took flight; the family jewels which had disappeared from under the eyes of the cultivated bourgeois too stupid even to notice that someone had swiped something, were in his pocket. He didn't bother to declare a right that he exercised in fact — behavior peculiar to the antisocial. The thief didn't have to explain himself; how did this watch get into your pocket, my good man? Where did you learn to write *our* language, sir? He told the hour by that watch; he spoke that language. Those were the proofs.

Sartre has told us how Jean's first childish offence oriented his destiny; at the beginning, there was a *blunder*: a child, pilfering, caught in the act; then, the label of "thief" stuck on his back,[1] and an obsession with the mark which the boy only manages to shake the day that, voluntarily this time, he deserves it. A first conditioned response, a cog setting into motion the whole mechanism: our thief

[1] A psychoanalyst would link this current expression to the phrase by which Sartre defines the poet's passive homosexuality: "A prodigious word turns him around and strikes him like a medal: buggered." [There is a word play here between "stuck on his back" — "colleé au dos," and "buggered" — "enculé." Translator's note.]

has become the essence of Thief, the Thief. And prison follows. Writing too.

Obviously, the historical truth is not so simple. On the one hand, there were the years of earliest youth when the Thief was taken under the wing of René de Buxheuil, blind poet, who had the boy instructed in the culture which he himself so blithely offended; the marvelous songs, mewed by the accordions of a Montmartre today much debased, which will be remembered for a long time:

> Tonight it's war on the butte
> All the urchins have declared it!

A more telling fact is that before prison doors shut on the adult Genet, reliable people swear to have seen him in Central Europe, in Prague, an assistant tutor of French. In May 1968, Genet declared to the young occupants of the Sorbonne: "I have one superiority over you; I am without culture." That is the biggest lie he ever told. The philosopher Lucien Goldmann, who does not allow himself to be fooled easily, told me of having been dazzled during their encounter two years previously: "He's terribly *informed;* he's got a lot more than a cultural baggage; he could be named to a chair of philosophy. I didn't expect that." A poet accursed if you like, but not a self-taught man.

In no sense do these observations detract from the esteem and admiration due him and about which he couldn't care less. Henri de Montherlant said that when a man has serious reasons for holding a grudge against humanity, it is proof of a natural goodness to be contented with laughing at it.

It is, then, particularly difficult to establish a "summary" of Genet's different prisons, from the reformatory to Fontevrault. Names rise up at random: Mettray, "which was my childhood," he says, and for the adult: La Santé, Tourelles, Fresnes.

At least the greater part of his work, if not all, saw the light of day in prison: at Fresnes, *Our Lady of the Flowers;* at Tourelles, the *Miracle of the Rose* which tells of experiences at Mettray and Fontevrault. Later, upon France's liberation, there followed Genet's. Sartre wrote in 1952, "For eight years prison doors have not closed upon him." Sartre and Cocteau had acted: Vincent Auriol, president of the Fourth Republic, had pardoned the Thief. His last conviction, if I am not mistaken, prolonged his detention for having "damaged administrative supplies." These "supplies" were paper bags in which the prisoners wrapped one thing and another, and the "damage" consisted in the poems that Genet scribbled on them. That was all.

In the last analysis, it matters little to us that the cycle of the great novels was not written entirely in the shadow of the cell walls, that intermissions which were both long enough and privileged enough to allow the acquisition and investigation of the rudiments of a culture had interrupted the periods of imprisonment. The most important thing is that, in order to permit its venomous rings to live and palpitate, the cycle of novels did require that their author be caged—for a duration of greater or lesser extent—in those various fortresses more closed than the leather sack in which Lou Culafroy's country lover imprisoned his serpents (which he "put in the feminine," saying: the *girls* won't harm you). Never, since the Marquis de Sade, has the immediate relationship between writer and incarceration been more glaring, more necessary. If François Villon expresses above all a defiance of society, John of the Cross the eroticism of a mystic in despair at being on earth, Sade a will to destroy by writing, Oscar Wilde a need to penetrate into the paradise of the youthful ephebes, Paul Verlaine the usefulness of being "confiscated" in order to endure eternally, they bear relationships to their prison holes which are far from being equally univocal, precise, and convincing.* Genet, who is Sade's equal in this respect, contains in himself the various motivating forces of all the others; but he goes further, exalting them sometimes to the point of incandescence. Just as there is a young Marx and a classic Marx, so there are two periods in the Thief's creation: the Genet of the years of detention who is the novelist and poet, and the Genet at liberty who is the man of theater and of action, taking a position for Black Power and giving interviews belonging to literature.[2]

Genet's defiance of society resembles that of Villon, but it does not arise against the background—like the gold background in illuminations—of Villon's fideist faith in *the final goals of man*. A vague religiosity may haunt the imprisoned Genet who puts the following line of Verlaine into Pilorge's mouth:

*[All the above are writers who experienced prison, and are discussed in Françoise d'Eaubonne's book, *Les Ecrivains en Cage.*—Ed.]
[2]Cf. *Le Nouvel Observateur*, June 1970.

Forgive me, my God, for I have sinned!

In addition, the contained flame of a mysticism without faith, born perhaps of that "desperate intelligence" found in the reflection of two lovely knees, runs from one end to the other of his work. But religiosity and mysticism by no means makes a religion; indeed, they are often opposed to it. Genet is lost to God and God to him, as is all of the twentieth century compared with the Middle Ages. Because of this loss his defiance of society takes on an acuteness all the more bitter—such acuteness is unknown to the most progressive of Christians—just as a ferocious light sharpens the shadow thrown by the ruined La Coste, Sade's castle, onto the naked bone of the rock of that region: it is the absence of a sky melted in flames which lends so much existence to the countryside. Only a believing Israelite who knows that the difference between "the one who believes in Heaven and the one who does not" is a Christian's problem and not a Jew's, could enter into this world of Harcamone.[3]

It is hardly necessary to speak of the origin of this defiance. The impassioned refusal opposed by Genet to the temptation of ever complaining, becoming tender, being moved or becoming indignant —refusal which goes so far as to label "imbecilic vandals" the reformers who managed to make the children's prisons disappear[4]— heightens ten times more than the most eloquent demonstration by Jules Vallès the abomination of applying such a fate to children; and this so many years after Oscar Wilde's *Ballad of Reading Gaol,* not in puritan England but in our sweet France with its prison names reminiscent of chivalry: Fontevrault, Clairvaux, Poissy.

"I arrived at the county jail with chains on my feet and on my wrists. I had been prepared by a very long and hard trip in an armoured police-train. There was a hole in the seat and when my gripes got too bad from the jolting, I had only to unbutton myself... There were thirty of us arriving. Half of the convoy was composed of men of about thirty. The rest ranged between eighteen and sixty."

[3]In *Lune d'hiver* (Flammarion, 1970) Claude Vigée explains that a rabbi was asked one day whether there is a future life. His answer: "Maybe there is one, maybe not, but all we know is that our present world has not even the slightest shadow of an existence."

[4]Fifteen years ago, on the program *Carte Blanche,* Genet was supposed to read a speech that finally was not accepted by the station. In it, he developed the argument that reformatories are necessary for preparing the best enemies of society.

Thus an adult, a young adult named Genet, leaves a Paris emptied like an egg, transformed by exodus into a "kind of Pompeii," and makes a pilgrimage to the black sources of memory: the memory of the little "settlers" with shaven heads, that "bad seed" whom stylish people helped the wardens of the Isle of Ré to chase along the Brittany coast in 1932. Here, no legend is necessary: the author of the *Miracle of the Rose* and *The Balcony* could well have run on hands and knees in those ditches scanned by the headlights of elegant cars. Eight years later, he is twisted again by colic, like John of the Cross, and chained, on his way to the jail that awaits him — for what misdemeanours? Housebreaking? Living off immoral earnings? Nothing resembling a murder or the hold-up of a mail train, in any case. Hundreds of others underwent the same treatment while being transferred, for the same kind of infractions of the civil law. For Genet, it is the memory of Mettray and Fontevrault that awaits him. And the caresses that he knew there. To be pronounced with the biting irony of Emmanuelle Riva in the film *Hiroshima mon amour: "At Nevers, she had a youthful love."*

We can go one better than the nineteenth-century tormenters of Oscar Wilde who took him to trial when he was forty. In 1935, the reporter Alexis Danan discovered a four-year-old child in a reformatory. He listened to the confidences of the war orphan who had been sent to the establishment through administrative error. Having ascertained the facts, the director had concluded philosophically: "This kid ought to be in a civil institution, not a penal one, but since they sent him to me, bah! I'll keep him." Indeed, he kept him so long that the child left destroyed for life.[5] Genet lived in this universe which he angrily refuses to baptise with the name of regret or pain: "Of all the state prisons of France, Fontevrault is the most disquieting..." The young housebreaker of 1940 takes a youth cure at the fountain of vitriol; it is through the quickly rediscovered rules and regulations of the state prison that he is going to attempt to live again his "green paradise of childish loves," that is: "the abolished reformatory, the children's work farm that has been destroyed." "When I was led to the reformatory at Mettray, I was fifteen years and seventeen days old." First apprenticeship of hunger in what the idyllic directory called a "large family"; the future

[5]Cf. the collected articles of Alexis Danan and Albert Londres in their *Oeuvres Complètes*.

victims of tuberculosis and rickety children, the offspring of that *bad seed* suffered from "the natural gluttony of childhood that was never sated, even by abundance." A fifteen-year-old was already a "big one" in the former abbey with its summer flower garden which was so easily transformed into a huge resting place ("and since then, flowers have been infernal accessories to me"). A child who escapes, of perhaps thirteen or fourteen, becomes a "doe"; there, among the roses, the wistaria, the trees of rare fragrance, the reformatory inhabited by little starvelings leads its secret life, filling the farmers around with disquiet. "Each peasant received a bounty of fifty francs per escaped inmate, so a real child hunt, with pitchforks, guns, and dogs, occurs every day and night in the Mettray countryside." One of them, Rio, set fire to a farm in order to steal a few clothes to replace his canvas breeches; he made it as far as Orléans. At sixteen, Jean cleared out in turn. He tells how the merest hint of a flirtation between himself and the one who brought him back earned the latter the hole which he left so thin and destroyed that the proud Stolkay "begged bread crusts and slops from the jerks." To cut short the future life of such bad seed is a pious work. "Our scrawninesses fight among themselves, and each one of them against hunger." The same punishment, twenty days in the hole, would strike the child Genet for having answered the warden who challenged him as he was lost in dreaming, in a game proper to his age: "What are you doing there?" "You can see for yourself, I'm going by." He was riding then on one of his dreams; twenty days in the cooler for the crime of equitation, that counts. Especially when the horse is imaginary. But it is one thing more taken away by the lucky Just: the one to be liberated is weakened, the punk will not grow old bones. You had to be a murderer, like Harcamone, to dare to adorn your cap with two sprigs of lilac; he had nothing to lose. And it is in this "castle of shadows" that the child Genet, stripped of all clothing upon his arrival and wrapped in a blanket, will listen for the rest of his life, as soon as he's settled in, to "the hammering on the floor of the heavy shoes moved about by forty or sixty little naked and flayed feet." It is there that he will savor, instead of the punishment prepared by imbeciles, "a grim happiness, heavy with carbonic gas."

The oppression of childhood is always the work of a society in which the male dominates. Ethnologists are aware of this fact: lacking other information in their research among natives, they manage to define women's place in the tribe according to the fate reserved its children. Man wants to perpetuate himself, but he hates what prolongs him; the Oedipus complex should be called the complex of Laius: it is the complex of the father who sees in his son his future murderer and rival for woman, for *his* woman. The increasing importance of the second sex has put an end to the more apparent aspects of such persecution; the rules of boarding schools, of secondary schools, and even the ways and regulations of the barracks have felt this; the work farms disappeared even before the vote was given to women, thanks to their constant access to the domains reserved to men in France before World War II. But what statistics can prove to us that the horror and the guilt to which such descriptions give birth are lived equally by readers of both sexes? Violette Leduc draws the correct conclusion: "Does it happen that he is indulgent? If he is, he's indulgent silently; thus, we believe that we are murdering the poor boy that he was." This *we* really belongs to the second sex.[6]

The monstruous stupidities with which the "lack of imagination" analyzed by Wilde has marked the heart and body of the greatest living genius of French letters, are perpetuated in the pathological elements of his present behavior. Conqueror, praised to the skies, the aging poet cannot stop avenging the "poor boy that he was"; and since there are no longer any wardens nor any reformatory, and since the petty larcenies perpetrated after leaving prison have never been enough to recommit an author before whom every magistrate blows low, he continues to chastise at random everything approaching him—although without excess, for he only manages to be vicious in literature. It is his revenge on an idiotic society, this mental confusion between an old warden and a friendship incapable of innocence as soon as it is addressed to him. Thus, during a dinner given in his honor by an unfortunate woman with great talent who admires him to distraction, the man in whom a "child who prefers himself to all else" (Sartre) survives, overturns his plate and bestrews the tiles with the remains of that poor little feast of good will. (Is her crime to have been a woman, like the mother who rejected him?) Something of the torturers of yore triumphs in the profound neuroses which such a gesture betrays; those torturers win out who tried so stubbornly to mark for life—preferably physically, but mentally too, why not? let's get on with it—the young flesh destined

[6]Violette Leduc, *La Folie en tête*. [English trans.: *Mad in Pursuit*].

to feed their petty bourgeois demon, until they could find better: for Fontevrault, Mettray, and other all-too-beautiful gardens were followed by the rosary linking Dachau to Belsen-Belsen.

Thus Genet cleared for himself a path on the fringes near to the one that guided François Villon: although Genet's way is more complex, both paths have the same origin in defiance. If Villon's appetites, although less unusual, were just about as difficult to satisfy in his century as were those of a poor and obscure Genet in ours, François chose just as deliberately to appease them by totally scorning the social—but not the divine—laws, rather than in the way reserved to intellectuals, those poor relations of the rich. Neither François nor Jean is a pure product of his social class or of his historical moment; but both, to about the same extent, bear loud witness against the iniquities of those two determining forces. And the undeniable traces of their deformation bear testimony too, since it is due to one of these factors that there are such traces, or at least, without such determining factors their lives would not have borne such bitter consequences.

Genet differs the most from John of the Cross in that he is fascinated—at least the first Genet, the one important for this study— by sainthood; he had not yet read in Sartre that sanctity is the "squalor of the soul." John of the Cross, on the other hand, is not at all interested in such squalor; he is filthy with great unaffectedness; his dirtiness radiates from him and perfumes more sweetly than the hygiene of our pasteurized century. Like Georges Bataille, Genet tries to make Evil into good, to assimilate it to the written word; he wants to canonize Divine who, although she does not write, is born of his writing. To make out of her a little "Saint Bridget of Hell," as Georges Bernanos said of one of his heroines who cuts herself to pieces with thrusts of the knife. Divine slices herself up over many pages, and she does it much better than Sade's Justine, for she uses intelligence. Did Pascal not teach us that we need as great a capacity "to reach nothingness as to reach the whole"? In fact; "What to do, in the midst of this situation? Revolt is part of the same world...and by no means leads to *the hour of greater illumination.*"[7] Unable to face up to the situation, obliged to be "in its midst," Divine takes the same attitude in her effort towards Nothingness as does a saint like John of the Cross who destroys himself

[7]Kostas Axelos, *Vers une pensée planétaire.*

to arrive at the whole; but in her it is a premeditated subterfuge; in
the author of the *Spiritual Canticle,* the movement may not be quite
spontaneous, but it is free, or at least, *more* free. "Let the Eternal
pass by in the form of a pimp," mocks Genet. Why not? Lautréamont
already showed Him to us in the bordello, losing one of His hairs.
We should see here an effect less of sacrilege than of modesty. And
it sounds, although situated poles apart from it, like John of the
Cross's identification of erotic pleasure with the embrace of the
Divinity. Genet, who is not a fideist, believes nonetheless in an
Absolute. For a while he wanted to entitle his *Miracle of the Rose,*
The Children of the Angels, from a Bible verse which once came to
his attention. He toyed with the idea that the "bad seed," stripped of
everything but rich in the potential crimes expected of their fru-
ition, were the "youthful descendants, learned from birth, of Angels
and women." And again, this key phrase: "The life I lead requires
as its condition that abandonment of earthly things which the
Church, like all churches, demands of its saints. Then this life opens,
forces a door that leads into the miraculous." Once again we find
those "windows opening into the realm of holy light" of which the
Kabbalists speak. Conclusion: "And sainthood can also be recognized by the fact that it leads to Heaven via the pathway of sin."
(Miracle of the Rose)

To formulate "Saint Genet" is already to enter into the realm of
comedy, even if that comedy be only in using martyrdom as a social
expression; Saint John of the Cross may be called Fray Juan and no
one will question his sainthood, just as a lawyer without his robe
and in a coat and tie is still a lawyer; the extent of their knowledge
and not their ceremonial titles is what is in question. The more profound relationship between the sixteenth-century monk and the
twentieth-century Thief lies elsewhere then: on the level of writing.
For writing is not an "expression" which serves as one means or another, as the vehicle of one passenger or another; it is a whole: when
we cease to be dualists, we stop believing in an opposition between
form and content. If these two poets had not defied their prison
experiences by an attempt at annihilation and humiliation even
more profound than those experiences *imposed* on them, if both
had not resolved to improve upon their condition and to choose
these horrors, would their voices send such corresponding echoes
to one another across the *untouchable wall?* And isn't it tempting to

imagine Genet as the author of these esoteric verses composed in solitary confinement:

> For well I know the fountain that pours forth and flows
> the night notwithstanding,
> That eternal and secret fountain,
> how well I know where lies its hiding place
> the night notwithstanding.
> ...I know well there can be nothing else so lovely,
> that heaven and earth are slaked by it,
> the night notwithstanding.
> ...I know well that its currents run rich,
> watering the hells and the heavens and the peoples
> the night notwithstanding.
> ...To Him it calls all creatures
> and they are sated by that water, but in darkness,
> for it is night.

A proud conduct of failure: this definition of the behavior of Genet-the-younger refers us back to Sade. There is justice in Jean too: objectively victim, he becomes, in the domain of language, the executioner of the honest souls who put him there. Like Sade, he seeks, "groaning," that Evil which suddenly becomes a Good. The author himself recognizes this in *Funeral Rites:* "If Evil excites such a passion it is because it is itself a Good." Nothing is more consistent with the spirit of Sade than this reversal of values. And here again there is a reflexive touch owed to prison; above and beyond the rapid and coarse utilitarian criteria which have led to life imprisonment, a prisoner of quality seeks to define in the midst of silence, of privation, of the reduction of man to his simplest elements, the metaphysical essence of all possible Good and of all possible Evil, without any relationship to how judges—and ruffians—may understand them. More lucid than Sade who despairs in his work of ever living the Evil he adores and which continually slips away from him, because Nature wants the worst, Genet loved that somber god even to the point of desiring his own failure: that is, he loved "the impossibility of living even to the systematic destruction of his own life."[8]

[8]Sartre, *Saint Genet: Actor and Martyr.*

It has been said of Sade that a writer takes up the pen for the first time in order to displease; cannot this also be said of Genet? But both of them, before this second motive, already had a burning desire: to please oneself, to give oneself pleasure, in the most auto-erotic sense of the term, and that precisely within the condition of prisoner, which the exterior world reduces on purpose to whatever is the most unpleasant, not only in the eyes of others but also in the eyes of the prisoner himself. To escape the horror of a moment that, like the hell of Theseus, is always the same, that "time reduced to the pure state" which Simone Weil reckons to be the very essence of damnation, first Sade and then Genet had to escape into the unlimited duration of the dream which is also the spatiality of the tale and of the poem, by means of the onanism which Cocteau so rightly symbolized in *Beauty and the Beast* by the magic glove that transports into other times and other places. This is perhaps what escapes Georges Bataille when, in *Literature and Evil,* he reproaches Genet with betraying his "sovereignty" by a refusal of communication. Communication had been refused to Genet in the name of the Just; according to his Cainistic logic,[9] it is his duty to himself to have "wanted" this absence of communication in order to assume fully responsibility for it; and, in fact, in this way he establishes a communication to the second power that consists in displeasing; similarly, Sade, in his need for victims, remains a humanist in comparison to the executioner by trade, or to the simple egotist. But it is nonetheless true that the necessity of fleeing an unbearable tension—with the help of the sustained masturbation of a scenario endlessly reworked, enriched, and which little by little becomes a novel—can be found at the base of this work; in short, it is in a greediness for pleasure either modest or sharp that this moral epic of asceticism in Evil began.[10]

[9]"Cain," second book in *Saint Genet.*

[10]In his *Saint Genet,* Sartre has written more than a masterfully important work; the book seems to us to be the cornerstone of a monument which no one since has dared to touch; it is impossible to speak of homosexuality—among other things— in the same terms since that work, although that is what almost everyone has done. However—and this fits in logically with the structure of the work since a perfect work must close on itself and *Saint Genet* does exactly the opposite—we find again that curious limitation which is so Sartrian, the total lack of importance given to pleasure as a motivating force. We are willing to admit that pleasure is as equivocal as is suffering; it seems, however, that not recognizing this factor may be, on a certain level, the price that superior people, who have constantly to observe them-

The two impulses are linked to one another, no doubt; the pleasure of defying and of scandalizing the invisible but by no means imaginary reader certainly accompanies the solitary pleasures that the fathers of Justine and Divine give to themselves. Their books are open letters to the judge, to the policeman, to the honest man outside; the two prisoners, reduced by incarceration to the dependency and revolt of childhood, think to defile the enemy with sacrilegious ejaculations, by doing hommage to murder and to the vices, just as the furious child shows by a revengeful piss that "the ego affirms itself by opposing." The creator does not innovate but rather transcends his experience of animality, of early childhood; in the two literary cases of which we speak, what the author chooses of this experience is the "polymorphous perverse," which is obviously dreamed. No doubt it is useless to try to establish the chronology of creation. But in this process, inescapably, just as sensation precedes perception, so the appetite for pleasure fans and renews the voluptuousness of a revenge against the authorities. "My victory is verbal," says Genet; Sade could have signed that.

What expresses best the fusion of these two motivating forces of the work, as much for Sade as for Genet, is that they give the same result: an ecstacy at the same time erotic and agressive which is translated so delightfully in the portraits of both their favorite heroes. There is a resemblance such that we could believe, always excepting a few particularities of style, that the authors had exchanged pens:

"Born false, hard, imperious, barbarous, egotistical, equally prodigal in his pleasures and avaricious in his usefulness, deceitful, gourmand, drunken, cowardly, sodomitical, incestuous, murderous, incendiary, thieving..."

Such is the portrait of the Duke of Blangis, one of the four monsters of the *120 Days of Sodom*. But a final touch is lacking:

"A resolute child might have frightened this colossus, and as soon as he could no longer employ ruses and betrayals to rid himself of his enemy, he became timid and cowardly..."

Now this:

---

selves to keep from becoming inhuman, must pay for their superiority. Sartre does not seem to realize any more than in *What is Literature* that even the greatest among us can be originally motivated by the need for pleasure; and that onanism, homosexuality and literature are, above all else, pleasures. Sometimes we wish that the most important French philosopher of our epoch would reread La Mettrie.

"Armand's face was false, cunning, cruel, surly, brutal. He was a brute... He laughed little and without candor... In himself... I think he elaborated his will to impose, apply and render visible hypocrisy, stupidity, spitefulness, servility and to obtain in this demonstration the most obscene success on his whole person."

That is from the *Thief's Journal.* But a last touch is lacking. It is a confederate who gives it: when Robert reproaches Genet with stealing only from old men, Armand inflicts on him a most Sade-like lesson in morality:

"It's not old men I attack, it's old ladies. Not men, women. And I pick the weakest. What I want is the bucks. A good job is the one you carry off."

And so we know that this Armand, fascinating by virtue of his very hideousness, is as "splendidly cowardly" as Mignon, as Stilitano; on the heels of Sade, Genet salvages cowardliness as an erotic attraction. In the case of Armand or the Duke of Blangis, the monster is only admirable because he escapes any possibility of being admired by the honest men on the outside. Harcamone, the wonderful murderer, still maintains some ties with humanity through the disinterestedness of his crimes; by his ignominious robberies, Armand cuts himself off radically from human kind. It seems a rather unexpected naiveté on Bataille's part to call such a taking of inhumanity's part a refusal of all access to communication. In fact, he never asks this question about Sade; Bataille recognizes that sovereignty has been conquered in Sade's writings, thanks to the latter's audacity at having known, in the face of the dangerous bursts of his own desires, how to pose the "unfathomable question that they ask in truth of all men" rather than forgetting these desires like everyone else. We know from Jules Janin and other romantic writers that all men are "sadistic"; and since Freud we know too that they are all "homosexuals"; it is strange that Georges Bataille does not see by this simple parallel that a communication—which may horrify both partners—is established, and indeed, must be established, between Genet-the-younger and his reader, just as between Sade and his: from this overwhelming revelation is born the sovereignty that Bataille contests in the modern writer."[11]

---

[11] This is not the only thing with which Bataille reproaches Genet. He thinks the admiration of Sartre is "in part exaggerated" and judges: "Nothing colder, nothing less moving, under the glittering parade of words, than the famous passage in which Genet recounts Harcamone's death..." Moving for whom? What does not touch

Genet may be linked directly to Wilde, as Sartre has shown in a passage quoted earlier in this work. Both, as the philosopher explains, want to penetrate into the edenic world of the ephebes who are "dressed in priceless stuffs and caress precious stones"; but each author uses very different means. Genet takes the material for an imaginary paradise where he knew a "grim happiness, heavy with carbonic gas," from the vile reality that surrounds him. Wilde, like Verlaine in his "Crimen Amoris," constructs a paradise out of erotic and literary memories in order to escape the very reality that Sartre maintains had "broken his back" at Reading Gaol. Wilde tries to persuade where Genet transgresses; the first entreats the world, the second supplants it by an image so transcendent that it could be said to belong to a universe of madmen. In the *Miracle of the Rose* Genet evokes "an adolescent...honest enough to remember that Mettray was a paradise." Bataille recognizes correctly the "pathetic" use of that adjective: "The Mettray house of correction was a hell!" Only he is wrong to believe in an evolution of Genet's "honesty" when the latter admits that Fontevrault is populated by wretches with rotten teeth who are cowardly, who stink, who bore him with their "unequalable stupidity," and in whom he no longer finds anything but "the outrageous caricature of the beautiful criminals that I saw there when I was twenty." Genet is thirty now, and Bataille draws rapid conclusions from the fact that Mettray and Fontevrault are populated and regulated in about the same manner; he forgets the most important, the phrase "when I was twenty..." The worst, like the best, gets worse with time; Genet does not recognize a mirage, he remarks upon an aging. And that is the great difference between the experiences of Genet and Wilde: the first enters prison at fifteen years and seventeen days old, the other at forty. Perhaps we ought to seek the radical opposition of their literary attitudes toward the prison universe in this fact, more than in their respective

---

Georges Bataille moved Violette Leduc deeply. She tells of her emotional upheaval in *La Folie en tête:* "I reread the *Miracle of the Rose.* Fever, thrills, shivers, the same as when I first read it nineteen years ago. For whom did I feel feverish? For Harcamone condemned to death. I reread Genet, I thrilled with pleasure. I will do so again in twenty years." The word "moving," the word "cold," are hardly the words of a *critic;* I am willing to admit that Bataille's objectivity is but a decoy; but a declared subjectivity that goes that far—what a want of decorum! [An excerpt from Georges Bataille's essay is to be found in this volume.—Ed.]

temperaments, more than in the social difference between a modish author and a corrupted youth raised by Welfare. Wilde never knew the atmosphere of the young hive that even the most hideous prison can assume for a child shut up with other children, nor the honey that can be drawn from it by a poet.

The difference, even the antithesis, between their works that came out of prison, is found even more in the moral attitudes of the two authors. Homosexuality is never taken into account in the experience which may be called "concentrationary" that Oscar Wilde had of Reading. At the time that the Labouchère law was abolished during a celebrated English debate several years ago, one of the adversaries of the punishment that was applied to homosexuals had humourously declared that to send one of them to a men's prison was equivalent to "putting a libertine into a harem to cure him of lechery"—but this question was never asked by Wilde. For Genet, the prison universe, if it did not determine his eroticism, was at least the athanor, the closed place in which the alchemist's Great Work is slowly prepared. "That ignoble matter which Wilde exerted himself not to see..." (Sartre) bore down on him nonetheless during his detour by way of the castle of Reading. What did he make of it? Certainly not a poem like Genet, for the *Ballad* is by no means a canticle to a matter transmuted by verbal magic like the one in which Genet finds his "victory." But Wilde gets something out of it nonetheless: a protest. Protest based on a discovery of this matter, and of the relationship that men carry on with it under compulsion. Another discovery is hidden like the yellow of an egg in the innermost part of the first; it is that "each man kills the thing he loves," and in this Wilde crosses Genet's path. (The latter's dream of murdering a handsome boy takes many forms in the course of his cycle of novels; Erik brings down a child; Riton kills Erik; in *Funeral Rites* Genet kills the lover he gave by procuration to a militiaman; Querelle of Brest kills the Armenian he is tempted to love, etc.) But despite this important discovery, Wilde leaves prison more a "moralist" than a poet, and in this sense he situates himself at the opposite pole from Genet. No doubt Genet is a moralist above all— in Cocteau's sense of the word—just as Sade was; but this phrase no longer means anything if we apply it indiscriminately to both Wilde and Genet. We can say in all fairness that Wilde remains conformist even in his nonconformism of Reading. The name "writer with a commitment" certainly fits him more than it does Genet-the-younger. Because the ignominy of cell life allowed him to pass through Narcissus's mirror, he speaks of "thanking God on my knees," as would a simple Verlaine. Even more, by his press campaign he obtained from the powers-that-be a reform in the penitentiary system toward more humanity and softness, thereby placing himself among those whom Genet calls "vandals"; similarly, Sade curses the reformers Pinel and Esquirol who had made impossible the grim paradise of the Charenton madhouse, where libertines could rape and murder the demented at the height of their passion. Nothing is further from the liberated Wilde than Genet's sentence in *The Child Criminal:* "Suffer a poet who is also an enemy to speak to you as poet and as enemy." Here, the antagonisms between the two individuals are revealed, much more than in the different manners—the first "pleasing and facile," the second violent and even violating—in which the two poets have chosen to aim at the same mark: to make of beauty a machine of war and thereby to inject a subtle poison into the world that has condemned the two of them. If Genet went incomparably further along that road it is because we can apply to him, more than to Wilde, the words with which Proust describes the diabolical Mademoiselle Vinteuil, a lesbian and parricide: "A sadist of her kind is an artist of evil, something a wholly bad creature would not be, for in that case the evil would not have been external, but would have seemed natural to her."

To understand exactly in what measure Genet wanted to be prisoner *before* rather than *after* his first adult conviction—for the childish condemnation, although creating that conditioned reflex of which Sartre has shown the mechanism, was neither so determining nor so rapidly effective as it might seem from reading *Saint Genet*—certainly, we would have to have more documentation on the "hidden life" of the writer. We could then decide the part played by the will to be exiled from the world which we have discerned in the course of this study in the very different behaviors of a Verlaine or of a Wilde. A psychoanalyst of the current type would reduce this "sullenness" (the term is Sartre's) to a will to punish the absent mother by fleeing her in the form of a Mother-Society; we know that the truth is not so simple. This particular wound of the abandoned child seems responsible rather for the "Phaëthon complex" to which so many children born to unknown parents are subject,[12] and which Genet describes in speaking of the mania of belonging to nobility from which the little orphaned "settlers" of Mettray suffer. Similarly, the missing genitor seems to have left a gaping hole in Jean's affectivity, a hole nothing can fill and in which he tried, for a time, to lose his thirst for an absolute called Evil.

However, perhaps there is less heroic theater in his repeated affirmation of having wanted everything that has happened to him than Sartre has found in it. Of course, the latter did not try to make Genet into a pure product of social misfortune who recovers his freedom in a choice made *after the fact* of that misfortune; that would be to make the capital work the philosopher has devoted to the poet into a rationalism which would be rather crude as a psychology. But, however crude this schema may seem, social misfortune remains one of the most determining factors of that knot of contradictions which is Genet — as it does for all of us — but in a more transcendent fashion for the writer than for us since he is at the same time objectively more *constrained,* and subjectively more *free.* Now, the examination of the real facts would undoubtedly lead us to attenuate the force of this judgment by rediscovering the part of choice, *at the origin,* in the misfortune and injustice that struck the Thief. If he benefited from a bourgeois education in his adolescence, even if only from a second-rate Homer, and if during his adulthood he can be found giving French lessons abroad, the machine thrown into gear by a theft from peasants would seem less fatalistic, less engineered by the world alone; it would seem that in this situation Genet would say with Kafka: "In the fight between the world and yourself, the world comes in second." He was incited, but not forced, by the need to go to the very limits of misfortune, because to stop halfway would be to forgive it. Indeed, it is because he is implacable that Genet wants to be a victim.

In Verlaine, there is nothing like this; prison would remain for him, really and objectively, a solution to an untenable situation: his murderous impulses, the alcoholism which stoked them, the tor-

---

[12]The tendency — which can become neurosis — of a child born of an unknown father to invent an illustrious parent, and to wish to prove it by enterprises conducting to catastrophe, is called a Phaëthon complex, in memory of the son of Apollo who, furious over his illegitimacy, wanted to drive the chariot of the sun and was struck down by Jupiter.

ment of his "bimetallism" made of Mons a refuge into which he threw
himself. Nothing further, apparently, from Genet's attitude. However, we do not know nor will we know for some time to what extent,
after the horror of years wasted in a reformatory, prison seemed to
the adult Genet—who was haunted as much by his memories of "infernal happiness" as by the bitter problem of his social insignificance,
of his inability to prove himself and to discover himself in his own
eyes—not an asylum but an intermediate solution, at the same time
as it meant the "return to the sources" that we have discussed.

We can see that Genet has garnered something in passing from
all the different antisocial writers encountered in these pages. Not
from any desire on his part, of course; there is really no relationship
between his appeal to a quintessence and the infantilism of a Verlaine who plays at being Villon. Like Phidias, Jean seems to have
borrowed from each author some characteristic to serve him in building a statue that is more like him than he is himself.

Some believed that Sartre had sterilized Genet's genius after 1952
by devoting to him a "preface" as heavy as a tombstone. Genet's
silence led them to speak of stupor. In fact, it was the condition of
being a free man and not the heavy and sumptuous commentary
that had, like a splendid court mantle, forced the sovereign's spirit
to lie idle (for don't children's tales teach us that the king is always
naked?). At the end of his work, Sartre remarked that Genet no longer knew very well why to continue writing; only the ridiculous
thrusts of the late François Mauriac and the late André Rousseaux,
if anyone had been able to take them seriously, would have been
enough to encourage Genet to continue his evil example. But glory
kills the scandalous; freedom and success had exerted on him the
same effect that the Church had so subtly attempted on John of the
Cross in awarding him the Prize of the Catholic Office: they neu-
tralized him. He needed long voyages, "erotic errings," according to
Axelos's expression. He needed "information" in Lucien Goldmann's
words, an education which he pursued as far as a diploma which he
obviously never presented, in order to discover at last, with a commitment of a libertarian type, new reasons for undermining the
social, and hence, for writing. In *The Screens,* he formulated a conclusion which is his most frightening one precisely because it summarizes the human condition—the letter kills the spirit, but the
spirit cannot survive without the letter, and that is why Being and

Existence will never be fused: *there are no absolute truths except ones about which one can do nothing.* That is why each ideal, political or otherwise, forms with the real the eternal couple of the criminal and his victim. Yes, we cannot not kill what we love! More than Wilde, he who pushed this discovery to the limit was certainly the Inclement Thief. As Violette Leduc says: "He is silently indulgent."

Our Lady of the Flowers

by Brigid Brophy

J'entends déjà tomber avec des chocs funèbres
Le bois retentissant sur le pavé des cours.*

Thus Baudelaire; and the *retentissement,* having reverberated down a century, was caught up and reissued by the opening line of Jean Genet's long poem, "Le Condamné à Mort":

Le vent qui roule un coeur sur le pavé des cours.†

The first thing to realize (and Sartre, it seems, doesn't realize the first thing—or most of those that come after) is that Genet virtually is Baudelaire. Not that he's—except in the deliberate re-reverberations—an imitator. Being Baudelaire means being as original as Baudelaire. Genet is, however, a Baudelaire of the twentieth-century, with the result that he writes finer poetry in prose than in verse. "Le Condamné" is tinged with Reading Gaolery. It is the prose of "Notre-Dame des Fleurs" which defines and realizes the most cogent mythology of poetic images since Baudelaire's.

Our present disesteem of writing (or, more probably, our insensitivity to it) is bitterly shown up by the fact that the English reviewers, approaching Genet as philosopher or sociologist, have scarcely noticed that he is a *writer.* This must be quite personally bitter to Mr. Bernard Frechtman, who has made a brilliant translation into American: clever when need be—when Genet, seemingly

"Our Lady of the Flowers." From Brigid Brophy, *Don't Never Forget* (New York: Holt, Rinehart and Winston; London: Jonathan Cape Ltd., 1966). Used by permission of Jonathan Cape Ltd.

*["Already I hear, falling with funereal blows, the wood resounding on the cobblestone of the courtyards." ("Chant d' Automne".)—Ed.]
† ["The wind that rolls a heart on the cobblestones of the courtyards."—Ed.]

defying translation, writes of himself as "exilé aux confins de l'immonde (qui est du non-monde)," Mr Frechtman ingeniously comes up with "...the confines of the obscene (which is the off-scene of the world)"—but rising above cleverness to positive inspiration as constructions and paragraphs pursue and come excellently close to Genet's very cadences. The tiny points where one demurs are probably the fault of one or other of the languages concerned. That "amours" comes out as "carnal pleasures" must be blamed either on French for not possessing a separate word for sex or on the United States for not possessing the English middle-class tradition that everyone has at least boarding-school French, a tradition with some horrible implications but which would in this case have permitted "amours" to stand untranslated except into italics—and would also have left the character called Mignon as Genet christened him, instead of which he is translated, and slightly watered-down, into Darling.

The fashion for scarcely noticing Genet's imagery is set by Sartre, who stands sentinel over this edition in a long introduction (consisting, in fact, of the relevant chapter from *Saint Genet*). True, Sartre has a section headed "The Images"; but he turns out to mean things like Genet's "will-to-unify," his desire to *"verify"* his *conceptualism"* and his Platonism—which "one would think...at times is a kind of Aristotelianism." He is noble and grotesque, this impresario who, apparently blind and deaf to the talents of his prodigy, nonetheless intuitively—and generously—feels there is *something* in him, and goes stumbling round and round while he tries to think what on earth it can be. (Brilliance of metaphor, melody of language —you can shout the answers; but he only turns in another muddled circle, trying with good will to catch what you're saying.) There he stands, the gangling and admirable professor, goggling through his global spectacles, making lunges with his butterfly net—and above him swoops, sombre and solid, dazzling in smoothed black and white marble, a vast, wing-spread, baroque angel of death.

Genet's images are all of death: to be more precise, all of funerals. His is the imagery of the *chapelle ardente*. It is in seductively beautiful bad taste. The book starts with a shrine of faces torn from the illustrated papers, photographs Genet has stuck to the wall of his prison cell and whom he takes as his imaginary lovers when he masturbates on his "straw mattress, which has already been stained by more than a hundred prisoners." The faces make a "merveil-

leuse éclosion de belles et sombres fleurs"—funeral flowers. All
these handsome young men are murderers who have been executed.
The heads, cut off in the photographs, have in fact been cut off by
the guillotine. For "the most purely criminal" of them Genet has
made frames—"using the same beads with which the prisoners
next door make funeral wreaths." The form of the book is a string-
ing together of images into a funeral wreath. It is part meditation,
part memory, part masturbation. The whole book is, according to
Sartre, "the epic of masturbation," but epic it is not: it is *not* a story,
though it includes episodes of masterly narrative; and it is about
sainthood, not heroism.

It was not Sartre who invented Saint Genet but Genet himself—
in this book where he is identified with the character named Divine:
"it is my own destiny...that I am draping (at times a rag, at times a
court robe) on Divine's shoulders." "Tantôt haillon, tantôt manteau
de cour"...but always female. Divine is an "il" always referred to by
Genet, and almost always by her own thoughts, as "elle." Only
when the narrative goes back to her country childhood does Divine
become for sustained passages "il," the boy Lou Culafroy; once she
has come to Paris, where she lives as a prostitute, sharing her attic
with a succession, an attic frieze, of handsome "macs," Divine is in
permanent travesty: literally so in a phosphorescent night-scene at
a drag party, and always so in imagination. On the very evening of
her arrival in Paris, she rises from a cafe table "wriggling in a spray
of flowers and strewing swishes and spangles with an invisible
furbelow." Having established that Divine is himself, Genet goes on
"I want to strip her of every vestige of happiness so as to make a
saint of her"—to make, in other words, Saint Genet, a saint in drag,
like a doll-madonna in a lacy skirt.

Calling the book an epic, Sartre has ignored the information
Genet gives: "I raised egoistic masturbation to the dignity of a cult."
The whole nature of the book is stated in the *cult*. Genet does everything, strings his entire wreath, with—in the Catholic sense—an
intention. His opening sequence is strung from a clutch of queers
with flowering, frocked or girlish names—"Mimosa I, Mimosa II,
Mimosa mi-IV, Première Communion, Angéla, Monseigneur,
Castagnette, Régine": a "long litany," he calls them, "of creatures
who are glittering names." These he threads (they themselves are
carrying "wreaths of glass beads, the very kind I make in my cell")
into a black funeral cortège in the rain. (The priest leading it be-

comes lost in an erotic fantasy.) The funeral is of Divine herself.
The book begins and ends with the death of Divine; in between, she
has betrayed herself to the police for a minor crime, and a murderer has betrayed himself and been executed. Genet is having a
masturbation fantasy, but he is also dedicating an altar. As he tells
us at the start, meditating before his shrine of assassins, "c'est en
l'honneur de leurs crimes que j'écris mon livre."

Noticing the insistence on hosts and masses, and the tributary
garland of the title itself (in fact Notre-Dame des Fleurs is the name
of the handsomest young murderer), Sartre mistakes the psychology
of religious observance for religious faith, leaps at the notion of
the ages of faith and hammers in his introduction at the idea of a
medieval Genet. It is a ghastly howler, of the sort liable to be made
by the tone-deaf. Anyone with an eye for a style—any antique dealer
or auctioneer—could have told Sartre Genet is baroque. His essence is that he's post-Counter Reformation. (It can even be demon-
strated scholastically. Divine's death-blood is "revealed with dramatic insistence, as does a Jesus the gilded chancre where gleams
His flaming Sacred Heart." The cult of the Sacred Heart was not observed before 1648.) Like the "litanies" and the "ex-voto dans le
goût espagnol" of Baudelaire's vocabulary, Genet's is the over-
blown, peony-sized language of devotional flowers that did not come
into existence until faith had been challenged from outside. It is
necessary, precisely, to *counter* the Reformation: you must screw
your eyes tight shut and *exclude* the outside world—that is, you
must *induce* the images.

As it happens, faith has been emptied out from this tight-shut
imaginary world. The idiom of rites and cults is employed to induce a state not of grace but of mind. Genet says nothing about religion, either way. It is his literature, not his faith, that is Catholic.
Linguistically and psychologically, the idiom of the erotic and the
idiom of the religious are the same; therefore the two are wholly
the same for Genet, who is utterly a psychological linguist. When
Notre-Dame des Fleurs is—"la bouche ouverte en o"—penetrated
by Mignon ("sa queue lourde et lisse, aussi polie et chaude qu'une
colonne au soleil"—the cult practised by Genet's imagination is
a phallic cult), he is Bernini's St. Teresa pierced to the heart of
ecstasy by an angelic spear. Indeed, one of Divine's lovers is a soldier
named Gabriel, whom Divine addresses as "Archange." And Genet
is an ecstatic—"mon âme de cambrioleur extatique." The *cam-*

brioleur is interchangeable with the saint. The confessional is interchangeable with the outdoor lavatory in the country (in both places "the most secret part of human beings came to reveal itself"), where the boy Culafroy "roosts" ("juché sur le siège de bois"), listening to the rain on the zinc roof and aggravating his "bien-être triste" by half-opening the door and letting himself be desolated by the sight of "the wet garden and the pelted vegetables." An invocation may in psychological fact be offered interchangeably to a divinity or a lover. (We all pray when we are in love—to the person we are in love with.) When Divine is arrested on the boulevard, she is singing the *Veni, Creator,* of which the essential item is the *Veni,* the inducing of a presence. For Genet, the essential item throughout is that rites are performed with an intention, gestures are, like masses, offered—whom or what for is not the point. First, induce the images. When they exist to be dedicated, you can offer them to whom you will, just as the "thou" of a sonnet can be equated with whatever initials you care to write at the top.

Sartre is for once construing Genet right when he traces to masturbation fantasies the peculiar technique of Genet's story-telling, whereby he admits to making up his characters as he goes along, dithers visibly about what form to make them up in, signals in advance that such a one will presently enter the book and sometimes leaves the reader free to imagine the dialogue two of them have on meeting. He is a resurrectionist, treating his characters like zombies. Even Divine, who is Genet, has to be led by the hand by Genet— to sainthood: "Et moi, plus doux qu' un mauvais ange, par la main je la conduis."*

The technique of ushering his characters into the book permits Genet to create effects of baroque theatricality, as if he were seeing them on to the stage down a *trompe l'oeil* avenue. Thus "Our Lady of the Flowers here makes his solemn entrance through the door of crime, a secret door, that opens on to a dark but elegant stairway." This is *trompe l'oeil* indeed, for having effected Notre-Dame's entrance into the book Genet continues "Our Lady mounts the stairway... He is sixteen when he reaches the landing"—and at this point the narrative merges into actuality; the character is on a real landing, about to knock and go into a room and murder an old man.

The rhythm, whether of masturbation or of Genet's prose, is de-

*["And I, gentler than a wicked angel, lead her by the hand."—Ed.]

signed to induce the images to take on enough solidity and durability
to be dwelt on. And it is interesting that Divine's sex life is lived almost wholly in the imagination. It is not only that most of the narrative is the product of Genet's masturbatory fantasy: even when the
narrative steps wholly inside the play-within-a-play, the sexual acts
with partners do not replace masturbation, on which Divine still
depends to "finish off." The acts with others do not advance Divine
towards direct sexual satisfaction; they serve to consolidate and
sharpen the contrast on the images—so that in the end the images
almost take off into a detached sex life, coupling and enjoying the
process on their own.

Indeed, it is the images rather than the characters that Genet
animates, which is why he is more poet than novelist. The independent life he charges them with is so erotic that it is no surprise
to find them combining; they themselves are the population of a
gallant and promiscuous society. Since the images combine, Genet's
mythology is metamorphotic. (This is a point Sartre half-takes; he
keeps using the word *metamorphosis,* but without much direction.)
In two sentences heavy with nineteenth-century—with Second
Empire—baroque, Genet includes and surpasses all the fusions of
image and the evocations of decor attempted so pretentiously by
Marienbad. Genet writes: "For low masses are said at the end of the
halls of big hotels, where the mahogany and marble light and blow
out candles. A mingled burial service and marriage takes place
there in secret from one end of the year to the other."

That is the conjurer's *trompe l'oeil* of the author who speaks of
"my taste for imposture, my taste for the sham, which could very
well make me write on my visiting cards: "Jean Genet, bogus Count
of Tillancourt."

The furniture actually lights and blows out candles by one of
Genet's most poignant devices, a fusion of images in the melting-
moment of a syntactical plus semantic paradox. When Divine and
her men leave the all night drag party, "the dawn was tight, a little
tight, not very sure of itself, on the point of falling and vomiting."
And when the boy Culafroy waits in a moonlit country garden,
among the washing, hoping the man he loves will come, "La lune
sonna dix heures."

Indeed, the entire language of *Notre-Dame des Fleurs* is built
up from the grammatical metamorphosis of "il" into "elle." From

this flowers the queer *argot*—which is used only by "male" queers; for Divine to use it would be as unseemly as "whistling with her tongue and teeth...or putting her hands in her trousers pockets and keeping them there." Even so, the metamorphosis is never fixed. It is a film Genet can run backwards at will—and which he does, when with the meticulous and dispassionate love of an early watercolourist recording exotic fauna, he describes that bizarre change of life that comes to queers at thirty, the moment when a beloved crosses over and becomes a lover. Suddenly Divine does whistle, does put her hands in her pockets—until she discovers that after all she "had not become virile; she had aged. An adolescent now excited her...."

I feel tolerably sure that this particular metamorphosis has a reflection in Genet's own name. (Is it his real one? He seems to hint not by calling his boy-self Culafroy. Accident or assumption as it may be, Genet is not the man to have failed to contemplate—to make a cult of—his own name.) Take him straight and he is *un genet,* a jennet, a Spanish horse—an image, to his mind, as another of his transformation scenes demonstrates, of virility: but put, as surely his own imagination often does put, a circumflex on the second *e,* and he becomes some kind of flowering gorse or furze—a companion to all those secondary characters named Mimosa who weave a decorative and feminine garland through the book.

Genet plays paradoxes and transformations not only with words and single images but with myths: Christian (Mignon goes to church to pray "Our Mother Which art in heaven...") or pagan (Genet is so queer that for him it is the sailors who charm the Sirens) or both (were Genet making Divine not in his own but in the image of the men who command his love, he would make her "with flat and polished cheeks, heavy eyelids, pagan knees so lovely that they reflected the desperate intelligences of the faces of mystics"). In describing Divine's love-making with Gabriel, he starts from one metamorphosis—"One night, the Archangel turned faun"—and is led, by an associative chain, into a sustained conceit in which he breathtakingly performs another: "...Gabriel avait acquis une telle virtuosité qu'il pouvait, tout en restant immobile lui-même, donner à sa verge un frémissement comparable à celui d'un cheval qui s'indigne. Il força avec sa rage habituelle et ressentit si intensément sa puissance qu'il—avec sa gorge et son nez—hennit de victoire, si impétueusement que Divine crut que Gabriel de tout son corps de centaure la pénétrait; elle s'evanouit d'amour comme une nymphe dans l'arbre."*

The most astounding metamorphosis of all is the one which transforms the images that activate Genet's personal erotic tastes (which few do and some cannot even expect to share) into poetry, poetry being, precisely, a universal imagery of eroticism, which provokes the imagination to an intangible but all the same completely sensual erection—a universal love-language which is, however, in fact understood by fewer readers than French and practised by fewer devotees than the most esoteric sexual perversion.

*["Gabriel had acquired such virtuosity that he was able, though remaining motionless himself, to make his tool quiver like a shying horse. He forced with his usual fury and felt his potency so intensely that—with his nose and throat—he whinnied with victory, so impetuously that Divine thought he was penetrating her with his whole centaur body. She swooned with love like a nymph in a tree."—Ed.]

Traps and Allegories: *Miracle of the Rose*

by Richard N. Coe

The Central Prison *(La Centrale)* of Fontevrault is an isolated community cut off from the rest of the world, cruel, intense, superstitious, hierarchical and ascetic — all in all, not very different from the mediaeval abbey, with its dependent monasteries and convents, that had originally occupied this same position. The convicts of the present are simultaneously the monks and lay-brothers of the long-dead past — an identification which destroys the intervening barrier of time, thus giving the whole prison a dream-like and sacred quality which Genet discreetly emphasises by setting the time of how own arrival there late on Christmas Eve:

> The prison lived like a cathedral at midnight of Christmas eve. We were carrying on the tradition of the monks who went about their business at night, in silence. We belonged to the Middle Ages.

This is the first introduction to the basic structure of *Miracle of the Rose*, which consists in eliminating the profane dimension of time by superimposing different fragments of experience in time one on top of the other, identifying them and allowing them to interpenetrate, so that the final reality that survives is timeless and, in the fullest sense that Genet gives to the word, "symbolic."

Much of this technique, this *"décomposition prismatique de mon amour et de ma douleur,"* as Genet terms it elsewhere, is Proustian in origin. Jean Genet evokes his adolescence at Mettray in much the same way, and with much the same purpose, as Marcel Proust evoking his own lost childhood at Combray. Proust has his famous *madeleine*, and other symbolic or magic objects and experiences which open the door on the enchanted gardens of involuntary mem-

"Traps and Allegories." From Richard Coe, *The Vision of Jean Genet* (New York: Grove Press, Inc.; London; Peter Owen Ltd., 1968), pp. 73-81. Copyright © 1968 by Richard Coe. Used by permission of Peter Owen, Ltd., and Howard Moorepark.

ory, and give the continuous past a total reality in the instantaneous present; Genet at Fontevrault meets and loves, first Bulkaen, a young burglar who, earlier in his career, has been at Mettray, then Divers, in whom he rediscovers an older Mettray-love of his own generation —and both these take him back in a rush of involuntary memories through the nightmares of his life in the open-prison Reformatory which, in the 'twenties and early 'thirties, had stood in the flowering countryside of Touraine. At times, the Proustian parallel is so exact that one almost suspects parody. The avenue of chestnut-trees at Mettray seems to correspond to the famous hawthorn path in *Swann's Way;* the failure of conscious efforts at memorizing a vanished part puzzle and torment Genet as much as they do Proust— as when Divers reminds him of another delinquent of their generation, one Villeroy, whom Genet remembers all too well:

> ...but a surprising thing happened: as he went on talking, the image I had retained of my big shot grew dimmer instead of clearer.

—finally, Genet himself describes his experiments with involuntary memory as an attempt "to redescend to the depths of time," at the end of which "I regress, with the Divers of old at my side, to a nauseating childhood which is magnified by horror and which I would never have wanted to leave."

However, if Mettray is to some extent a Combray-through-the-Looking-Glass—and it is understandable that Genet, comparing his own childhood with that of the wealthy, spoilt and hypochondriac young Marcel, must have felt a pretty violent sense of alienation—the parodic element is never dominant. Genet, at this period at any rate, is far too deeply involved in his own experiences, and in his own search for spiritual liberation, to waste much time on the experiences of others, however similar. If *Miracle of the Rose* has a number of affinities with *In Remembrance of Things Past* (including the interventions of the narrator, and perhaps some deliberate elaboration of style), it is also in many significant ways different. (It is characteristic that when, in *Pompes Funèbres,* there is an exact equivalent of the *madeleine* episode—the sudden glimpse by the Narrator of Erik half-hidden in a curtain, evoking a whole panorama of childhood—the childhood evoked is not Genet's own, but Erik's, which Genet *"veut revivre à sa place."*) *Miracle of the Rose* differs from Proust in the fragmentation of its technique, in its total lack of interest in consecutive narrative, but above all in the super-imposing of a *third* plane of experience over and above the Proustian levels of past and present. This is the plane of the *sacred,* of existence which is still technically *in* life, but in fact, outside life, space and time alike—the level of experience which is symbolized by Harcamone. Harcamone, from the mystic solitude of his condemned cell, is already "beyond life"; he lives "a dead life," he experiences "the heartbreaking sweetness of being out of the world before death," and this state is literally, for Genet, "supra-terrestrial [. ...] one of those states which might be called magical [. ...] a new mode of being." Harcamone has, in fact, through his transgression and later through his condemnation, attained that level of sanctity, isolation and total detachment from profane reality that Divine aspired to, yet failed to reach—the level at which all miracles are possible. Genet, Bulkaen and Divers exist simultaneously on two planes in time and space: Harcamone, on three. Consequently it is Harcamone who dominates the rest ("he himself soared above that world"), and not only dominates it but, being himself a symbol, gives meaning to all the other symbols which compose the worlds of Fontevrault and of Mettray.

To begin with, if the prison itself is a mystery, a sanctuary, if it is a daemonic stronghold of "former powers," and if its prisoners are giants and heroes that move as in a dream, it is *because of* Harcamone. Genet has no illusions about the profane reality of his fellow-inmates: "Now that the prison is stripped of its sacred ornaments, I see it naked, and its nakedness is cruel"—and his rational lucidity, which never ceases to run concurrently with his visionary dreams, is merciless in its assessment of their "unparalleled stupidity." Yet, just as in the mediaeval monastery, the presence of one saintly ascetic in his tower could shed an aura of glory over the whole community, so the presence of one unrepentant murderer in his condemned cell can lift the prison, and all its convicts, even its governor and warders, into the dimension of angels and eternity. The ladder of "ascension downwards" leads from Mettray to Fontevrault, from Fontevrault to Harcamone. At Mettray, Genet sees Fontevrault as "the perfect expression of his truth"; at Fontevrault he feels the whole building, walls, watch-house, cells and all, ready to be lifted up bodily and sent to drift away eternally among the stars. Harcamone, in the solitude of his fourth dimension, can walk through doors and walls; and in the vision which Genet has of him, his chains are garlanded with blossom and his heart is the Flower of

Flowers. For Harcamone is not only the symbol that gives meaning to all the other symbols, but he himself is symbolized by that most banal, most mysterious and, in the circumstances, most deliberately inapposite of symbols: the Mystic Rose.

At the head of Genet's long catalogue of particular symbols comes the flower; and at the head of the list of flowers stands the Rose. But —and this is essential—not the rose considered *as a rose,* but the Rose-as-a-symbol. Genet's roses, in other words, are the mirror-images of roses; they are pure-appearance, they are intellectual or spiritual artifacts. They appear among his pageantry of symbols because they have a precise symbolic function to perform; *not* because they are roses. On the whole, Genet would probably be happier if there were no real flowers in the world at all; in an ideal existence they would all be artificial. Fashioned of wax or velvet, and rather crudely botched together at that. If Sartre's report is reliable, Genet once entrusted him with a secret: he detests flowers. Animals also, although to a lesser degree. It is striking that, except for cats and an occasional heraldic lion or brachet, animals have no part to play in his poetic vision of the world. "Don't you like animals?" asked an effusive cat-lover once. "I don't like people who like animals," was Genet's reply. The retort is characteristic. Genet is anything but a nature lover; he belongs to the town, to the underworld of the city; and one of the most poetic descriptions in his writings is "the excursion down the rue Lepic," at dawn among the dustbins of the Butte Montmartre. Not that he *cannot* describe nature—there is an excellent Spanish landscape in *The Thief's Journal* —but in general he is not interested. His immediate ideal, in contrast to the harsh severity of his cell, or the foetid poverty of his life as a down-and-out,[1] is never Rousseau's or Lawrence's Nature but rather a somewhat childish conception of luxury—the sort of sumptuous and elephantine opulence that Osbert Lancaster has char-

---

[1] Even in the *Journal,* Genet rarely makes us conscious of the physical misery of his early life; he is much more concerned with its moral degradation. For comparison, it is interesting to read Orwell's *Down and Out in London and Paris;* or, more especially, Christopher Jackson's *Manuel* (London, Cape, 1965). The parallels between the Chilean adolescent criminal, Manuel Garcès, and Genet as he appears in the *Miracle,* are remarkable. Another writer with first-hand experience of reform-school and prison life is Albertine Sarrazin; however, the various prisons of *La Cavale* (Paris, Pauvert, 1966) appear as havens of comfort compared with those depicted by Genet. For a description of the interior of Fresnes or Fontevrault under the Nazis, see B. Marshall's *The White Rabbit.*

acterized as *le style Rothschild,* and which is still to be found in some
of the more expensive brothels in Cairo (it is also characteristic of
"La Féria" and of *The Balcony*): "…a luxurious apartment, adorned
with gold, the walls hung with garnet-red velvet, the furniture heavy
but toned down with red faille curtains"—a luxury which is fundamentally middle-class and urban.

For Genet, the city—the city of brothels, palaces or prisons—is
something familiar and reassuring: human, at any rate, made *by*
man *for* man. Not so nature. Nature is fundamentally hostile, a
domain of animate, untamable symbols, alive with a life which is not
human but "magical," and which can only be penetrated by accepting an alien domination—by surrendering to those heraldic and
uncanny forces. In *The Thief's Journal,* there is a strange and
significant passage in which Genet is hiding in a cornfield, while
attempting to make a clandestine crossing of the Czech-Polish
frontier. At this crisis, the whole of nature—the golden fields, the
fir-trees, the birches—is transmuted into a single heraldic symbol:
Poland, with its two-headed eagles and all its history; and Genet
himself, before he dare penetrate that realm, must himself cease
to be a human individual, and stylize his own reality: "I would penetrate less into a country than to the interior of an image."

More than any other phenomenon in Genet's world, Nature is at
once magical and hostile and two-dimensional. It is legendary rather
than real, like the treasure-islands and cannibal kingdoms of boy-
hood. Even Genet's favourite season, autumn—the "perpetual autumn" of Fontevrault, the "intense and insidious" autumn of Mettray,
the damp, dead leaves of the Tiergarten, amidst which Erik meets
the Headsman, the constant fogs of Brest or the mists of Antwerp,
which give the city "its sad character and its sordid maritime poetry"
—even the autumn seems "artificial and terrible." And yet autumn
is the season nearest to Genet's own emotions, the most familiar to
him, the least oppressive. As a true, if belated, romantic spirit in the
vein of Ossian and Sénancour, his melancholy, his "despair," if it
finds peace anywhere in the world, finds it among the dripping of
dank branches and the mouldering of dead leaves. How infinitely
foreign to him, then, are the bright flowers of summer—blossoms
that belong to the *bourgeois* world of prospertiy, normality and
suave summer seasons on the Cote D'Azur!

And yet, the flowers are everywhere: not only roses, but wisteria, dahlias, marigolds, gladioli, monkey-puzzles, catalpas, primroses, geraniums, daisies, lilies, carnations, cherry-blossom, mignonette, peonies, rhododendrons, may-flowers, forget-me-nots, camellias, magnolias, thistles, chrysanthemums, holly, pansies, Japanese bamboos, laburnums, daffodils, laurels, edelweiss, iris, mimosa, lilac... A symbol is a sign which leads from one world to another; and from one world to another; and flowers, precisely because they exist *in* Genet's world, yet are not *of* Genet's world, are the symbol of symbols. Not that normally they signify anything *exact;* rather, their symbolic power lies in their violent negativity. For the very reason that they are *not* of Bulkaen's world, or Divine's, or Divers', they become capable of *reflecting* that world. They are *not* life — not Genet's life: therefore they become precisely the symbol of all that is not-life. They are transformed into the image of death. They are *not* sordid, therefore they mirror the sordid, they give it reality, but in a new dimension... thus when Darling picks his nose, "from his nostrils he plucks acacia and violet petals." In the *bourgeois* world, flowers are associated with the Gardens of Paradise; their innocence and beauty are the very Mettray, "in the blossoming heart of France," and of Hell; they are the "infernal accessories" that replace the walls of the open-prison, and they are more powerful and more dangerous than the walls, because their power inherits the magic of another world. The young delinquents are only too well aware of the evil aura of this barrier of flowers: "We were victims of a foliage which was seemingly harmless, but which, in response to the least daring of our gestures, might become electrified."

Flowers are not obscene, and therefore they become the symbol of obscenity; they are feminine, therefore they signify the male, the "tough," the criminal, the murderer; they are bright and luminous, and thus they are identified with darkness and with night; they are conventionally beautiful, consequently they become the mirror-images of ugliness, like the flower that is Mario's blackened thumbnail. For, in the mirror, significances are transmuted, and the most intimate bond between an object and its essential meaning is the bond of opposition. It is the characteristic of the Saint — the adventurer among forbidden and sacred temples — that he is perpetually forced to "love that which he abhors...." To Genet, flowers are repellent; consequently he is sacred in proportion as his world is made of flowers. Conversely, the power and the beauty of flowers is enhanced and magnified in proportion as they symbolize degradation and brutality—the granitic ugliness of convicts, murderers and traitors:

> *There is a close relationship between flowers and convicts.* The fragility and delicacy of the former are of the same nature as the brutal insensitivity of the latter.

Whether or not we care to label this negative symbolism as cynical or perverse, the fact remains that it lies at the very root of Genet's whole poetic imagination—and that it is effective. The very titles *Our Lady of the Flowers* and *Miracle of the Rose* are powerful and evocative in precise ratio to the failure of these novels to deal with Ste. Thérèse de Lisieux or St. Francis of Assisi. From a purely literary point of view, we can see some reason for Genet's revolt against the platitudes and the wishy-washy aestheticism of some of the later symbolists—not Mallarmé or Rimbaud, but Joséphin Péladan, perhaps, or François Coppée. There are powerful elements of aestheticism in Genet himself, but—as we shall see—these elements, even if they lead him to some paradoxical conclusions in ethics, are never obsessive enough to cloud his intellect, and he is as deeply concerned as Sartre or Ionesco to understand the meaning of art, and to re-define the traditional concept of beauty in the context of a post-Hiroshima sensibility. In this attempted re-definition, the violent contradiction implicit in Genet's floral symbolism is extremely significant. There are, however, two other factors which contribute to explaining Genet's peculiar obsession with flowers: the first is the accident of his name, the second the accident of his homosexuality.

As a poet, Genet is fascinated by words (it is to be observed that all his flowers have names as resonant to the ear as their petals are resplendent to the eye); and as a mystic, he is intrigued and more than a little awed by the magic of names. In the majority of primitive religions, the Name-of-God has ritualistic significance; it is in itself a symbol, a poem, an incantation endowed with supernatural powers. This mixture of superstition and ritual poetry is passed on by Genet to most of his characters and embodied in their names, or more often in the fabulous and usually beautiful nicknames that traditionally get attached to the more notorious French criminals. These names—the queers, Divine the Gay-time Girl, Mimosa I, Mimosa II, Mimosa the half-IV, First Communion, Angela, Milord,

Castagnette, Régine: the convicts, Jennot-du-Matin (= Genet himself), Lou-Daybreak, Riton-la-Noïe, Bebert the Legionnaire, Black Jim, Laurent, Martinelle, Bako, Dédé from Javel—are like flowers: their mysterious efficacy springs from the dynamic contrast between the poetic enchantments that the words suggest, and the ugly realities which they serve to mask. That such names have a magic-symbolic power, Genet has no doubt; they constitute a sort of electric hedge about their possessor. To betray them to a potential enemy is to increase one's vulnerability, and Adrien Baillon is as hesitant to reveal, even to *Darling Dainty-Foot,* the secret of his marvellous sobriquet, *Our Lady of the Flowers,* as is the superstitious Buganda tribesman to allow himself to be photographed— and for identical reasons.[2] In view of this, it is not surprising that Genet sees manifold significances and symbols in the imagery of his own name: *Genet,* the small but high-spirited horse of the Spanish light cavalry —but also *Genêt,* the flower of the ancient Kings of England, the golden broom.

It is strange that, in *The Thief's Journal,* where Jean Genet discusses his affinity with the golden-flowered *genêt* of the Morvan, the normal relationship between object and symbol is reversed. In the case of Harcamone, the Rose is the symbol of the man; in the case of the broom, Genet is the symbol of the flower: "I am alone in the world, and I am not sure that I am not the king—perhaps the sprite—of these flowers." Further on, Genet makes bold to suggest that, through this family relationship, as it were, which he has with one particular species of flower, "I can regard all flowers without pity; they are members of my family." I suspect that this is no more than a piece of rather specious whimsicality—certainly its tone is at variance with the less anodyne, if rather more perverse visions of *Miracle of the Rose.* Even so, the phrase "regard *without pity*" is characteristic; and the probability still holds that part at least of the poet's fascination with flower-symbols is due to the coincidence of his name.

So far, we have been considering some of Genet's most pervasive symbolism in terms of its poetic function in relation to his imagination. But Genet is in addition a self-proclaimed and practising pas-

[2]In Genet's later works, particularly in his plays, his names change character, becoming less mystic-poetic, more intellectual. Thus Diop *(The Blacks)* suggests the double-vision of Descartes' *La Dioptrique;* Diouf, the combination "Dieu" plus "Ouf!"

sive homosexual, and the whole of his creative vision is profoundly influenced by this fact. In other words, there are few symbols, religious or otherwise, in *Miracle of the Rose* or any of the other novels which are not at the same time fairly precise images of a certain type of sexual motivation. The majority of these sexual symbols — and there are dozens of them: hardness, brightness, ice, brittleness, fragility ("...the *porcelain* of which the boy was made...", gravity (particularly in relation to voices), the burglar's jemmy, the guitar, the "java" (a modern dance), jewels, the Renaissance court-page, the soldier, the sailor, the acrobat, the murderer, the *voyou,* the cyclist, the archangel, the athlete, the gaucho, the Negro, the "pimps and apaches with a smoking butt," the dagger, the revolver, the mast of a sailing-ship or galley, the snake, the violin, the belt and belt-buckle, the statue, the machine, the stone towers of La Rochelle... etc., etc.—all these are straightforward erotic images evoking the violence, the virility, and the more-or-less symbolic sadism which the passive homosexual ideally desires to find in his lovers. But Genet, as the essentially feminine partner in the union, can experience *himself* as none of these things; nor, on the other hand, can he sublimate himself and his own desires in terms of a traditionally feminine symbolism—water, waves, the mother, the gateway, etc.— since he is not a woman, but only a man-playing-at-being-a-woman. Of the very few recurrent symbols that incarnate, not his desire for the triumphant male who is to subdue him, but rather his own reaction, the most important is that of the flower—and above all (once again) the Rose. The surge and pressure of his desire he visualises, not as a knife or sword to penetrate, nor as water to be thrust apart and plunged into, but as something between the two: as the expansion and unfolding in colour and richness of the richest and most voluptuous of flowers: the Mystic Rose. Yet the Rose is by no means only yielding—"sweeter and more fragrant than the rose petals of Saadi"—but ever inseparable, in the vision, from its stem: hard, thorn-protected, as unfeminine as barbed wire or a hempen rope. "This indifference like a steely metallic stalk"—the symbol of Genet himself.

So, in the *Miracle,* the central, unifying symbol of the Rose is of considerable complexity. "The rose means love, friendship, death... and silence!" Harcamone, the murderer, is the Rose of Death; yet the warder he kills is known as "Bois-de-Rose"—the Rose-Wood used for coffins. The Rose is head and heart and sex—cut off from its stem, it falls as heavily to the ground as the head beneath the knife of the guillotine; it is mourning, it is mystery, it is passion; it is Genet's lovers, and it is Jean Genet himself crushed beneath their love. It is beauty that symbolizes its mirror-opposite, evil and ugliness, it is the paradox, it blossoms at once in the profane and sacred worlds. It is the Head of Christ and the Crown of Thorns. It is Proust's *madeleine,* unlocking memories of Mettray. It is the miracle; it is profanation, transgression and ultimately—in Genet's special sense—sanctity:

> ...a door opened by itself and we saw before us a red rose of monstrous size and beauty.
> "The Mystic Rose" murmured the chaplain.
> The four men were staggered by the splendour. [...] They were in the throes of drunken profanation. With their temples throbbing and their brows beaded with sweat, they reached the heart of the rose. It was a kind of dark well. At the very edge of this pit, which was as murky and deep as an eye, they leaned forward and were seized by a kind of dizziness. All four made the gestures of people losing their balance, and they toppled into that deep gaze.

The Thief's Journal

by Philip Thody

Partly because of its intellectualisation, *The Thief's Journal* is Genet's best known and most immediately accessible prose work. It was the first to be openly published in France, has appeared in England in Penguin Modern Classics, and was included, in François Truffaut's film *Fahrenheit 451,* in a pile of major European literary masterpieces about to be destroyed by fire in the name of social stability. It is shorter than any of the novels, requires less imaginative effort from the reader, and appears to offer a convenient summary both of Genet's main ideas and of the most interesting period of his life. He himself states that its three basic subjects are "theft, treason and homosexuality," and it provides a detailed account of the various humiliations which he chose to endure in his wanderings through Spain, Yugoslavia and the Low Countries during the nineteen-thirties. There is also extended discussion of sainthood, and at one point Genet provides Sartre with the starting point for a central passage analysing his relevance to the present day when he writes that he is an "impossible nullity." Compared to *Our Lady of the Flowers* and *Querelle of Brest,* however, *The Thief's Journal* is a fairly conventional literary work. Although Genet speaks at one point about persisting in "the rigour of composition," the book actually goes back to one of the earliest and least rigorous of all European literary genres: the picaresque novel. Appropriately enough in this respect, much of the action is set in Spain, and Genet's own character, like that of the traditional picaresque hero, does not evolve. Yet whereas the predominant characteristic of Gil Blas was

"The Thief's Journal" by Philip Thody. From *Jean Genet: A Study of His Novels and Plays* (Briarcliff Manor, N.Y.: Stein and Day Publishers, 1968) pp. 141-54. Copyright © 1968 by Philip Thody. Reprinted with permission of Stein and Day Publishers and Hamish Hamilton Ltd., London.

a sturdy common-sense, Genet describes his misadventures from the standpoint of a poet and a metaphysician. This is visible even when he talks about the activity which gives the book its title and which, since homosexuality is not a criminal offence in Europe, led to his various prison sentences: theft.

Thus he gives practically no details about how or what he stole, and although he speaks with considerable enthusiasm about his relationship with a professional cracksman called Guy, his book offers few tips to the apprentice burglar. He does not elaborate on his interesting if controversial remark in *Miracle of the Rose* that it is quieter to walk on one's heels than on tip-toe, and provides no examples to illustrate what he calls the heroic aspects of robbery. The act of stealing so excites Genet's thieves that some have to defecate immediately they have stolen, but this is not because of the physical dangers which theft involves. It is because they feel acutely aware of the moral challenge they are offering society, and the most detailed account which Genet provides of theft in *The Thief's Journal* concentrates upon the feelings which he had while breaking into people's homes. In this, he provides an interesting gloss on G. K. Chesterton's essentially common-sense view that the burglar has an intense respect for the idea of private property, and merely wishes to alter its distribution. What interests Genet is the "long shudder" which runs down his back when he realises that he is going to steal, and the feeling that he is "steeped in the idea of property," at the very moment when he is "looting" it. His choice of words is extremely significant here, for he talks not about a transference of property, as a Chestertonian burglar might, but about its destruction. The word *"saccager,"* that he uses in the French text, definitely implies this, and takes on its full meaning in the light of an analysis of theft in *Saint Genet, actor and martyr*. Let us imagine, says Sartre, a Chinese miniature originally brought back from the Far East by its present owner's grandfather. It is stolen by a thief, who immediately converts it into a pile of dirty bank-notes, which disappear as he spends them on drink, women, gambling and fancy clothes. Whatever his intention, the thief has converted a very specific object, with innumerable family associations, to nothing. It is because he destroys property, and thus defies the moral principles inculcated in him as a child, that Genet feels such awe and terror when he is stealing. It is perhaps because the theft of objects from houses causes him such intense anxiety that he gives so few details about it, and he is much more forthcoming about the money which he stole from some of his homosexual clients. Indeed, the anecdotes which make up the central story-line in *The Thief's Journal* are far more concerned with Genet's homosexual friends or with his life as a beggar than they are with the actual title of the book.

At the beginning of *The Thief's Journal,* Genet is already living as a beggar in Spain, sharing his food and pleasures with a vermin-ridden outcast called Salvador. He then makes the acquaintance of a more enterprising youth called Pépé, who calmly asks Genet to wait outside a public lavatory while he goes inside to masturbate in order to calm his nerves before an important card game. In spite of this apparently traditional precaution, Pépé loses, and kills another player who tries to snatch the money. Before escaping, he hands this money over to Genet, who runs off to join another of his friends, Stilitano, the original one-armed bandit. The last we hear of Salvador is when Genet has one of his rare attacks of generosity and sends him money to comfort him in gaol. In this respect, Genet treats him very much better than he does Pépé. Instead of sending him money when the latter is in Monjuich gaol, Genet treats himself to a sumptuous lunch, rejoicing in the thought that his friend is now languishing in prison and reflecting that by this particularly nasty action he has finally "freed himself from moral preoccupations."

Salvador's replacement by Stilitano is a definite improvement as far as the interest of *The Thief's Journal* is concerned. Sartre describes Stilitano as "cowardly, empty and feminine," and in this respect he is typical of all the "splendid males" whom Genet presents with such irony in his work. Like Divine, however, Stilitano has a kind of genius for transforming humiliation into victory by the same technique of carrying a situation to the point where he triumphs through the total abolition of conventional standards. Thus, on one occasion, he is walking with Genet through Barcelona, when he mistakes a group of "real" men for a bunch of homosexuals whom he can jeer at with impunity. He starts on his insults, only to be greeted with a serious challenge to fight. He escapes from this situation by holding out the stump of his amputated arm and saying: "After all, fellows, you're not going to fight with a cripple." Genet calls this "vile hamming," but also writes that it so ennobles Stilitano in his eyes that "the absence of the hand was as real and effective as a royal attribute, as the hand of justice," and this apparent contradiction throws an interesting light on his attitude towards Stilitano and towards the reactions which he knows that his reader will have. What he is saying is, in fact, that he knows Stilitano is an absolute bounder, and admires him all the more for it. A similar duality recurs when he talks about Stilitano's clothes, remarking that they achieve "a harmony in bad taste" which he describes as "the height of elegance." Stilitano, he writes, "had unfalteringly chosen a pair of green and tan crocodile shoes, a brown suit, a white silk shirt, a pink tie, a multicoloured scarf, and a green hat," and as he walks along by his side Genet can feel his own body moving in sympathy as Stilitano's crocodile leather shoes "creak with the ponderous body of that monarch of the slums" *("monarque faubourien")*. The fact that Genet keeps a completely straight face when he talks about Stilitano only adds to the humour of his presentation, and in this respect *The Thief's Journal* gains from being a more straightforward and less obviously tormented work of art than *Our Lady of the Flowers*. In his first novel, he still gave the impression of being at least partly taken in by the Mignons and Notre-Dames of his world, and to be laughing at them only because his obsessions and sexual preferences could not quite overcome his intelligence. In *The Thief's Journal,* at least as far as Stilitano is concerned, he is totally liberated from the prestige of the *mac,* and therefore all the funnier when he writes about him.

Cyril Connolly was so impressed with Stilitano that he claimed, in his review of the English translation of *The Thief's Journal,* that the interest of the book "wanes, like that of a school story after the dare-devil has been sacked" when Genet loses Stilitano and leaves Spain. This is not quite fair to the book, for Stilitano does turn up again later in Antwerp, where he is doing a little honest pimping (his woman, a luscious blonde called Sylvia, hugs Genet's arm very tightly to show how glad she is to meet one of Stilitano's friends, and almost makes poor Genet feel sick), and even manages to steal a police motor cycle. When he does finally disappear, his place is filled very effectively by the two figures of Armand and Bernardini, who reflect an aspect of Genet's personality which had already expressed itself in the creation of Norbert and Mario Daugas in *Querelle of Brest:* the longing for solid, massive, brutal men, by whom he will be at one and the same time both dominated and reassured. Psychologically, this longing bears witness to a curious mixture in Genet's personality between a basic masochism and an intense longing for a father figure, and contrasts in every way with his attitude towards Stilitano and Mignon. His aim as far as these two characters are concerned is, as Sartre emphasises, to underline how deceptive their masculine appearance really is, and there is a brilliant passage in *Saint Genet, actor and martyr* which links this *"malice pédérastique"* to the common homosexual practice of *fellatio*. In his creation of Armand and Mario, Genet's aim seems to be different: to invent, within a sexual relationship, the security which he had never known as a child. Like the Mother in *The Screens,* Armand has an attitude of total permissiveness towards other people's actions, and this also gives him a place in Genet's imaginary reconstitution of a family: neither Armand nor Saïd's mother would have abandoned Genet at birth in anticipatory punishment for the crimes they knew he was going to commit.

It is not, however, as raw material for psychological analysis that *The Thief's Journal* offers its greatest interest, and there are two important objections to interpreting any of Genet's books in this way. Such an approach presupposes that authors do express through their work a childhood crisis which still dominates their creative process even when they are in their late thirties; and it offers no guide to the aesthetic value of what they write. From a more exclusively literary point of view, *The Thief's Journal* offers three main areas of interest: it describes an experience of physical and psychological humiliation; it gives an account of life among beggars, thieves and homosexuals in the nineteen-thirties; and it explains how the political and social structure of society appears to a man totally excluded from it. Intellectually, it raises the important question of whether, in his later work, Genet began to interpret his experience in the light of Sartre's ideas rather than of his own original feelings.

Genet's account of his life in the nineteen-thirties insists on the theme of humiliation in two ways: in the details which he gives about begging for food, cleaning out police station lavatories, and serving as a kind of whipping boy to Stilitano and Armand; and in the images which he uses to evoke the kind of experience he was trying to achieve. It is his images which are most consistently interesting, for after his description of Divine's life and of his own experiences at Mettray, even the most harrowing account of life in a Jugoslavian prison sounds a little flat. When, however, he compares his feelings of exile and humiliation to life on the planet Uranus, where the atmosphere is "so heavy that the ferns there are creepers; the animals drag along, crushed by the weight of gases," he shows that his achievement as a writer depends not on what he actually did but on his ability to transmute his personal vision into effective terms. Stellar or planetary images clearly attract Genet, for he twice evokes the light still reaching us here on earth from a dead star to express the emotion which he feels for his dead friends. When he speaks of Uranus, it is to evoke a "forlorn planet" where, amidst hideous reptiles, he will "pursue an eternal, miserable death in a darkness where leaves will be black, the waters of the marshes thick and cold." There, like his hero Querelle, he will "recognise with increasing lucidity the unclean fraternity of smiling alligators," and experience the same "monstrous participation in the realms of great muddy rivers and deep jungles." When Genet uses this kind of imagery to speak both of his imaginary characters and of himself, he goes beyond the private mythology which expresses itself in the theme of the double in *Querelle of Brest* or in the snake worship and pyromania that recur in his film *Mademoiselle*. Instead, he creates in literary terms a universe like that of Hieronymus Bosch, in which man's horror of himself takes the form of an identification with the most repulsive and inhuman animal shapes. When, in Spain, he was *"un pou avec la conscience de l'être"* ("a louse and conscious of being one"), he was so far separated from the world of normal emotions and experiences that he did almost lose his humanity. It is this experience which, recorded in parts of *The Thief's Journal,* gives the book its greatest originality.

In contrast, Genet's treatment of homosexuality in *The Thief's Journal* is less complex than in any other of his works. He does not create characters like Divine or Querelle, but concentrates either on describing his own relationship with Salvador, Stilitano or Armand, or on reporting how the Barcelona homosexuals behaved. As in his account of Stilitano's clothes, it is difficult to believe that he is not being deliberately amusing when he tells how Theresa the Great used to take her knitting and a sandwich when waiting for clients at one of Barcelona's most celebrated public urinals, or when he describes how the Barcelona homosexuals, the "Carolinas," went in "shawls, mantillas, silk dresses and fitted jackets" to place a "bunch of red roses tied together with a crape veil" on the site of one of the dirtiest but most beloved urinals that had been destroyed after the riots of 1933. He provides further light on his creation of Divine when he writes that the Carolinas' "shrill voices, their cries, their extravagant gestures" seemed to him to have "no other aim than to try to pierce the shell of the world's contempt," and his insistence on the contempt which homosexuals expect to receive from other people suggests that he chose this type of sexuality because it fitted perfectly into his aim of exiling himself from society and being despised. It is in every way a mistake to look to him for support in any rational or liberal attitude.

In spite of his refusal to question conventional bourgeois values, Genet is nevertheless quite ready to satirise the attitude which ordinary members of society take towards its outcasts. At one point in *The Thief's Journal,* for example, a group of French tourists visit Barcelona and take photographs of the community to which Genet belonged. He describes them as carrying on "an audible dialogue, the terms of which were exact and rigorous, almost technical," and in which they discussed, "without thinking that they might be wounding the beggars," the different aesthetic effects which their appearance created.

> "There's a perfect harmony between the tonalities of the sky and the slightly greenish shades of the rags."
> "...something out of Goya..."
> "It's very interesting to watch this group on the left. There are things of Gustave Doré in which the composition..."
> "They're happier than we are."
> "There's something more sordid about them than those in the shantytown, do you remember, in Casablanca? There's no denying that the Moroccan costume gives a *simple* beggar a dignity which no European can ever have."
> "We're seeing them when they're all frozen. They have to be seen when the weather is right."
> "On the contrary, the originality of the poses..."

Genet claims to have felt uncomfortable, on this occasion, less for his own sake than for that of Lucien, his "little fisherman from Le Suquet" to whom he later dedicated one of his poems. He nevertheless projects on to Lucien some of the obsessions that went to the creation of Divine when he writes of his being "dizzily swept to the depths of the nameless" by the way in which the tourists directed "the cruel lenses of their cameras" towards him. Genet undoubtedly portrays the tourists with critical hostility, in the same way that he attacks society for requiring beggars to produce what he calls the "humiliating 'anthropometric card'" to prove their identity. Nevertheless, there is both bad faith and intellectual inconsistency in his criticism. He did, after all, choose to behave in this way, and derived what can only be called, in view of his aspirations to sainthood through humiliation, spiritual benefit from experiences which the scornful attitude of society alone made possible.

The Thief's Journal is the only one of Genet's prose works to show any awareness of the political situation in Europe either before or after the Second World War. In his earlier works, he had been concerned with war only in so far as it satisfied his two main interests of homosexuality and treason. In *Our Lady of the Flowers,* war in general was "the red blood that flows from the artilleryman's ears...the lightfoot soldier of the snows crucified on skis, a spahi on his horse of cloud that has pulled up at the edge of Eternity," but like the specific war which Genet evokes from time to time in this book, it is interesting only because of the associations which it has with sex. The political atmosphere of the nineteen-thirties is evoked only very indirectly in *Querelle of Brest* when Genet appears to be criticising the policy of appeasement by writing of Gil having *"cette face crucifiée des nations qui refusent la lutte"* ("the crucified countenance of nations who prefer not to join in the struggle"), and in *Pompes Funèbres* the occupation of France is significant only for the opportunities it provided for treason. It is true that *The Thief's Journal* in no way sets out to deal directly with politics. The reference which Genet makes to the threat of war which hung over Europe while he was actually writing his book in the nineteen-forties is brief indeed, for he merely notes that warlike preparations involve "no longer the high-sounding declarations of statesmen but the menacing exactness of technicians." Nevertheless, this evocation of the pre-Krushchev phase of the Cold War is extremely effective, and for all his supposed lack of interest in what was happening in the higher reaches of society, he had also felt the political agitation which accompanied the growth of Fascism and the events leading to the Second World War. In the same way that he had had the impression, in Hitler's Germany, that he was in "a camp organised by bandits," and would be breaking no law if he stole, he had also been aware of the atmosphere which preceded the outbreak of the Civil War in Spain. "Under all the tinsel and idiotic gilding," he writes, he could see "the angular and muscular force which, suddenly taut and erect *(bandant soudain)*, was to bring the whole thing down a few years later."

It might be argued, of course, that such statements do not really reflect how Genet actually felt in the nineteen-thirties. After all, he was writing *The Thief's Journal* some ten to fifteen years after the events which it describes had taken place, and he may well have projected on to his past experience some of the political ideas picked up from his new friends on the intellectual Left. Nevertheless, his general account of how he saw society before the Second World War has a ring of accuracy and sincerity which suggest that he may well be describing real feelings. Thus he remarks that all he noticed of the complex social order around him was its "perfect coherence." "I was astounded," he continues, "by so rigorous an edifice whose details were united against me. Nothing in the world was irrelevant: the stars on a general's sleeve, the stock-market quotations, the olive harvest, the style of the judiciary, the wheat exchange, flower-beds ...This order, fearful and feared, had only one meaning: my exile." What makes this disclaimer of detailed social awareness so interesting is the development of Genet's later career as a dramatist, for after his first two plays, he openly concentrates on political themes. *The Balcony,* in particular, deals with one of the most important events in the nineteen-thirties: the transference of power, in Stalin's Russia as well as in Franco's Spain and Hitler's Germany, from working-class revolutionaries to efficient police forces. What *The Thief's Journal* seems to indicate is that part of Genet's original inspiration for this play stems from three aspects of his own personal experience: his encounter with the "oppressively perfect" police system of the Central European states; the erotic attraction which he felt for policemen, which gave them virtually a mythical status in his eyes; and his diffused, unintellectualised awareness of what was happening in the nineteen-thirties. For all his sexual sophistication, his view of the world seems at that period to have been that of a child: an undifferentiated awareness of an incomprehensibly complex authoritarian structure. But in the same way that a child is often more sensitive than an adult to the general atmosphere around him, so Genet may well have had a similarly intense vision of something which he could not express until much later in his life. It is perhaps this, among a number of other factors, which accounts for the excellence of his third play.

The Thief's Journal is dedicated to Sartre and Simone de Beauvoir, and reads at times like a rationalisation in Sartrean terms of the more instinctive attitude which Genet had expressed in his earlier novels. The distance which Genet realised he had travelled since *Our Lady of the Flowers* is indicated by a comment which he makes in *The Thief's Journal* on the composition of his first book in La Santé prison. He began to write, he says, not because he wanted to relieve or communicate his emotions, but because he hoped, "by expressing them in a form that they themselves imposed," to construct a moral order whose nature he himself did not yet know. Writing was thus, in the first instance, a means of self-exploration and self-knowledge, and an attempt to discover just what attitude he did have towards the laws which had condemned him and which he had chosen to defy. Once he began, in the early nineteen-forties, to live outside the criminal community, and to associate with intellectuals like Cocteau and Sartre, he seems to have been encouraged to rationalise this attitude much more systematically, and to understand why, as he remarks in *Querelle of Brest,* he had throughout his youth looked at the world through lowered eyebrows. In dedicating *The Thief's Journal* to Sartre and Simone de Beauvoir, he seems to be approving in advance of the basic theme in *Saint Genet, actor and martyr.* Sartre's study began appearing in *Les Temps Modernes* in 1950, some eighteen months after the publication in book form of *The Thief's Journal,* but since extracts from *The Thief's Journal* were published in July 1946, the question of a direct textual influence of Sartre's essay on this book must be ruled out. Nevertheless, Genet must have known from his many conversations with Sartre what attitude his friend was likely to take, and Sartre himself had indicated his approval of Genet's basic choice as early as 1947, when he dedicated his essay on Baudelaire to him. In returning the compliment, Genet was to some extent underwriting what he certainly realised would be the starting point for Sartre's essay, however devastating he may have found the whole essay when he finally saw himself stripped naked.

Genet had, of course, spoken in his earlier works of what he calls in *The Thief's Journal* his "identification with the handsomest and most unfortunate criminals." *Pompes Funèbres,* in particular, is full of autobiographical remarks about his choice of evil and disappointment in it. It is nevertheless in *The Thief's Journal* that he talks about clarifying the meaning of his choice to be a thief, and presents it as a "moral adventure" in which he preferred to commit crimes in France because he wanted to accuse himself in his own language. It is in this book that he insists upon his desire to be guilty and condemned, and describes how, when he felt tempted to rebel against the perfect coherence of the rest of society, he was held back by "the ingrained habit of living with my head down and in accordance with an ethic contrary to the one which governs the world." It is also here that he speaks of the way in which prisons were constructed for him and "have their foundations" within him, and thus either anticipates or echoes Sartre's view that he was the creature not only of his own choice but also of the predestination by which society selects its criminals and outcasts at birth. Indeed, *The Thief's Journal* does more than provide almost suspiciously perfect evidence for Sartre's views. It even reflects some of the ambiguities and obscurities of *Saint Genet, actor and martyr,* for like Sartre himself Genet seems constantly uncertain as to whether his fundamental choice was admirable and justified or not. In his essay, Sartre oscillates between the common-sense view that Genet "is making a great to-do about a few acts of solitary or mutual masturbation" and the more romantic view that Genet's work "re-establishes the poetic truth of crime," and this duality recurs in *The Thief's Journal* as it does in the earlier novels. Similarly, both Genet and Sartre appear undecided as to whether *The Thief's Journal* is carefully constructed or not. At one point, Genet speaks of "persisting in the rigour of composition" while nevertheless stating elsewhere that he is presenting his memories *"en vrac"* ("loose, or in bulk"), and Sartre refers to the "rigorous, classical unity" of Genet's works nine pages after he has gone out of his way to say how carelessly they are put together.

While in this particular respect there is obviously no question of an influence of Sartre on Genet, there are other texts by Genet which had definitely expressed a neo-Sartrian attitude towards existence some time before *The Thief's Journal* was published. When Genet notes in *Pompes Funèbres* that *"nous souffrons de ne pouvoir fixer notre chagrin,"* the reflexions on the impossibility of actually holding an emotion there, and examining it as if it were an object, seem to come directly from *L'Etre et le Néant*. Similarly, when he remarks of Juliette that *"une bonne ne fait pas de projets pour sa fille,"* it is as though he were offering an example to illustrate the thesis which Sartre put forward in *Matérialisme et Révolution* in 1946:

that only members of the bourgeoisie bring children into the world because they have a specific role for them in mind. Gil Turko's fear in *Querelle of Brest* that his parents have no real affection for him because his birth was the result of an inefficient douching — *"Je suis né d'une giclée qui n'a pas réussi"* — also parallels Sartre's views on the essential contingency of conception and physical birth. He notes in *Saint Genet, actor and martyr* that "Genet's origin is a *blunder* (there would not have been a Genet if someone had used a contraceptive)," and he is equally unromantic in his own autobiography when he describes his father as "shedding the few drops of sperm that go to make a man." In Genet's plays, with their consistent attack upon the values and institutions of bourgeois society, the resemblance between his own ideas and those of the man who has done most to make him famous becomes even more marked.

The Glory of Annihilation: Jean Genet

by Jacques Guicharnaud
(in collaboration with June Guicharnaud)

While Beckett continues to sing, in muted tones, of the desperate effort to exist and to voice an obsession with the irremediable past, Jean Genet, in a great flourish of lyricism, has gradually become the master of ceremonies of a frenzied plunge into annihilation. Seemingly paradoxical, his theatrical works give the impression of a sumptuous structure, huge and complex—an ornate temple, baroque in its way and sometimes even "pop," whose saint of saints, both the pretext for such extravagance and the goal of the characters, is quite simply nothingness. From play to play this has become increasingly clear, until today a formula that might be applied to the whole of Genet's works is Archibald's description, at the end of *Les Nègres,* of the spectacle that has just unfolded: an "architecture of emptiness and words."

At the roots of this venture is a dual assumption, which Genet initially expressed in a letter appended to his first performed play, *Les Bonnes.* To begin with, and closely related to Artaud's theories, is Genet's disgust with Western theatre, especially its frivolity and triviality: at most a quality entertainment, such theatre is nonetheless mere entertainment. What Genet would like is something similar to Oriental theatre, or at least what we know of it—theatre in which ceremony would replace the masquerade, and symbols the characters. Or, as he writes, "there is nothing more [theatrically] effective than the elevation" during Mass. Religious mystery and communion are the two necessary components of true theatre. Beauty would replace faith, but a beauty that "must have at least the power

"The Glory of Annihilation: Jean Genet." From Jacques Guicharnaud, *Modern French Theatre from Giraudoux to Genet,* revised edition (New Haven: Yale University Press, 1975), pp. 259-76. Reprinted by permission of the publisher.

of a poem—that is, of a crime." Together with this aesthetic mystique is a second principle, that of theatre as a vanishing dream: "A performance that does not act on my soul is vain. It is vain if I don't believe what I see, which will stop—which will never have existed—once the curtain falls." This is an extreme expression of theatricalism and of the paradox of two simultaneous states of consciousness, assimilating the spectator to the regular customers of Irma's brothel in *Le Balcon:* during their visits, each customer, by means of a sumptuous disguise, becomes his own ideal of social and sexual grandeur, but during the ceremony, "they all want it to be as real as possible ...except for some indefinable thing making it all not real." To his higher demand for mystical—or magical—effectiveness Genet adds an equally unyielding demand for illusion and the negation of reality.

Critics have put great emphasis on the ritual aspect of Genet's theatre. And, indeed, his plays are both the presentation of a rite and a rite in themselves. First of all, Genet uses theatre—and often the novel—as an instrument for evoking or exorcising his most private fantasies. Adorned with all the marvels of lighting, make-up, and theatrical costuming, the inhabitants of his sexual imagination assume shapes, are objectified, and become real. The beauty of the prisoners in *Haute Surveillance,* the incarnation of Blood, Tears, and Sperm in three young men in *Le Balcon,* the muscled femininity of Arthur in the same play, the steely eye and disarray of the handsome Sergeant of *Les Paravents,* all show that the universe of Genet's plays is, as it were, his private Hollywood, where he can be both the creator and the prey of his own gods. On this level the ceremony is elementary and similar to the secret rites of adolescents who seek satisfaction by making obscene drawings, thus conferring "existence" upon imaginary, ideal, and forbidden creatures. Yet Genet's method transcends childishness because of his awareness of the ambiguity of such incarnations: he knows that they are merely theatrical figures, performed myths, not living realities. The statue of Galathea remains a statue, and Pygmalion has merely an illusory satisfaction.

On another level the plays tell a story, in which the characters take part in a ceremony that is meant to procure for them some particular satisfaction. In Genet's first play, *Haute Surveillance,* the rite is very primitive, since the symbol is inseparable from the act: seeking to identify with great criminals and thus commune with them in love, Lefranc commits a murder by strangling young Maurice. In *Les Bonnes* the situation is more complex: the murder of Madame by her two maids Claire and Solange never takes place, and the play ends with the suicide of Claire, who is "playing" Madame—a suicide that is the equivalent of both an expiation and the symbolic murder of Madame. Similarly, at the end of *Le Balcon* the defeated revolutionary, Roger, dressed in the costume of the Chief of Police, castrates himself, thus symbolically mutilating the man responsible for his defeat. In *Les Nègres,* where the purpose of the ceremony enacted onstage is to free the Blacks not only from the Whites but from the image they have of themselves because of the Whites, the symbol ends by dispensing with even the vicarious act: the black actors who, masked, represent an image of the Whites are sent off to hell, but they are presented to the audience as actors and quite simply leave the stage. Thus, from *Haute Surveillance* to *Les Nègres,* Genet has gradually changed the ceremony into a symbol, going from the realism of a ritual murder to a metaphor that is openly offered as a metaphor.

While this gradual evolution might appear to be a weakening of dramatic force with increased recourse to abstraction, it in fact has given Genet's works greater theatrical power. Despite the rhetoric and *préciosité* of the dialogue, *Les Bonnes* and *Haute Surveillance* are dramaturgically no great departure from traditional theatre (for which reason Genet almost repudiated *Les Bonnes*). When it was first performed, *Les Bonnes* could easily have been taken for a social protest against the oppression of servants or for a high tragedy of serving maids. As for *Haute Surveillance,* it might well have been seen as, above all, a documentation of the stranger aspects of prison life. With *Le Balcon* and especially *Les Nègres,* phantasmagoria and masquerade eliminate the realism and at the same time address the plays directly to the audience. In her final monologue Mme. Irma, speaking to the spectators, puts them on the same footing as the characters and declares that the illusions of her brothel are merely a reflection of the illusions of our own lives, which are made up of rites that we take seriously but that are even more deceptive than those of the Balcony. In *Les Nègres* the spectator finally becomes an actor who does not witness a ceremony but actually takes part in it: at least one white spectator must be seated in the theatre so that his reflection may be seen onstage in the form of the grotesque masks of the Queen, the Missionary, and so on. The black actors who are not masked play constantly with their two audiences—the white masks and the spectators. They mock them both, threaten one by way of the other, and frankly insult the spectators by obliterating their image when they send the white masks off to hell. The play ends with all the black actors grouped together, apparently freed and separated from the spectators, who, after having been "used" throughout the play, are relegated to a solitude in which nothing any longer offers them the satisfaction of being reflected, of being set up as formidable images.

Although Genet's plays differ with regard to the spectator's degree of involvement in the theatrical rite, they have this in common: that the performed rite or rites, whatever their purpose, are always based on the acting out of a role, on the characters' attempt at identification with what they want to become or want to destroy. Lefranc plays at being a great murderer by strangling Maurice, in order to belong to the world of Yeux-Verts and perhaps to that of the super-murderer Boule de Neige. Claire and Solange, making ready for the murder of Madame, play at being Madame and Claire. The regular customers of the Balcony play at being a bishop, a general, and a judge. The Blacks play at being Whites and also at being Blacks such as the Whites imagine them to be. Thus the characters become reflections, images of something other than themselves—but no more than reflections, for there is always that distance of unreality required by the customers of the Balcony. On the other hand, these reflections have a real effect when the identification has actually been achieved in the eyes of others: when they are really taken for the Bishop, the General, and the Judge, the customers of the Balcony —led by the Chief of Police and Irma, who has become the Queen— make possible the defeat of the revolution; and Claire, who has become Madame in the eyes of Solange playing the role of Claire, is really poisoned. But the characters or actors never completely take the place of those whom they reflect or symbolically embody. The real Madame doesn't die from Claire's poison; at nightfall Irma is still the head of the brothel, and Roger, the revolutionary who castrates himself, castrates only himself: "I still have mine," cries the Chief of Police with satisfaction; "though my image is castrated in all the brothels in the world, I remain intact. Intact, gentlemen."

Library
Highland Comm. College
Highland, KS 66035

One can only conclude that in the long run the rite is ineffective and vain.

As early as *Haute Surveillance*, Genet showed the ritual murder to be a failure. Of course Maurice is really killed, but Lefranc, objectively a murderer, does not manage to correspond to the image of himself that he wanted to have in the eyes of Yeux-Verts. Genet recognizes that a rite, by definition, is trickery, since it is a deliberate representation of something other than itself. Hence the "tragedy" of *Les Bonnes* is that the gesture of the two maids, seeking desperately to identify with their mistress so that they can manage to kill her, must result in suicide for one of them and in prison for the other. In a different tone, *Le Balcon* can end only in mockery, since, in an offhand manner and by way of Irma, both spectators and characters are dismissed and sent back to their daily illusions. As for *Les Nègres,* the play is frankly presented as a deception: the game of mirrors, insulting to all, is ultimately shown to be merely an entertainment without any real significance; all the sumptuous imagery and the whirlwind of language and gestures actually have been not only a warning but, essentially and taken as a whole, a masque meant to conceal some obscure event that was truly happening offstage and that was the concern only of the Blacks in the mystery of their drama and their rebellion. A divertissement in the etymological sense of the word—that is, an action designed to turn away or distract—*Les Nègres* recalls those royal betrayals in which, while the jesters were dazing the guests by amiably mocking them, outside the palace a massacre was taking place. Faced with this particularly complex game, the spectator is tempted to wonder whether it is true that every evening, during the performance, a real act is committed by the Blacks while the white audience lets itself be taken in by the sorcery of a sham ceremony in a theatre. But, obviously, the act committed off-stage is real only in relation to the spectacle; it is another sham, more threatening than the spectacle but just as imaginary.

Thus this most ritual of all theatre remains theatre. That is to say, contrary to true ritual—or, as it were, a true Mass, however black—the symbol does not represent a transcendent and actual reality but becomes an aesthetic absolute in itself. Having proclaimed his dream of a theatre-Mass—that is, a ceremony during which the bread would veritably become divine flesh—Genet is the first to acknowledge the inevitable failure of that transubstantiation. His plays as a whole, and not merely the beautiful and sordid sexual objects in which they abound, are wishful thinking and are presented as such. Genet may have once dreamed of what a Mau Mau theatre might be, but he well knows that the magic it implies can be only imaginary in the world of today. Our world is such that when we stick pins in the effigy of an enemy, he doesn't necessarily collapse of a deadly disease. Genet is not an enchanter, a surrealist magician, or an illuminist. His works—fictional, poetic, or dramatic—have little to do with a primitive attempt at working magic. They are quite simply a search for personal salvation—his own and that of his characters—and while the terms are very special to him, it is a really modern salvation: asserting one's authenticity within the social and political world.

In Genet's universe that outside world always remains essentially the same, even though it sometimes changes color, as it were. Madame sips champagne with her lover, who has just been released from prison, while Claire poisons herself. The Chief of Police, still "intact," closes himself into his sumptuous tomb "to wait for 2,000 years," while Roger castrates himself. The colonists in *Les Paravents* and the Whites in *Les Nègres* may have fled or been sent off to hell, but the principle of authority remains unchanged: the Arab soldiers in *Les Paravents* have set up their own police state; the Blacks in *Les Nègres* foresee the coming of a "black" state. Both states—the overthrown and the new—are necessary and hateful. They interest Genet only to the extent that they allow his chosen (that is to say, wholly cursed) characters to define themselves.

Les Nègres and *Les Paravents* clearly show the stages involved in that search for an authentic definition. The first stage is the liquidation of authority as it exists in the world of established Good: for the Blacks, the Whites, and for the Arabs, the colonists. Here Genet is in a sense cheating, for he portrays those established groups by way of expressionist masks representing a historically dated reality: his queens, his missionaries, his generals, his big landowners, English or Dutch, are in fact allegories of nineteenth-century colonialism, contemporaneous with Queen Victoria or Lyautey. Their kind of oppression is of course a reflection of ours today, but a degraded reflection, out of phase with the times, showing ours as nothing but a dying memory of past conquests. In *Les Nègres* Genet's portrayal of the Whites as a cliché of anti-colonialist liberalism allows him to point up not simply the Blacks' revolt against authority, but, more importantly, and on the periphery of White authority (which is so easy to satirize), the *inner* drama of the black rebellion; for the mysterious and threatening act committed offstage is a drama between Blacks.[1] In short, the drama is less the rebellion than the inner life of the rebellion. Similarly, while *Les Paravents* shows first the elimination of nineteenth-century colonialism and then the gory battle against the present reality (the Foreign Legion and soldiers of repression), its real tragedy has to do with the Arabs themselves. True, it is in relation to the missionaries, the big landowners, the academicians, the Foreign Legion, and the police that the revolt is made possible, but what the play really suggests is the question of how not to reproduce what one hates. Revolt, for Genet, is valid only if it remains a revolt—hence the tragedy. In the end, one order is replaced by another, and authority and oppression remain or merely take on new forms: Madame alive, the Chief of Police immortal in his tomb, and the Algerian rebels in their new roles of judges and organizers are all necessary to his thesis. For it is only in the negation of success—that is to say, in defeat or renunciation, in suicide instead of murder, in the vicarious mutilation of the hated image, or in the most extreme realization of baseness—that the protagonists achieve the authenticity which Genet calls "glory."

Glory is a word that occurs frequently in the works of Genet, and one which has innumerable connotations for the French. Among other things, it evokes, on the one hand, the fate of the Christian martyrs and, on the other, the ambition of Corneille's heroes. And these two connotations are closely linked: glory results when a being has completely achieved his destiny, his inner purpose, or the demands of his faith, in his own eyes or in the eyes of God or man. It means that a radiance emanates from his person, and Genet's imagery ("shining," "radiant," "illuminating") is not far removed from that which bestows a halo on the saints or from the "glow" and "brightness" by which the heroes and heroines of Corneille make themselves visible. The only ambition of Genet's protagonists is to be seen or to see themselves in that dazzling light conferred by self-realization. It is their definition of salvation. It is also Genet's. And what better means is there than theatre for imposing that image of

---

[1] The ambiguity of the whole thing lies in the fact that Genet speaks forcefully to the spectator, only to say that it is actually none of his business.

himself on larger and larger crowds—an image that finally becomes his truth through having been relentlessly asserted.

A play by Genet may be a ritual, but the purpose of that ritual is not to prod us into action in order to improve the lot of maids, blacks, or Algerians (Genet is hostile to all liberal reform, finding it an insult), or to strike us down magically in order that the oppressed may more easily win their freedom. Its purpose is to bestow halos on the oppressed and, by the same token, on him around whom oppression has crystallized—Genet himself. For Genet is Genet, and his intensely personal works are, above all, a description of the author's destiny. While Genet sings of the evil and misery of an entire antisociety, it is upon himself that his song confers glory or himself that it annihilates.

Genet and his characters are, of course, all prisoners of definitions or humiliating images that have been imposed on them from the outside, and their prison provokes in them the angry rebellion through which they transcend such definitions. At the very start, however, *Haute Surveillance* showed that to transcend one's lowly state and rise to the level of a great hero required more than just wanting to, or even performing acts similar to those of the heroes; one had also to be marked out by a kind of grace. It was in *Haute Surveillance* that Genet disclosed his personal dilemma. Rejected by established society, who saw him as a pariah, a petty thief and homosexual prostitute, he accepted that rejection but only to go beyond it toward a more grandiose state of evil or misery. Yet such glory through excessive evil was also refused him. Genet is not and never could be a hero of crime, but he has discovered still another possibility: the acceptance of both rejections and a continuous effort to sink ever deeper into a social and moral no-man's land—the realm of absolute negation.

It is doubtless from this perspective that Genet's most recent play, *Les Paravents*, should be considered. And, retrospectively, that play throws light on his earlier dramatic achievements. Men, as seen by Genet, aim at dazzling the world with a powerful and beautiful image of themselves. If the image fits in with the established Good, Genet holds it up to ridicule, although he pays poetic tributes to certain killer-images of that established order: the Executioner, Chief of Police, Soldier—those who destroy in the name of Good being both the adored and hated brothers of the criminals branded by Evil. If such an image is at war with the established

Good, in the name of crime or destructive revolution, it is glorified
by Genet through lyricism and all the resources of the imagination.
In both cases Genet is the savage or ecstatic bard, but he can be only
a bard: he himself is out of picture; he is the cursed poet, doubly
cursed, and his poetry is one of substance with his malediction.
Having, at the end of *Haute Surveillance,* revealed that double
curse in Lefranc's cry, "I'm really all alone," it would seem that
from play to play Genet managed to "assume" his double solitude
and out of it finally created the main character of *Les Paravents,*
Saïd, whose long pilgrimage is a difficult and rigorous descent into
the zone of dual rejection and, in the end, complete annihilation.

Indeed, Saïd's glory in *Les Paravents* is not that of the great
criminal, king of the prison, whose walk to the guillotine is an
apotheosis. His glory is that of the traitor. Presented from the very
beginning as the poorest and most abject of all, it is by forcing his
abjection to the very extreme that he ends by "shining"; it is because he is finally executed by his own people that he, more than
any other character, has completely achieved his destiny. When the
curtain falls, the dead are waiting for him to arrive; but he will not
arrive, for his death is an absolute death. Ironically, the dead themselves say that he is "among the dead": on earth as in heaven or hell,
absolutely nothing of him remains, except the legend of his achievement.

Les Paravents has over ninety characters but is entirely organized
around the great adventure of Saïd and his wife-shadow, Leila, the
ugliest woman in Algeria—so ugly that she has to wear a hood to
hide her face. It is in relation to this adventure that the numerous
events of the play—crimes, rebellions, repressions, revolutions,
murder—all drawn from the substance of the recent war in Algeria,
take on their meaning. There can be no doubt that on a certain level
the play is on the side of the rebels and includes a vicious, although
rather ambiguous, satire of the colonists. That the French Army and
the Foreign Legion are handled too roughly[2] is open to question:
Genet raises the Lieutenant and the handsome Sergeant to a level
of poetic heroism that shows how both attracted and repelled he is by
his own characters. He glorifies them, but for their almost Nazi
nihilism or for the foul things they do, and he poeticizes them in
the name of Evil. However, he rejects the Algerian revolution as

[2]For this reason the performance was interrupted by violent manifestations in
May and September 1966.

soon as it sets up its own order. In other words, by using but transcending a political issue that is still an extremely sensitive subject among the French and Algerians, Genet deliberately situates his play in the living reality of the most current collective passions, thus, beyond any ambiguity, pointing up the stand he takes, or what might be called his personal heroism. Well anchored in the present historical reality, he describes his ethic—a refusal of the world.

In this respect the play is both the outcome of a search that has abstract philosophical depth and the integration of an individual drama into concrete reality. In all probability the intellectual exchanges between Sartre and Genet contributed to this development; in fact, one sometimes gets the impression that Genet is becoming what Sartre said that Genet was aiming to be. But whatever the influences that came into play, Genet has arrived at the historic embodiment necessary for a theatre "of ideas" to evolve from abstract allegory to living drama, a process to which we have already alluded in the case of Claudel.[3] Thus with *Les Paravents,* and within the framework of history, the philosophical implications of Genet's works become clear: they lead straight to nothingness, but a nothingness *hic et nunc.*

There is, at the outset, Genet's desire to exalt an antisociety through poetry, describing it in all its horror, but with the flourishes of a rhetoric that gloriously parodies the French "beau style." This antisociety is necessarily relative to our own society and is, so to speak, a negative of it. It is the world of thieves, murderers, perverts, prostitutes, rebels—or of blacks, since *we* are white, and of slaves, since *we* are masters. "Going into a brothel," says Carmen in *Le Balcon,* "means rejecting the world." That is to say, going into crime is like going into holy orders: it is a sign of renouncement. Carried a step further, renouncement becomes not only social but universal: from *Haute Surveillance* to *Les Paravents* (and no doubt with all the "whirligigs" Sartre speaks of in his *Saint Genet*) one moves into that more complete negation. While society and antisociety reflect one another as photograph and negative, within each of the two groups there is also a play of reflections in which everything is merely appearance—that is, in which the real dissolves. This is the general meaning of *Le Balcon,* where not only is the General, for example, reduced to "nothing [nothing other than the

[3]See above, pp. 69-70 [of Guicharnaud, *Modern French Theatre*].

image of what he is not, since he is not really a general] reflected
ad infinitum" in the mirrors of one of the studios at Mme. Irma's,
but the play itself is presented as an illusion that merely reflects,
in the form of a reverse image, the illusion of our own world. As for
Les Nègres, once the ceremony is over, even if the Whites have been
symbolically eliminated, the curtain falls on the group of Blacks
contemplating the white catafalque seen at the beginning of the
play: if they continue to exist, it will be in relation to their revolt
against the Whites. And even if the dialogue and final reunion of
Village and Vertu have been considered "the first gleam of hope
in Genet's dark theatre,"[4] their dialogue emphasizes the fact that
the existence of the Blacks remains relative: Vertu reproaches Village for being like all men—that is, for "imitating"—and concludes
by saying, "There's at least one sure thing: you won't be able to wind
up your fingers in my long blond hair"—as if she can't manage to
picture herself except in relation to a kind of Mélisande. Turning
one's back on someone, even as a sign of liberation, means taking
him into account. The identity of antisociety can be affirmed only
in contrast, by means of reflection, even if that reflection be rejected. Hence there can be no absolute identity or authenticity. In
fact, the only "reality" is nothingness—a nothingness, as Sartre
points out, perhaps not very different from Mallarmé's Void while
he was in the process of composing his incompleted text *Igitur,* and
indeed Mallarmé needed a mirror in which to look at himself in
order to be sure he existed.

Genet's last works are filled with symbols of emptiness: the tomb
(no doubt recalling Franco's) into which the Chief of Police dis-
appears at the end of *Le Balcon;* the sheet stretched over the chairs
in *Les Nègres* ("architecture of emptiness"), under which the expected coffin is missing; and, most of all, the many absences that
punctuate *Les Paravents*—the suitcase of wedding presents that
turns out to be empty, at the end of Tableau 1 and, again, the gendarme's empty suitcase in Tableau 13; Saïd's empty pants dancing
alone in the third tableau; the giant empty glove in the fourth;
the nonexistent farmyard of Leila and Saïd's mother in the third;
and Leila's blanket reduced to a single hole in the ninth. Actually,
all of Genet's works move in the direction of emptiness, but especially *Les Paravents,* which picks up devices, motifs, and even char-

---

[4]Martin Esslin, *The Theatre of the Absurd* (New York, Doubleday Anchor, 1961),
p. 163.

acters from his earlier novels and plays. In the sixteenth tableau of *Les Paravents* (when one discovers that nothing of Leila is left on earth, and that only her hood remains among the dead) there is one of the most violent metaphors of this theme: in a long speech the dead Sergeant tells about how he died and describes the moment when, with "vacuous eyes," he evacuated into a hole. The scatological metaphor may be unbearable for many spectators—indeed, it is meant to be—but it is no less valid for all that: at the very moment that, empty-eyed, he empties his bowels, the Sergeant loses his power, "the beauty of [his] warlike gestures," in the same way that at such moments a general would lose his stars. The glow of the image of the hero as hero dies out not only for himself but for others. Since the end of this play reveals a glory of another kind, however, Genet pays his character the tribute of killing him off then and there, without giving him the time to become again the mythical Sergeant haloed by his murders and bloody deeds.[5] One might say that the Sergeant died a "beautiful" death, its beauty being not that of the guillotine or torture but that of emptiness. That is why, in death, he makes contact with Saïd, who of course is much further along the road to annihilation than he is, for annihilation is the result not of some final circumstance but of a long progression.

During *Les Paravents* the main characters are destroyed one after another, and while the survivors manage merely to replace a hateful order by one equally hateful, the dead find themselves in a common limbo, where they are all smilingly reconciled. Only Saïd and his wife succeed in going even beyond death to nothingness. Just as there is a hierarchy of established society and a hierarchy in the world of crime, so there is a hierarchy in death, the summit of which is complete absence. Situated directly under that glorious spot is Saïd's mother, for it was she who did her very best to help her son in his journey toward nothingness, foreseeing and summoning that nothingness, which is the cause of her barking like a dog and her wild laughter that fills the Algerian night. She herself remains this side of the final achievement—as one might say that Mary does not have quite the perfection of Jesus—but among

---

[5]For the performance Roger Blin and Jean-Louis Barrault didn't hesitate to give the Sergeant's speech the marvelous theatrical setting Genet was after: the two greatest ladies of French theatre today, Madeleine Renaud (playing the fantastic prostitute Warda) and Maria Casarès (playing Saïd's mother), both among the dead and in extravagant costumes, serenely transformed themselves into sumptuous armrests to hold up the squatting Sergeant while he told and mimed his story.

the dead she has the right to a throne. Thus, after having sung of an antisociety, Genet, with *Les Paravents,* managed to impose the image of an antitheology.

"I know of no other criterion for the beauty of an act, an object, or a person than the singing it arouses within me," said Genet—or, rather, wrote Genet, since the quotation comes from a speech written for the radio but never delivered. This statement may not be the key to Genet's works, but it does clarify them: Genet sings, and he calls what he sings *beautiful.* In fact, all the philosophical "whirligigs" in his works add up to an aesthetic. In the wake of Baudelaire and Rimbaud, Genet renames the world through his song—that is, through his words—thus creating beauty.

Among thousands of examples of his aesthetic theory, consider the flute player in *Les Paravents,* who at one point appears playing his flute with his nose. A rather banal metaphor of poetic alchemy, this episode illustrates an idea that has been well known since Baudelaire, the Romantics, and, even before them, Boileau (with his "odious monster").[6] Here "the air breathed out of two holes in a dirty nose" becomes sweet music. But elsewhere in the play, and more precisely, Genet affirms the power of semantics itself: in Tableau 9 Leila almost drops a glass, keeps it from falling, and says, "Stop being an ass or I'll break you. ... And what will you be then? Bits of glass...bits of broken glass...little fragments...little pieces of glass...debris. *(Solemnly)* Or, if I want to be kind, chips... sparkling splinters." Genet discovered (or rediscovered in the wake of the *poètes maudits*) that beauty is a question of vocabulary; he also saw that the trouble Baudelaire took in *La Charogne* or Rimbaud in *Les Chercheuses de poux* was unnecessary, that one has merely to give the name "glory" to all that is ignoble and the transformation is complete. Shakespeare and Corneille knew all about the trick, although they used it in their own ways and less systematically. But since they lived in a pre-Sartrean and pre-Lévi-Straussian period, they were unable to take Genet's short cuts.

If Corneille comes to mind apropos of Genet, it is not only because the two are linked by a particularly glorious vocabulary, but also, and above all, because the characters of both playwrights achieve their personal integrity through a systematic *abuse* of the

[6]*Art poétique,* Chant 3, line 1.

vocabulary they use to describe themselves. In both writers language is baptism—that is, name-giving: the spectators or listeners must give in when a character says, "I am thus and so" or "this object is called thus and so," even if what they perceive is quite the opposite. Of course, another comparison is also suggested: "this is my body...this is my blood," The Gospel, Corneille, Claudel, and Genet all use the same hocus-pocus, in which madness, quackery, and mysticism meet, but which is fantastically effective, even after three centuries of rationalism. In short, one might say that Genet, for his own special purposes, reaffirms the reality of the Word.

An early nineteenth-century caricature shows Victor Hugo and the whole Romantic school on the back of a Pegasus-dragon, under the banner, "Nothing is beautiful but ugliness." Today the engraving may seem ridiculous, yet Hugo's assertion of the beauty of the grotesque was no less contradictory than Genet's exaltation of the beauty of crime, sordidness, and abjection. Leila in *Les Paravents,* who is so ugly that she is not allowed to live without covering her face, is worthy of the same homage as Quasimodo in *Notre Dame de Paris.* Saïd's thefts and betrayal are worthy of as much "admiration" as Cleopatra's revenge in Corneille's *Rodogune.* In all civilizations ugliness and crime have often been the object of poetic glorification. In this respect Genet is a traditional writer; he merely draws the extreme inferences of that tradition.

Genet's very language is comprised of both ugliness as such and traditionally poetic elements which paradoxically affirm the beauty of that ugliness. As Jacques Lemarchand remarked in his review of *Les Paravents,*[7] "the dirty words used by Genet," which shock the spectators, are spoken "by the very people who should use them, and if they spoke in any other way, we would no longer believe in them." In other words, much of Genet's vocabulary and syntax is borrowed directly from the violent slang used by the models for his characters, and such slang may be said to have its own beauty. But sometimes the characters suddenly stop using those realistic words and change to an artificial language, eloquent or poetic, which seems to be a parody of a lofty French style. In this way the characters themselves become the bards of their own crime, baseness, or misery. They steal from the world they reject, or which rejects them, a language that is not their own but with which they adorn them-

---

[7]*Figaro Littéraire,* April 28, 1966.

selves—just as they physically deck themselves out in stolen clothing or in shoes they happen to find. For Genet adorns his antiworld with more than language. The entire spectacle (costumes, makeup, decor) is meant to dress his characters and his favorite themes in their Sunday best, as it were.

The contrasts in color and the garish lighting of *Haute Surveillance,* like the Louis XV furniture, the lace, and the profusion of flowers in *Les Bonnes,* add to those sort of "No Exit" plays a feeling of chapels—one austere, the other very chichi—which serve to enshrine the murders. The brothel and costumes of *Le Balcon* are so extravagant that what might have been merely picturesque becomes a monument to universal illusion. With *Les Nègres* and especially *Les Paravents,* the scenic festivity becomes even more original and significant. In honor of the rebels or the crimes, an architecture rising in tiers is constructed onstage, the various levels serving not only to grade—that is, to promote or demote—actions and groups of characters, but to put them really on display—a display of the worst possible taste: black suits and yellow shoes, grotesque masks, excessive makeup in the expressionist manner, clashing and gaudy colors, an overabundance of rags and tatters, the mismatched motley of patched garments.

The screens themselves, in *Les Paravents,* savagely and sketchily painted, are more than a mere functional device for quick changes and stylized decor: they give the play its title, and since, in their naive fakery, they enshrine each action, they "unreal-ize" the whole play by reducing it to a decoration. In fact, the play itself is basically a setting (the screens) plus a song (culminating in Ommou's cry at the end of the play, "Long live the song!"). It is presented to the spectator as nothing more than a great architectural and verbal decoration, a huge facade, a gigantic creation of the imagination, like the illusion of a cathedral built in honor of nothingness.

In the middle of *Les Paravents* unfolds one of the most shattering scenes in today's theatre. Right after Kadidja, the leading woman revolutionary, has been killed, she invokes Evil: "Evil, marvelous Evil, you who stay with us when everything else is shot to hell, miraculous Evil, you're going to help us. Please—standing up, I beg you, Evil—come and impregnate my people. And they'd better not be idle!" Then one after another the Arab rebels arrive, and Kadidja asks each one what he has done. Briefly they answer: one has picked up weapons, another has raped the daughter of a colonist, a third has screamed "kill the bastards," a fourth has torn out a heart, a fifth has ripped open a stomach, and so on. They spread out onstage and each one, with a color-spray gun, quickly draws on one of the white screens what he has done. In a very short time the stage is decorated with horrible, improvised pictures representing weapons, fires, torn limbs, and other attrocities This gigantic "happening" points up the general meaning of Genet's works: ritual invocations, hate, crime, and evil are all hurled at the spectator, but the frightful acts recalled by the Arabs are twice removed, in the form of images, for, more than the acts themselves, there is the beauty that emerges from their horror. In other words, the real massacres fade out behind the spots of color that represent them. And those spots of color are, in the end, merely spots of color.

If Genet shocks, it is certainly because he has set himself up as the poet of our possible collective massacre,[8] and also because he cries out his hatred of our well-being, affirms the presence of Evil within Good and of antisociety within society, and identifies us with what we prefer to ignore or repress. But his works transcend mere provocation or denunciation. Rejected from all sides, Genet rejects the world; or, rather, he empties it. Caught up in the frustrating mirror-play of reflections ad infinitum, haunted by the most personal fantasies, Genet, in *Les Paravents,* while keeping all the elements of that private universe, moves beyond them toward an authentic heroism or, as has often been said, toward a kind of saintliness: "I want you to refuse the brilliance of darkness, the softness of flint, and the honey of thistles," says Leila to Saïd in Tableau 13. And this going even beyond evil and misery is probably Genet's cruelest insult of all, for we realize that the great flourish of glory and heroism and the harsh poetry of renunciation have only one purpose—to conjure us away altogether, characters and spectators alike.

[8]Indeed, Robert Brustein believes that Genet "may well go down as the dramatic artist who presided over the disintegration of the West" (*Theatre of Revolt* [Boston, Little, Brown, 1964] , p. 411).

Genet: The Struggle With Theater

by Bernard Dort

Much is said about Genet and very little about his works. If anyone comments on them, it is in order to return to Genet the character, to exalt the legend of that "foundling, thief, beggar, convict, homosexual...and artist." In short, there is no end to the canonizing of "Saint Genet." Every critic thinks he is obliged to retrace, for himself and in his own way, the path traced once and for all by Sartre. Impossible to pass this checkpoint. Genet's works refer back to Genet the character and this character exists only for these works. As a result, all critical discussions seem ridiculous and vain: did Sartre not say everything which could be said about Genet the artist as a hero of our time and the antithesis of the revolutionary Bukharin, and hadn't Genet himself already put the finishing touch on his portrait in *The Thief's Journal?*

To be sure, one of his central preoccupations was the fashioning of his image. His novels are so many imaginary autobiographies, so many trick mirrors aimed at making this image shine forth. But Genet did not stop there. As early as *The Thief's Journal,* he also showed us the other side of these mirrors. Perhaps it was precisely Sartre's book which allowed him to cross that barrier behind which his critics are presently entrapped. He acknowledged it himself: "It took me a while to recover. I was almost unable to continue writing. Sartre's book created a vacuum which allowed a sort of psychological deterioration. This deterioration permitted the meditation which led me to my theater."

"Genet: The Struggle with Theater," by Bernard Dort. Translated from the French by Ruth Goldfarb. From *Théâtre réel* (Paris: Editions du Seuil, 1971), pp. 173-89. Used by permission of Georges Borchardt, Inc. Some footnotes have been deleted.

The Theatrical Metamorphosis

With the exception of *Deathwatch,* still very close to his novels, and *The Maids,* all of Genet's theater is in effect posterior to *Saint Genet, Actor and Martyr.* Since that time, Genet has not written, or at least has not published, a novel. Thus his activity as playwright coincides, in the main, with a mutation. Genet the writer detached himself, thanks to Sartrian meditation, from Genet the character. While retaining the same themes, his production has changed its structure, its function and perhaps its meaning. This is precisely what the critics, by trying to outdo one another about the writer as a character, have hardly noticed: in the studies by Claude Bonnefoy[1] or Jean-Marie Magnan,[2] the place devoted to theater remains small, and the plays are generally evoked only by reference to the novelistic universe. But it is through an understanding of the distance which separates his plays from his novels that we can understand Genet's theater: And not in forcing the latter back onto the former.

A first observation imposes itself: Genet's universe has widened. In his novels, it was limited to the closed milieu of the prison or the back rooms of Pigalle cafes where the queens of *Our Lady of the Flowers* make fun of each other. On the stage, note how it expands vertiginously: first restricted to a prison cell *(Deathwatch),* then to the bedroom of Madame where the Maids act out their servitude and their sham revolt (at first, Genet wanted the action to take place in the back staircase which leads from the master's apartment to the maids' rooms), it has expanded to encompass the whole space of a city, from the brothel to the headquarters of the revolutionaries, including a phantom Royal Palace *(The Balcony),* then a fictitious continent: the Africa of *The Blacks,* and finally a real country: Algeria fighting for its independence, which continues the "balcony" of the kingdom of the dead. And the temporal concentration which was the rule—for example, in *Funeral Rites,* Genet's long meditation, when he returns from the morgue, on the death of Jean D.—is

---

[1]Claude Bonnefoy, *Genet* (coll. "Classiques du XXe siècle," no, 76, Editions universitaires, Paris, 1965).

[2]Jean-Marie Magnan, *Essai sur Jean Genet* (coll. "Poètes d'au jourd'hui," no, 148, Seghers, Paris, 1966).

followed by the unfolding of a chronicle of moments and events (from colonization to independence) in *The Screens.*

Must one rush to conclude that, as Claude Bonnefoy writes, "Genet is becoming a Socialist"? Doubtless, "in *The Maids,* the master-servant relationship already doubled and disturbed the love relationship uniting the servants with Madame. *The Balcony, The Blacks, The Screens* are critiques of prejudices, of justice, power, oppression, and colonialism. But they are criticisms only indirectly since Genet gives everything at once and shows the situations in their complexity. It is up to the spectator to draw the conclusions." By making Genet the playwright a politically committed writer, one risks understanding nothing about his theater and, in addition, justifying certain of the inane attacks of which he is the object.

On this point Genet is explicit: he did not write his plays to attack or defend anyone whomsoever: "One thing must be written: this has nothing to do with an argument on the lot of domestics. I suppose servants have their union—that's no business of ours."·"If my plays help Blacks, I do not worry about it. I don't believe it, however. I believe that action, the direct fight against colonialism, does more for Blacks than a play." Moreover, he is suspicious of all theatrical projects of the sort. They seriously threaten to turn against the cause which they mean to defend. Because "this is what a conciliating conscience never stops whispering to the audience: *The problem of a certain disorder—or evil—which has just been resolved on-stage indicates that it has really been abolished since, according to the dramatic conventions of our time, theatrical representation can only be the representation of a fact. Let's go on to something else and let our hearts swell with pride since we sided with the hero who strove for, and reached, the solution.*" The point is thus to do something else entirely and not to pretend to resolve, dramatically, the problems of the world. "No problem presented should be resolved in the imaginary especially as the dramatic solution serves an established social order. On the contrary, let the evil on the stage explode, show us naked, leave us haggard if it can, and with no recourse outside ourselves."

Didacticism or Magic?

One can always turn this categorical refusal around and see in Genet the playwright if not a committed writer at least a realistic one, which is very different. Noting that, in a play like *The Balcony*, "many of Genet's traditional themes, *the double, the mirror, sexuality* and especially, the superiority of the 'pure and sterile' dream and, at an extreme, of death, over effective but 'impure and compromise-spotted' reality, have been relegated to the level of accidents of the second order," Lucien Goldmann maintains that the works "have overall a realistic and *didactic* (in the Brechtian sense of the word) structure."[3] For him, "the play's subject, perfectly clear, almost *didactic,* is, as a matter of fact, constituted by the essential transformations of industrial society in the first half of the century." *The Balcony* would thus be a vast realistic parable in which Genet would have (consciously or unconsciously) "transposed onto a literary plane [...] the great political and social upheavals of the 20th century and in particular, for Western society, [...] the miscarriage of the enormous revolutionary hope which characterized the first decades of the century." Lucien Goldmann sees the best proof of this in what he considers to be the central action of the play: "the ascension of the Chief of Police and the Proprietor of the house of illusions"—individual incarnations, he says, of what a sociologist would have designated more largely as technocracy, incarnations which are not, however, accidental since the two characters represent its two essential aspects, the organization of business and the power of the State—"to a prestige previously reserved for the Queen, the Judge, and the General."

Such an interpretation is surely very ingenious. It nevertheless gives rise to serious objections. First of all, it fails to mention certain characters in the play: for example, the Beggar (of the eighth tableau) and the Slave (ninth) who in Paris were played by the same actor. This double character who seems to have only a secondary role performs an essential function: alone, with the Court Envoy, not to undergo a metamorphosis and not to accede to the dead glory of the "images" of the house of illusions, he doubtless represents the poet, indeed Genet himself ("famous for my songs, sir, which are hymns to your glory"). Next, it reduces the work to a socio-historic outline which is much too broad and imprecise to allow one to af-

[3]Lucien Goldmann, "Une pièce réaliste: *Le Balcon* de Genet," *Les Temps Modernes,* no. 171 (June, 1960). Having written this study before the publication of Goldmann's long essay entitled "Genet: A Sociological Study" [which is included in this volume], I was unable to take into account here the much more extensive and precise analysis to which Goldmann devoted himself.

firm, as does Goldmann, that we are dealing, in *The Balcony,* with the "first great Brechtian play in French literature," an example of "epic and didactic theater," whose object would be to relate "on a *typical level* an *essential evolution.*" Goldmann admits as much himself in passing: it is only on the level of "their manifestations in the superstructure" that *The Balcony* describes the great historic transformations for us. Thus, it would be more fitting to speak about a simple naturalistic fact, on a very large scale, than about epic Brechtian realism. For, unlike Brecht, Genet does not seek to show the causes of such transformations: he is content to show the effects — effects which are, in appearance, irreversible. Finally, an attempt at a Goldmannian decoding neglects a fundamental element of the dramatic structure of the work: its ceremonial character and the constant use which Genet makes of theater within theater. Perhaps Goldmann could reply to this last objection that such a theatrical game is precisely the sign of the reification of modern industrial society. Let us admit that a similar analogy remains quite vague, and would doubtless apply to any society.

Contrary to this sociological interpretation, there is another which entails seeing in Genet's dramatic works the very realization of the "metaphysical theater" of which Antonin Artaud dreamed. In fact, Genet and Artaud share the same admiration for the theater of the Far East and the same wariness with regard to Western dramatic art degraded to the point where it is now but a pretext for diversion or an instrument of propaganda. For the one as for the other, the object is to restore to theatrical representation its ceremonial character and to make it once again an act, to restore to the stage, that "place closely related to death, where all liberties are possible", its dignity. Thus, it is not a mistake to refer to Artaud when one speaks of Genet. Geneviève Serreau,[4] for example, cites Artaud calling for, rather than "the long habit of entertainment spectacles," "a serious theater, which, overturning all our preconceptions, inspires us with the fiery magnetism of its images and finally acts upon us like a spiritual therapeutics whose touch can never be forgotten."[5] Genet's theater would thus not have value "except by a magic, awful link with reality and danger." And it is

[4]Geneviève Serreau, *Histoire du "nouveau théâtre,"* (coll. Ideés Gallimard, Paris, 1966).

[5]Antonin Artaud, *The Theater and Its Double* (Grove Press, New York, 1958).

true that certain sentences in *The Letters to Roger Blin* resonate like echoes of *The Theater and Its Double.*

Let us leave aside as of secondary interest the question of the influence which the writings of Antonin Artaud could have had on Genet. If comparisons impose themselves occasionally, they remain rather vague and, above all, have virtually no explanatory value. For Genet's approach remains fundamentally different from Artaud's. Geneviève Serreau acknowledges this: Genet's refusal is much less radical than Artaud's. Far from rejecting all Western dramaturgy as "a theater of idiots, madmen, sexual perverts, grammarians, grocers, antipoets and positivists," Genet goes still further: he pushes this dramaturgy to its furthest limits, he down shifts and plays with it to the point of exhaustion. His theater remains a textual theater.[6] Although he makes much of the spectacle, nowhere does he attempt to bring the spoken word back to its origin, "to the brink of the moment when the word is not yet born, when articulation is already no longer a cry but is not yet discourse, when rehearsal is *almost* impossible and with it language in general."[7] Likewise, it is less the body which Genet wants to expose on stage than its disguises; far from having to retrace this "blood-route by which he penetrates into all the others each time his organs in full power awaken from their sleep," the actor, according to Genet, never ceases to declare his pretence. It is neither a character copied from life nor his own body which he shows on stage; it is a collection of masks and shams, a perpetual illusion. One can even say that Genet takes precisely the opposite course from Artaud: while the latter takes exception to rehearsal, in that it is repetition, diminution and disguise, Genet makes it the very object of his theater; he stages it and exalts it. His theater is, in the literal sense of the word, a theater of representation: not only theater *within* the theater, but also theater about the theater. A doubly theatrical theater. Let us add however that a like operation does not exist without putting representational theater itself into question. Genet celebrates it only better to destroy it. Thus, by a singular chronological reversal, could Artaud take up where Genet left off.

[6]Artaud on the other hand emphasized the need for a "physical language, this materialized, soldified language by means of which theater is able to differentiate itself from speech."

[7]Jacques Derrida, *L'Ecriture et la Différence* (Le Seuil, Paris, 1967), p. 352.

A "Celebration of Nothing"

Does Genet himself, in the forewords to his plays, his *How to play* ... or the *Letters to Roger Blin,* give us therefore the key to his theater? In these texts, at once detailed and broad, one preoccupation is constantly expressed: that of making theater a ceremony, a celebration, "the Celebration." There again, we rejoin Artaud. And that Genet scarcely believes possible any more than a single performance of *The Screens* ("A single performance properly staged ought to suffice") is quite close to the refusal of rehearsals that Artaud opposed to Western theater. But the two approaches are nevertheless funadmentally divergent: while for Artaud theater "puts itself, whenever possible, in communication with pure forces," for Genet, it should, on the contrary, remain a celebration without content: "People say that plays are generally supposed to have a meaning: not this one. It is a celebration whose elements are disparate; it is the celebration of nothing." And if for the author of *The Theater and Its Double* theatrical activity, that "sort of primary Physics, from which Spirit has never disengaged itself," seeks to bring up to date, in the game between the stage and the audience, an essential truth, for the author of *The Screens* it remains the prisoner of the facticity which is the very mode of operation of our life in society. More exactly, this facticity is its very being.

To be sure, Genet never ceases to object that the stage stands in opposition to life: "Without being able to say exactly what theater is, I know what I won't allow it to be: the description of everyday gestures seen from the outside." Here one is talking about another domain and nothing can be transported, as is, from daily existence onto the stage: the actors must not allow themselves to slip back into "the gestures they use at home or in other plays," their actions here must surprise, flash ("the actor must act quickly, even in his slowness, but his speed, like lightning, will amaze") ... In short, onstage, everything must be *different.* Genet even excludes the possibility of lighting a cigarette, not from a fear of fire, but because the flame of a match cannot "be imitated on-stage: a lighted match in the audience or elsewhere is the same as on-stage. To be avoided." And no more than the theater is a reflection or a copy of reality, it cannot be the teaching of a moral lesson or the delivery of a message. Genet denies that *The Screens* signifies anything whatsoever: "My play is not the apologia for treason. It takes place in a realm where morality is replaced by the esthetics of the stage." Here we are going around in a circle. Dodging the affirmation of any truth (that of the world or of an antiworld) which would be exterior to it, would Genet's theater have any function other than the affirmation of a certain esthetic order, a certain theatrical truth? One can contest this view and see in the insistence with which Genet refuses to go beyond the opposition between the stage and everyday existence, between the theater and life, a kind of mask and something like a disguise, theatrical as well, of his own thoughts. It is now perhaps time to return to Genet's themes.

A House of Illusions

At the base of his works and his life itself there is an experience which we can justifiably term theatrical. This passage from *The Thief's Journal* is a corroboration: "In order to weather my desolation, when I withdrew more deeply into myself, I worked out, inadvertently, a rigorous discipline. The mechanisms were more or less the following (I have used them since): to every charge brought against me, unjust though it were, from the bottom of my heart I would answer 'Guilty.' No sooner had I pronounced this word, or the phrase signifying it, when within myself I felt the need to become what I had been accused of being."

It is here that theater is born. To oppose the world, Genet does not assert himself as he is; he transforms himself first into the person that others see in him. He is thus not going to show us, on-stage, men as they are or as they should be: he will put these people on stage the way we others, the audience, suspect and accuse them of being. Neither the Maids nor the Blacks are really servants or black people: they are maids as their masters imagine or fear them to be, Blacks as we, more or less racist Whites, imagine them. Genet clearly stipulates this: he wrote *The Blacks* in order that it be performed before Whites and for them: "This play, written, I repeat, by a white man, is intended for a white audience, but if, which is unlikely, it is ever performed before a black audience, then a white person, male

or female, should be invited to every evening. [...] You will play
for him. Throughout the entire performance, a spotlight should
be focused on this symbolic White. But what if no white person accepted this entertainment? Then let white masks be distributed at
the door to the black spectators. And if the Blacks refuse the masks,
then let a dummy be used."

Can one still speak about characters here? The word implies an
autonomy, an individual reality which the majority of Genet's
characters lack. Let us note, for example, that they are generally
nameless. A first name serves to designate them, or rather the in-
dication of their social role does so: here are the Chief of Police, the
Envoy... *(The Balcony),* the Policeman, the Gendarme, the Lieutenant, the Sergeant... *(The Screens).* Far from being individuals,
they appear as allegorical figures, as roles. Jean Genet calls them
"Images" or "Reflections." Let us not make a mistake here: this
reduction of the character to a type, this absorption of the individual
by a function is not, as is usually the case, a means of satire. The
point is not to fill the stage with caricatures. On the contrary, Genet
is bent on warning us: "One more thing: do not perform this play as
if it were a satire of this or that. It is, and will thus be played as,
a glorification of the Image and the Reflection. Its significance,
satirical or not, will appear only under these circumstances." While
he may have a Policeman or a Thief take the stage, it is not in order
to glorify the one and make fun of the other: he exalts them both to
the same degree. "The soldier scenes are meant to exalt—and I
mean *exalt*—the Army's prime, its chief virtue: stupidity." He never
knowingly reduces this or that character: if he reduces him to his
function, it is not to shrink him but rather to enlarge him through
this function. His theater is first of all celebration. Never "did I
look down on any of my characters—be it Sir Harold, the Gendarme,
or the Paratroopers. You can be sure that I have never sought to
understand them, but, having created them, on paper and for the
stage, I do not want to deny them. What binds me to them is something other than irony or contempt. They also helped to shape me.
I have never copied life—an event or a man, the Algerian War or
colonialists—but life has, quite naturally, caused various images to
come to life within me, or has illuminated them if they were already
there—images which I have translated either by a character or an
act."

On stage are thus assembled all the Images of what Genet could have been,[8] all the attitudes that society could have forced him to adopt. Perhaps theater is precisely that, for him: this house of illusions where you finally become what everyone else wants you to be. A perfectly ordered place where being and seeming, the character and the role coincide totally. At least Genet never ceases to dream about such a play of larger-than-life marionnettes, of "Über-marionnettes" to borrow Craig's expression, in other words of "actors plus fire, minus egoism."[9]

We find the image of such a supremely theatrical universe in the world of the dead in *The Screens*. They are only artificial dead people: they did not succumb to a physiological, a real death; they rather became their own Images. Death was for them only a means of realizing themselves as Reflections by becoming completely unreal. It is with the most disconcerting ease ("Well now!—That's right!—Well! What do you know!—That's it! And people make such a fuss about it!") that they reach their full theatrical existence. By breaking through a white paper screen, they penetrate the stage within the stage: into the very heart of the theater. There, they can shine, like Gordon Craig's Über-Marionnette which "will not compete with life—rather it will go beyond it. Its ideal will not be the flesh and blood but rather the body in trance—it will aim to clothe itself with a death-like beauty while exhaling a living spirit."[10] There they are immutable, perfect. As Genet already noted in *The Thief's Journal*: "If they [these heroes] have achieved perfection, behold them on the brink of death, no longer afraid of the judgment of men. Nothing can spoil their amazing success." Besides this, these fancy-dress dead people are also spectators: they take an interest in what goes on below, in Saïd's and Leila's existence; they await their arrival (but—we will come back to this later—neither Saïd nor Leila will reach the realm of the dead). Thus they are the entire theater: at once pure resplendent objects, without a flaw or a doubt, unveiled and transparent, and spectators contemplating the scene. In them, beneath the light of full illumination demanded by Genet ("Finally, if I am so insistent about the bright lights, both the

[8]The Lieutenant: "It's not a matter of intelligence; but rather of perpetuating an image more than ten centuries old, that grows stronger and stronger as that which it represents crumbles, that leads us all, as you know, to death." *(The Screens)*

[9]Edward Gordon Craig, *On the Art of the Theatre* (Heinemann, London, 1911), p. ix.

[10]Craig, *op. cit.*, p. 84.

stage and house lights, it is because I should in some way like both
actors and audience to be caught in the same illumination, and for
there to be no place for them to hide, or even half-hide"), theater
fulfills itself: here reigns, really and totally, "the esthetics of the
stage."

A Double Betrayal

Nevertheless, if ever one considers not only this privileged place
but the whole of Genet's theatrical universe (both the text and the
representation), this reign seems less total. It is doubly contested,
on the stage itself and by the audience at the same time.

Unlike Pirandello, for example, for whom stage acting at a second
level is the expression of an essential truth which people do not
manage either to articulate or to live in their day-to-day existence
but which they can grasp in the practice of drama, Genet never
ceases to emphasize the artificial character of such acting. He gives
the secret away. In *The Blacks,* Archibald is responsible for calling
us back to reality and he does not fail to do so: "We shall increase
the distance which separates us—a distance that is basic—by our
pomp, our manners, our insolence—for we are also actors. [...]
We're being observed by spectators. Sir, if you have any intention
of presenting even the most trivial of their ideas without caricatur-
ing it, then get out! Beat it!" The point is not to find truth in the
theater but on the contrary to exalt the false, the artificial which are
the portion of all theater. We, the audience, condemned Blacks to
be Negroes, servants to be Maids, etc. They are thus going to play
Negroes and Maids for us: "On this stage we are like guilty prisoners
who, in jail, play at being guilty." And the Balcony, the house of
illusions, does not directly represent a whole society, as Maya, the
metaphysical prostitute of the interwar playwright, incarnated the
image of all women, was Woman herself; it is society which enters
into the game of the Balcony, which submits to the sham of theater.

Jean Genet denies that the figures of his dramatic universe are
endowed with a general symbolic value. I have already emphasized
this: the stage, for him, cannot be a place where a real problem is
exposed and resolved, where a "perfected social order" is rebuilt.
On the contrary, it is a mask. The dramatic ceremony simultaneously conceals and reveals the essential: men's activity, their concrete

struggle, their refusal of society, if not of nature. Take *The Blacks;* while there takes place on-stage the imaginary execution of a white woman, who is in fact only a Black disguised by other Blacks who have become Negroes ("let the Negroes negrify themselves"), back- stage, far in the wings, farther still, the real action transpires: the execution of a Black guilty of having treated with the Whites ("Bear in mind that it's a matter of judging and probably sentencing and executing a Negro. That's a serious affair. It's no longer a matter of staging a performance. The man we're holding and for whom we're responsible is a real man. He moves, he chews, he coughs, he trem- bles. In a little while, he'll be killed.") The theater was "only there for show." What changes, what really happens, is out of our reach. On stage, the Blacks/Negroes are condemned to an endless repeti- tion: "We are what people want us to be, we will be that way until the end, absurdly," while elsewhere, somewhere else, something happens: not only a real execution (because the traitor "has paid. We'll have to get used to taking responsibility for blood—our own."), but an accession as well: "While a court was sentencing the one who was just executed, a congress was acclaiming another. He's on his way. He's going off to organize and continue the fight," a struggle which, they tell us, will reach the Whites in their "flesh and blood selves."

Theater can only *betray* reality, in the double sense of the word. It hides it to the extent that it can be only theater, that is to say a play of images turned towards the viewer and reflecting his own illusions. It reveals it since, in the final analysis, it denounces itself as theater: it cannot but repeat the same words and gestures in a ceremony pushed to the point of absurdity.

In *The Screens,* Genet does not content himself with superim- posing a false stage upon real wings: it is on the stage itself that he has played the theater and its antithesis, life. Thus the stage for *The Screens,* even more than for *The Blacks,* is divided into different levels whose number successively increases (in the seventeenth tableau the screens are arranged on four levels). It could even be said that the entire action of *The Screens* is contained in the pro- gressive differentiation of these levels. In the beginning everything happens on the ground. The characters group and define themselves by means of a double movement: the ascent of most of them, which is literally an accession to the theater, and the descent of the couple formed by Saïd and Leila. The former became, more or less, their

Images: their being is completed in the radicalization of their appearance. Thus they all find themselves, colonist and colonized, in that kingdom of the dead which is, in effect, the very domain of theater. The couple Saïd-Leila takes the opposite path. Far from affirming themselves as pure effigies, Saïd and Leila continue to deny themselves, to draw back. With all their might, they refuse to stand still, to become something. For them, the point is "to go to the end," not to perpetuate an image but to destroy all the images that can be made of them. To refuse any hold to anyone at all, because, as Saïd says, I must "keep rotting until the end of the world in order to rot the world." Thus, neither Saïd nor Leila will ever reach the theatrical realm of the dead. They will come to know a real death: the death which is the negation of life—the work of negation endlessly pursued. When she dies, Leila does not reach the heights of the set: she literally sinks within herself. And her death denies all theater, all ostentory facility: it is an obliteration, a destruction of the character (a character intimately linked with death: at the performance of *The Screens* given by the Odéon-Théâtre de France company, Leila, while still alive, was already fading away: a cloak of dirty linen hid her face from us). Nor does Saïd join the others who await him: like Leila, he is really going "to the dead."[11] He *exits* in death, unusable for everyone, having become a person and nevertheless present everywhere like an inexhaustible force for negation. Through Saïd and Leila, Genet's theater opens itself to question: it throws doubt upon the overly easy metamorphosis of people into characters, of characters into Images. He takes exception to any "dramatic solution" which "kowtows to an established social order." This time, it is indeed "evil [which] explodes onstage, shows us naked, leaves us haggard if it can and with no recourse outside ourselves." Leila says deliberately: "I know where we are going, Saïd, and why we're going there. It is not just to go somewhere, but so that those who are sending us there remain tranquil on a tranquil shore. We're here, and we're here so that those who are sending us here realize that they are not and that they're not here." Saïd and Leila shatter the interplay of reflections (between

[11] Here are the last lines of *The Screens:* "The Mother: Saïd!...I'll simply have to wait for him...Kadidja *(laughing):* Don't bother. He'll no more be back than will Leila.
The Mother: Well then, where is he?
Kadidja: With the dead."

characters and Images, between stage and house) which was, for Genet, all of theater.

The Last Celebration

Genet's dramatic works are the product of a merciless battle with the theater. First, Genet consents to theater; he is entirely in accord with it; he goes it one better in artifice. The stage becomes the scene of a ceremony where the social comedy is exalted in its most fragile appearances. Everything is ennobled and transfigured, even the most mediocre and ridiculous characters, frozen in their roles. Thus the reign of "the esthetics of the stage" is absolute. But this approach does not produce its own truth. Pushed to the limit, to the absurd, it self-destructs and reveals its emptiness to us. The Images show their reverse side, black like destruction and death.

It was necessary to entrap the audience. One had to give them this celebration where, promoted to the dignity of allegorical figures, they gorge themselves on their own reflections so that, at the end, they may recover their lucidity and see themselves, with neither mask nor disguise, perhaps in order that they, in their life itself, will recognize death at work. Just as in his novels Genet had, after a fashion, stolen beautiful language and, under the pretext of transfiguring the deeds, gestures and words of his "folles," pimps and murderers, given it to them in order that they might defile it forever and render it unusable for us, here he uses theater, in other words the most noble vehicle by means of which our society exhibits itself, only better to destroy it and, in the final analysis, to attack, by a spectacle, the society which needs such spectacles.

Here one thinks of the *potlatch* of certain primitive peoples which are at once offerings, celebrations and destruction. Genet's theater is a *potlatch* of the representation that our society makes of and for itself. And the catharsis it affords us is like the reverse of classical catharsis. After having provoked pity and fear, far from "bringing about the purgation proper to such emotions" (Aristotle), it opens instead onto the fear and pity of a naked existence: that of the poorest of the poor, the least endowed of the disinherited, that of a man whose life and death are synonymous. Releasing us from the comedy of a society which never ceases to contemplate itself, Genet introduces us into what one could call the silence of the "wretched of the earth."

Having started from a fascination with theater, his dramatic art is finally a negation of theater. For what it exposes on stage, that "place where reflections do not dwindle away but rather where flashes collide," is the theater itself. Thus Genet clears the slate: he gives us the last and perhaps the most fascinating of celebrations of our old theater. Nothing will escape, unless it be reality itself, unyieldingly rebellious, to all theater.

Jean Genet: The Theater of Hate

by Raymond Federman

Jean Genet has but rarely expressed himself openly on contemporary theater; but, to judge from his own dramatic output,
from the notes he often prefaces his plays with, and from the deep
interest he takes in their interpretation—as proof: the publication
of his *Letters to Roger Blin* concerning the staging of *The Screens*
in Paris—it is clear that he holds in some contempt the greater part
of contemporary theater.

Genet rejects such a theater because it betrays its origins and, as he
himself said in a letter to Jean-Jacques Pauvert (published as a post-
face to the original edition of *The Maids*): "Nothing can be expected
from a profession that is exercised with so little seriousness or self-
communion. Its point of departure, its raison d'être, is exhibitionism." In other words, Genet, throughout his works, is opposed to all
theater—even if it claims to be avant-garde—that satisfies too easily
the majority of the spectators and only brings to the playwright, as
to the actors, the zealous admiration of that part of society whose
vulgar instincts he flatters. A good example of this kind of exhibitionism is Peter Weiss' *Marat/Sade:* a fascinating theatrical experience, no doubt, but a play without either dramatic value or poetry
(Genet would say), and whose bourgeois success depends more on
the pseudo-spectacle that it offers than the power (which it doesn't
have) to involve the conscience of the spectators.

To be sure, Genet isn't the only one to indict what Sartre called,
long before him, "bourgeois theater"; Beckett, Pinget, Arrabal, the
"Living Theater," Ionesco—even if the creations of the latter (O

"Jean Genet: The Theater of Hate" by Raymond Federman. Translated from the
French by Frank Abetti. From *Esprit* 38: 391 (April 1970), pp. 697-713. Reprinted
by permission of the author.

irony...) seem more and more to satisfy bourgeois tastes—they too, even if only in their plays, have put into question the whole experience of the theater. But Genet cannot be tied down to any movement or school. He is the only one of his kind, and we will even dare say that he dominates contemporary theater by the originality of his plays and especially the subtlety with which he manipulates the essence of the theater.

After the fashion of Antonin Artaud in *The Theater and its Double,* Genet states that many modern plays have a tendency to divide men instead of making them communicate, even if only for an instant, in a kind of sacramental celebration. The goal of the theater, according to Genet, is precisely to give to the spectators a deeper sense of themselves, a more acute consciousness of their relationships with one another, even if these relationships are founded on a moral and social evil.

In this respect, Genet runs counter to a widespread tendency of the theater, and his plays become not only the vehicle of his ideas but also the means to give back to the theater a superior and more meaningful orientation. His plays arouse an intellectual enthusiasm in the spectator and, what is more, give each one the feeling of participating in something new, extraordinary: the spectators are as if transfigured; they become a sect. To sum up, Genet has attempted to return to what he considers the primary source of the theater: the *rite,* and more specifically the *mass* which awakens the feeling of communion so essential to all great theater.

Nothing is more dramatic than the elevation of the host; the mass unites the faithful in a bond symbolized by the bread consumed during the holy meal. Genet suggests (in the same letter to Pauvert) that good theater is of the same order:

> On a stage almost the same as our own, on a platform, the end of a meal was to be reconstituted. As a result of this single fundamental idea, which is hardly found any more, the greatest modern drama was expressed every day for 2,000 years in the sacrifice of the mass. The point of departure disappears under the profusion of ornaments which affect us still. Under the most familiar appearances—a crust of bread—a god is devoured. Theatrically, I know of nothing more effective than the elevation.

But, more than the rite itself, it is the *effectiveness* of the rite which fascinates Genet, just as in his works he is in search of the effects of beauty rather than beauty itself. For him, without doubt, one of the functions of art is to substitute the effects of beauty for those of religious faith, unless it is the converse, in the manner of Baudelaire: to substitute the effects of beauty for evil, a function which only the act of communion can accomplish.

Again in the letter to Pauvert (the one text for an understanding of his theater), Genet gives the example that Sartre related to him, of an instance where this feeling of communion was displayed in the middle of a theater audience. It happened in Germany in a prisoner of war camp, at Christmas:

> Some soliders, mediocre actors, had staged a French play evoking I don't know what theme—revolt, captivity, courage?—and the distant Fatherland was all of a sudden present not on the stage, but in the audience

The feeling the Christmas holiday aroused, to which memories of France were added, united all the spectators in a single poignant desire to see again the country from which they had been separated for such a long time. And Genet adds:

> A clandestine theater, where one could come secretly, at night and masked, a theater in the catacombs would still be possible. It would suffice to discover—or create—the common Enemy, then the Fatherland, to preserve or rediscover.

The existence of a Fatherland, whether it be France, the Church, the family or an experience shared by a group of men, is the necessary basis for the advent of this communion at the theater. The evocation of the fatherland, like the elevation of the host during the mass, unites those present in a common emotion. The emotion is magnified by the contribution of individual responses which dissolve to create a homogeneous body of feelings belonging simultaneously to each and to all. That is the essence of the rite.

But for Genet—and here we touch on the paradox crucial to his theater—the evocation of a fatherland is not possible. He doesn't have a fatherland; and even if he can evoke it for others it will always remain distant to the extent that it exists. Nor does he have religious faith, even if his works rely on a whole system of liturgical images. Nonetheless, he uses these concepts in his plays, but by inverting them: the native land (the "fatherland") becomes its opposite, the foreign land; religious images serve the cause of sensuality and sexuality. Thus, the emotions aroused in the spectators, calculated to unite them in a spirit of communion, become the opposite of love: hate.

The idea of an "inverted" fatherland takes on the form, therefore, of a "common enemy"; the role of the theater, then, consists in laying bare the causes of this hate, thereby uniting in a single group all those who recognize the enemy—just as one can offer a convincing argument, for example, by repeating that the only reason the free world has to justify its existence and its wars is the fight against communism.

Genet has never formulated a dramatic theory, the point is therefore not to find in his theater a coherent and precise system, but the idea of such an enemy is suggested throughout his works, and made explicit in a passage of the letter to Pauvert:

> I don't know what theater in a socialist world would be like, I understand better what it would be like in the land of the Mau Mau, but in the Western world, more and more affected by, and turned towards death, it can only refine itself in the "reflection" of a comedy, of a mirror-image of a mirror-image which a ceremonious game could make exquisite and close to invisibility. If one has chosen to watch oneself die deliciously, one must proceed with rigor, and arrange the funereal symbols. Or choose to live and discover the Enemy. For me, the Enemy will never be anywhere, there won't exist anymore Fatherland, whether it be abstract or interior. If I am moved, it will be because of the nostalgic memory of what it was. Only a theater of shadows would still touch me.

Even if only briefly set forth here, this idea of the enemy is amply substantiated in Genet's plays. The discovery of the enemy constitutes the plot of *Deathwatch, The Maids, The Blacks* and is implicit in the complex structure of *The Balcony* and *The Screens.*

Genet's theater is in fact based on this idea of discovery, that is, on a very often unexpected and shocking revelation. The discovery is that a situation is other than it seems, as it often happens in Latin theater of the decadent period or in Elizabethan drama. Understood in this sense, the discovery seems to be a modified version of the Aristotelian conception of the tragic awakening, since in this case the burden of consciousness is placed on the audience; the spectator bends under the tragedy, while the hero on stage is freed from his destiny. That is one of the subtleties Genet introduces in the conception of the tragic.

In *The Thief's Journal,* Genet says that the tragic hero is never conscious of the implications inherent in his condition, even if he believes himself to be his own enemy. Genet writes:

> Tragedy is a joyous moment. Joyous feelings are carried in the smile, in a liveliness of the whole body and face. The hero doesn't know the seriousness of a tragic theme. If he glimpses it ever, he must never really see it.

The enemy is in the relationships with others (or with the gods in Greek tragedy) and not inside the hero. Thus, as Genet says:

> The tragic hero delicately flouts his destiny. He accomplishes it so politely that the object this time is not man, but the gods.

It is in this way that Genet's plays reveal the common enemy and, in doing so, evoke and reaffirm the fundamental reason for the hate between men or between opposing groups—blacks against whites, mistress against maid, oppressor against oppressed, pimp against prostitute or, to use Genet's vocabulary, "caïd" against "mec."

Genet's plays, therefore, do not aim at purging hate, except in the case of Genet himself, if we are to believe Sartre when he says that for Genet writing is a form of personal catharsis. That is why it is false to state—despite certain critics—that a play like *The Blacks* was written to exorcise from whites a false image of blacks. Such an argument is tantamount to saying that Genet is a moralist and that exorcism constitutes the moral intention of his plays. To be sure, it is the only way a bourgeois audience is able to accept Genet's theater: by replacing it in the context of their own morality. But to attribute to Genet the intention to do good is rather odd; because those who see the moralist in him do nothing but apply to his works the traditional idea that all great art is moral art in the sense that it teaches us to live better—a strictly humanist point of view, and which excludes all works of art that give us a bad way of life; for example: Sade, Huysmans, D. H. Lawrence and many others, that is, all those who in the interest of moral security have been taxed with decadence and thereby placed out of the reach of young girls of good families.

In this sense, Genet isn't moral since his plays express evil and hate. What Genet shows on the stage isn't there to be rejected, but to be accepted, even if we loathe doing so. He wants us to devour the message of his plays, to digest it as well as possible, even if it is detrimental to our moral *good* health.

Ezra Pound often said that only "bad art" is immoral. From such a point of view, Genet is certainly moral, but independent of any humanist concepts of good and evil. If a moral philosophy is to be found in his works, it can only lie in the idea of obedience to the rules of conduct which govern human relationships. The term "equity" is the one that best describes this condition of morality in Genet. Any other attitude is false and can only logically lead to estheticism. If we accept this definition as a point of departure to judge the morality or immorality of Genet's art, it will be moral to the extent that he stages events which allow authentic human relationships to be established, in evil as in good. And if these events imply hate, servitude, lubricity, and not nobleness of soul, justice and temperance, can not one then reply to his detractors that it is high time someone had the courage to lay bare this other side of our existence?

The goal of Genet's theater is therefore to awaken in the spectator a common feeling of hate for the Enemy, whatever it may be. And it is this feeling which makes them communicate, not in love nor in joy nor in faith, but in hate and fear. However, this form of communion can not take place everywhere because the enemy is not the same everywhere; moreover, there is the problem raised by the different kinds of theater audiences. That is why Genet refused to let *The Blacks* be performed in Poland. There aren't any "blacks" in Poland, therefore no enemy—at least not that one. Genet explains what he means in a letter to Jerzy Lisowski, one of the Polish translators of *The Blacks:*

> I am opposed to such a performance for the following reasons: you understand that even if a few days before their execution condemned men—real ones—could act out, in the prison courtyard, in the presence of their judges and their executioners, a play dealing with the perfidy of their relationships with one another and with their executioners and judges, the dramatic emotion that such a performance would give rise to would have nothing in common with what ordinarily takes place at the theater. However, it happens that Blacks—real ones—are under the blow of the heavy sentence passed by the righteous tribunal composed of Whites—real ones, they too. These Blacks are thus in the above-mentioned situation: real condemned men face to face with their judges and their executioners.

And Genet adds a post-scriptum:

Except for miners, there aren't any Blacks in Poland; but this isn't a play about miners.

In the play, in fact, the spokesman for the Blacks, Archibald, says about the same thing when he cries out:

> On this stage, we're like guilty prisoners who play at being guilty.

If the sin, the hate or the shame evoked on stage are not shared by the spectators, the play has missed its point. That is why Genet insists that at least one white spectator be at each performance of *The Blacks;* the tribunal must always be present, even if only symbolically, in the form of a mannequin. In other words, the white spectators must be ill at ease; they must feel deeply that the play is against them, whence the necessity of the white in the theater, or else, as Genet says in his introduction, the message of the play is lost:

> This play, I repeat, written by a white, is destined for a white audience. But if, improbable as this may seem, it were to be performed one evening before a Black audience, it would be necessary to invite a white—male or female. The organizer of the spectacle will solemnly receive him, will have him dressed in a formal costume, and will lead him to his seat, preferably at the center of the first row of orchestra seats. The play will be performed for him. A projector will be aimed at this symbolic white during the whole spectacle.

It is clear, therefore, that the true subject of the play—and in fact of all Genet's other plays—is constituted by the events that act as a starting point for the permanent relationships of one man—or group of men—with another. The form in which this subject is incarnated is ritual. But, for Genet, what counts above all is the theater, the dramatic interplay—ritual effectiveness. Archibald expresses it in this way:

> To us too. They tell us we're grownup children. In that case, what's left for us! The theater! We'll play at being reflected in it and slowly we'll see ourselves—big black narcissus—slowly disappearing into its waters.

And elsewhere:

> Negroes, I am losing my temper. Either we continue the re-enactment or we leave.

So, rather than show on stage the real relationships of one group

of men with another, Genet gives symbolic images of these relationships. Because the function of the theater, according to him, is to
unite the author and spectator through the play; in order to do this,
the characters must be made to be mere metaphors of what they are
supposed to represent. That is why Genet has to invent for his characters a tone of voice, a bearing, particular gestures, those belonging to the rite. In the letter to Pauvert, he explains this in the following manner:

> I tried to obtain a disparity which, if a declamatory tone is permitted,
> would bring the theater in the theater. I thereby hoped to obtain the
> abolition of characters—who only exist by virtue of a psychological
> convention—in favor of signs as far as possible from what they are
> supposed to mean, but yet connected with their meaning in order to
> unite by this solitary link the author with the spectator.

The rite, with its rhythm and structure, is the motivating force behind Genet's plays; it gives them order and movement like the god
of the ptolemaic system of the universe with its nine spheres. A rite
is a series of fixed acts whose goal is to perpetuate the essence of an
original event in the life of a people—an event situated in a fairly
vague past—establishing a relationship between the people and the
supernatural. The goal of the celebration of such a rite is to evoke
the supernatural presence of a divinity who is thereby incarnated in
the formal gestures of the faithful, who renew in this manner their
link with him. In this frenzied state that the rite gives birth to, the
worshippers become the god. However, the goal set by the rite is not
an evolutionary process, but the state of ecstasy in which it results.
The rite is there to preserve and perpetuate in its raw form the original contact with the supernatural, a contact which exists outside the
march of time, of what has been, of what will be; times gone by are
not distinguishable from times to come; the ritual ceremony takes
place in an eternal present.

Most of Genet's commentators acknowledge the presence of the
rite in his plays, but without really asking what its function is. Some
of them try to draw a parallel between Genet's theater and Artaud's
ritual incantation. We are more of Roger Blin's opinion, who finds
Genet's theater closer to that of the Ancient Greeks than to Artaud's
conception, closer, in short, to myth. Indeed, Artaud saw the theater
as an act that in no wise distinguished the real from the imaginary;
a real event can have as much effect as the theater if it has a certain

measure of cruelty. In this sense, the true form of theater desired by Artaud took shape in the *happening*. Genet parts company with Artaud because, for Genet, on the contrary, the theater is above all an imaginary world, irreconcilable with reality. Thus, even the participation of the spectator is as imaginary as the actions he watches on the stage. The spectator knows that the character in the play is not really the husband of the woman to whom he pretends to be married; and he knows that this man will not really kill that woman or himself, either on stage or off. All that is illusion, yet he reacts as if he believed in it. But his feelings must indeed be imaginary, otherwise he would jump out of his seat screaming when the man cuts the throat of his wife or kills himself. That is how Genet's theater is closer to myth than to ritual incantation.

Genet uses the mythic aspects of the rite by introducing in his plays a manifestly fixed, although arbitrarily chosen, set of events; their goal is to perpetuate an established and real relationship, by no means between men and gods, but between men. As Archibald says, the rite of *The Blacks* wishes to evoke the relationships between Whites and Blacks as they are seen by the former, who use this as a pretext to subjugate the latter. Therefore, rejected by Whites, the Blacks want to play to the very end the role that has been assigned to them. In life as on the stage, they are required to perform their second nature in the middle of the social comedy put on by whites:

> Archibald: This evening we shall perform for you. But, in order that you may remain comfortably settled in your seats in the presence of the drama that is already unfolding here, in order that you be assured that there is no danger of such a drama's worming it's way into your precious lives, we shall even have the decency — learned from you — to make communication impossible. We shall increase the distance that separates us — a distance that is basic — by our pomp, our manners, our insolence — for we are also actors.

Blacks act out the comedy on stage because they have been compelled to do so in life. But in one sense, they reveal and mask at once the truth of their condition. They aren't just Blacks, they are actors. The malaise comes from our knowing that actors are also something other than actors; thus the imaginary role they play neutralizes the imaginary feelings of the spectators. Even if the *actors* are about to make communication impossible, to protect the spectators from the reality of the true condition of the actors, this communication — or rather this relationship — will be established on the human level, on the level of reality, that of Whites and Blacks. It is thus that the metaphorical relationships between actor and spectator are subtly manipulated by the mediation of the rite to become the real relationships between Whites and Blacks.

Genet uses the same technique in *The Maids* to denounce the odious relationship between master and servant, mistress and maid. Ritual acts serve to define this relationship, but there too, by a reversal in the situation — the maids play the role of the mistress to have some perspective on their own condition — they become the spectators of their own enslavement, whence their hate towards themselves which leads to the tragic outcome.

All this may seem to be a contradiction between act and gesture, between the real action and the imaginary seduction of the spectator. But in fact, Genet trades on this contradiction. That his plays are imaginary doesn't bother him; on the contrary, it is a quality particularly suited to the theater; because, if the play is imaginary and, as a consequence, the reaction of the spectators imaginary, then he can betray us because unreality and evil are on the same plane and therefore reconciled in the mind of the spectator. At least for the length of the show, the spectators are obliged to accept evil, to accept themselves as evil, if only in the unreality of their imagination. Genet attracts the spectator into evil just as the participants in a religious rite are drawn into becoming the god they worship.

If we accept this idea that Genet's theater is based on the rite, the fact must still be emphasized that it isn't religious in the traditional sense of the word, even if the conception of the rite of communication which Genet applies to the theater is similar in form to a Greek religious rite or to that of the Church. Genet knows no God; it is beauty that he substitutes for the divine presence in the rite. He has said so himself:

> Without doubt, one of the functions of art is to substitute the effectiveness of beauty for religious faith. At least this beauty has the power of a poem, that is, of a crime.

This is the kind of beauty that is important to Genet; not its charm outside of all possible utility, but only that utility of specific interest to him, or, in his own words:

Poetry is the art of using dung and making you eat it.

In his study of Genet, Sartre says that to name a thing is to determine its essence. To call a prison a palace, a thief a prince, a prostitute a lover, is to make the prison, the thief and the prostitute things of beauty. That is how language becomes a means to beautify ugliness. It allows the poet to ennoble the subject-matter of his poems, to mask the vulgarity until the moment chosen to reveal it. One cannot help but think of Baudelaire. But if for Baudelaire language serves to transform ugliness into beauty, he never uses it as a trap. As for Genet, he uses language as a seductive ornament to attract the reader into the heart of his poem and, from there, reveal all its vulgar falseness which was only there to hide the toneless matter which it covered. It is a means to make the reader (or spectator) admit what he ordinarily tries to remain ignorant of. It is in this sense that poetry is a warning, a crime. Genet exemplifies this idea in a passage from *Our Lady of the Flowers:*

> Quite some time before, the appearance on the village road of a bride wearing a black dress, though wrapped in a veil of white tulle, lovely and sparkling, like a young shepherd beneath the hoar frost, like a powdered blond miller, or like Our Lady of the Flowers...whom I saw with my own eyes here in my cell one morning, near the latrines— his sleepy face pink and bristly beneath the soapsuds, which blurred his vision—revealed...that poetry is something other than a melody of curves on sweetness, for the tulle snapped apart into abrupt, clear, rigorous, icy facets. It was a warning.

By means of this labyrinth of words, by this exquisite corridor of sensuality, Genet leads us into the heart of poetry and beauty, or, as it is the case in the first scene of *The Screens,* to the center of the dramatic illusion (which can be equated with beauty) when the suitcase, which is supposed to be full of marvelous gifts for Saïd's young wife, opens suddenly to reveal that it is empty.

Verbal embellishment is, however, only one method of revealing beauty. Another consists in surrounding it with a certain fatality, a certain rigidity which gives it a power beyond that of pleasing the spectator. Beauty, as Genet conceives it, is the installation of necessity in the domain of the contingent. It is, as Sartre has said, "organization." The creation of the beautiful object or act, of the beautiful person, does not depend exclusively on the materials they are made out of, but the way in which these materials are treated. For Genet, beauty is effective because it creates an inevitable, irrevocable bond between those who contemplate it. Certain objects, certain people have the power to decide the fate of those who watch them. It is because beautiful objects urge to action (more often bad than good) that Genet considers them fatal, especially when they lead to an irrevocable crime (which, for Genet, is a purely esthetic act). Such is the case of Green Eyes, in *Deathwatch,* who finds his crime irresistible — in placing his hands around the neck of the young girl he has begun an act that could only end in murder. Genet abhors unfinished acts. Green Eyes' crime is therefore purely esthetic; it is neither passionate nor dirty. Similarly, the death of one of the sisters in *The Maids,* the murder of the white woman in *The Blacks,* which is repeated every evening on stage (or rather off stage), the murder of Saïd in *The Screens,* all these crimes, despite their social or racial implications, remain purely esthetic acts; if passion or vengeance are mixed in, they are as soon dispelled by the act itself.

We have seen the role of the rite and beauty in Genet's theater, but we should note that these two elements do not function separately. One acts on the other and each plays a vital role in the creation of the illusion of communion in the spectators, the ultimate goal of such a theater. We will go so far as to say that the rite and beauty, for Genet at least, are almost identical; both are minutely articulated and organized structures. Thus the aura of fatality which seems to envelop beauty in a nimbus, and make it irresistible, stems from the almost hieratic fixity of the ritual acts of the play. That is, in fact, the productive function of the rite. Conversely, the rite depends on beauty to lure the spectator, and lead him into the heart of an experience that he did not wholeheartedly wish for. It is Archibald, once again, who explains this paradox to the audience of *The Blacks:*

> You see, ladies and gentlemen, just as you have your lilies and roses, so we — in order to serve you — shall use our beautiful, shiny black make-up. It is Mr. Deodatus Village who gathers the smoke-black, and Mrs. Felicity Trollop Pardon who thins it out in our saliva. These ladies help her. We embellish ourselves so as to please you. You are white. And spectators. This evening we shall perform for you.

All that is obviously a lie, a bit like the tulle over the bride's dress which tears and unveils the black dress underneath, because the promise aims at drawing the spectators into the world of the play, in order to finally reveal the Enemy, to the greater discomfort of everyone.

It is because men don't want to recognize the hate that binds them to each other, like the love in the act of communion that they have to be made to see, feel and admit by ruse. Genet presents first, therefore, a familiar world to the audience, even if it is somewhat distant from them, and lastly lays bare a part of that world which they would hardly dare imagine different or even possible.

Such a technique is the basis of all Genet's plays; we should note, however, that in *Deathwatch* and *The Maids,* it is used less universally. In Genet's theater there is a distinct progression from the relationship between *caïd* and *boy* (as we see them in *Deathwatch*) to the more universal themes of *The Balcony* and *The Screens.* But if we examine more closely the example of *The Blacks*—a play which offers itself as a rite accomplished by Blacks for the amusement of white spectators—that is where we discover all the subtlety of Genet's technique. Originally, it is the Whites who make the Blacks sing and dance; it is therefore expected that the play be performed for them. The central theme of the rite is constituted by the rape and murder of a white saleswoman by one of the members of the troupe—ejaculation of sperm and then blood. The murder is perpetrated each evening before the beginning of the performance like a kind of sacrifice. The corpse of the victim is then brought to the theater in a Cadillac and placed on a catafalque at the center of the stage. The reason for the crime: to provide a justification for the continual persecution of Blacks by Whites. Archibald explains the situation to the other players:

> Bear one thing in mind: we must deserve their reprobation and get them to deliver the judgment that will condemn us. I repeat, they know our crime...

The Blacks are therefore guilty men playing the role of guilty men before their judges; they exist on the fringe of white society and want to show very politely what they think is the cause of their exile and oppression. But the Blacks give a caricatural picture of whites in the grotesque faces of the members of the court who sit on a dias. These white puppets, in turn, impose a false image of Blacks on the stage. It is this doubel distortion that Genet is going to disturb during the play.

On the one hand, therefore: Blacks project their own vision of the world of Whites on the stage in the key figures of the Queen, the Judge, the Bishop, the Governor, and the Valet; on the other hand, they make them play their own vision of Whites coming to Africa (to be understood: controlling the Black ghettos of modern cities) to con-demn and enslave blacks for their crimes against Whites. However, it is not entirely correct to say that Whites have banished Blacks to the fringe of their society because of the murder of one white man or woman—even if Richard Wright, in *Black Boy*, states that Whites have the need, periodically, to attack and kill a Black, and that, for this reason, they use the murder or rape of a white woman by a Black as a pretext to attack him and his kind. It is rather that Whites have created a situation in which Blacks have no choice but to be Blacks, not because they have acted in such a way to deserve it, but because they are *black* in a white world. Genet's point of view is the same when he presents the criminal, the homosexual, the thief, the servant, etc.

Sartre adopts a similar attitude in *Anti-Semite and Jew* when he explains that man is always caught in a situation which defines his possibilities of action. It is neither the history nor religion of the Jew which makes him a Jew, but the fact that he finds himself in a situation where he is treated like a Jew and, sooner or later, learns that, to survive, he must react in a way expected by those around him.

That is exactly the situation of Blacks in the world of Whites. They are expected to act in a certain way—the black way. An image is imposed on them from the outside which determines what they must be. To be sure, it is a situation found, in one form or another, in all civilizations. For a long time, Jean-Jacques Rousseau's conception of the good savage has kept (civilized!) Whites in total ignorance of what primitive societies are really like. It is this same image, transposed to our own age, that colonial or pseudo-liberal governments (of what are today called democracies) have to face, and who refuse to see what is happening in the world that they have invaded or let develop in the middle of their own.

Whites have a distorted, therefore dangerous, vision of Blacks, because they refuse to consider them differently than according to the image they have of them. They refuse to admit that Blacks exist independently of themselves. Thus the dramatic conflict rises from the effort of Blacks to rid themselves of the false image imposed on them, and which the Whites want to perpetuate—a desire for liberation, expressed in splendid terms by one of the characters:

> Sir, I apologize. I'd like to glorify my color, just as you do. The kindness of the whites settled on my head, as it did on yours. Though it rested there lightly, it was unbearable. Their intelligence descended upon my right shoulder, and a whole flock of virtues on my left. And at times, when I opened my hands, I would find their charity nestling there. In my Negro solitude, I feel the need, just as you do, to glorify my exquisite savageness....

Although Blacks want to glorify their color (and their savageness), it is with the opposite intention that the show begins: the players tell the audience that they are there to offer their guilt to the white tribunal. Thus the two distorted visions of the two groups confront each other, clash together in a struggle for supremacy which reaches its apogee in the oratorical contest which opposes the Queen and Felicity. But finally, after Newport News enters on stage to announce the conviction of a black traitor, it is a triumph of Blacks over Whites when they reveal that there isn't any corpse in the catafalque. The Whites, therefore, have no reason to condemn them and, just as the judge in *The Balcony* depends on the criminal to exercise his function, Whites depend on Blacks. Thus their existence is no longer justified. They are therefore killed, lyrically and symbolically ("To the slaughterhouse... Next!... To hell," exclaims Archibald in killing them off), and solemnly leave the stage. But this shouldn't be taken seriously since the role of the Whites was held by Blacks. Real Whites don't die; it is only their image that the Blacks have torn from themselves; thus the play can be considered an inverted ceremony of exorcism.

However, that isn't the real subject of the play. The real drama took place in the wings during the performance. A real Black was tried, convicted, executed for having given in to the "white temptation." He betrayed in a suspicious manner a secret conspiracy of Blacks against Whites. Another Black was sent to replace him and will continue his work. The revelation of this second intrigue is like the white tulle which, when torn, reveals the black dress: poetry is a warning, a crime.

This revelation destroys both distorted images—that of the actors playing the role of Blacks and that of the Blacks playing the role of Whites—and unveils the real nature of the relationships between Whites and Blacks. That is the discovery that the white audience is underhandedly forced to make, that is, that there is an authentic, active conspiracy against them for world domination. They are therefore torn from the imaginary world of the play and from their imaginary feelings to face the fact that Blacks and Whites are irrevocably set against each other in mortal combat, a battle which the Whites seem to lose without ever being fully conscious of the nature of the conflict. Blacks are revealed to Whites as the Enemy. They are no longer actors playing the role of condemned men but dangerous and insidious adversaries—real enemies.

This unexpected revelation breaks the bond of servitude which united Blacks and Whites in order to substitute one of hate which separates the two groups into two united blocs. Paradoxically, it is this shock which serves as a driving force and inspires the feeling of unity, of communion in the Whites. They now share a feeling of fear mixed with hate towards Blacks who feel the same thing towards them. The white spectators have fallen into the trap which Genet set for them by the beauty of his language and the false elegance of his theater. They undergo the shock, united in horror, under the hypnotic influence of the performance—the illusion—of the play. They should have interpreted Archibald's words better:

> Dammit, do the best you can. Invent—if not words—then phrases that cut you off rather than bind you. Invent, not love, but hatred, and thereby make poetry, since that's the only domain in which we're allowed to operate. For their entertainment....

It is precisely for their amusement that Genet has drawn Whites into the rite of hate, a hate for Blacks which they surely wouldn't have recognized before the performance. That is Genet's technique in all his plays: to force the audience, whether it be white, bourgeois, imperialistic or moral, to admit its hate for, respectively, the Black, the criminal, the servant or the homosexual.

In all Genet's plays, the intention and method are the same: to destroy the distorted image in order to unmask the Enemy and reestablish the relationships between men on a real foundation, which, for Genet, is always hate, never love. It is at the expense of love that hate is justified, and in this sense, Genet is a moralist and an artist in a unique and grandiose way. Because the role of the artist in every society is to awaken the consciousness of the rest of its members to problems which they would be tempted to ignore. In our so-called civilized society a large percentage of people—said to be the minority—are totally ignored. In the Middle Ages and the centuries that followed, the distinction between rich and poor, believers and unbelievers, oppressed and oppressors were more clearly defined. In our modern society we have made this distinction more subtle, more hypocritical: men like Genet, who have known this other aspect of our world, who have had the courage of their own hate, can in turn lead us there, even if it means dirtying our hands and our souls.

Genet, His Actors and Directors

Odette Aslan

Genet and His Directors

When Louis Jouvet solicited a play from Genet, he had just returned to France after four years on tour in Latin America. In the course of his career, he had chiefly staged Molière, Jules Romains and all of the plays of Giraudoux. Having failed at the Conservatory as a student, he returned there as a professor. If his advice did not seem very orthodox in his time, in retrospect, it appears to be rather traditional. Working with Copeau, he wanted to renovate the classics; he created a scandal with his interpretation of *The School for Wives (L'Ecole des femmes);* however, at the Théâtre de l'Athénée he was working for a "high society" public unwilling to abandon the restraints imposed by the social code. He always strove to please and did not permit himself daring innovations. With Genet, when he received the manuscript of *The Maids,* he advanced on tiptoe. He rejected the first manuscript, indicated a revision, and was opposed to the idea of men in drag playing the women's roles. Adopting a reassuring tone in the production's program notes, he emphasized "the confidantes' tragedy," reducing the drama to bourgeois conventionality and the characters to delicate young girls suffering from their humble condition. As for the text, it seems that Jouvet tried to make Genet work at the rehearsals as he had done with Giraudoux. He made him modify a phrase, a passage, a scene several times. Flattered by this first theatrical experience, Genet probably conceded more than he wanted to. Faced with his employer's experience, he had not as yet found the quick argument needed to

"Genet, His Actors and Directors" by Odette Aslan, translated from the French by Elaine Ancekewicz. From "Genet et ses metteurs en scène," "Genet et les comédiens," in *Jean Genet* (Théâtre de tous les temps, 24) 1974, pp. 24-33. Reprinted by permission of Editions Seghers.

counter an interpretation that was leading the play in an incorrect direction. He would later express his regret concerning this.

Twenty-five years later, working with Victor Garcia, Genet had nothing to say. He watched none of the rehearsals and attended the performances in progress. Garcia deliberately did not adhere to the stage directions which he judged outdated. He did not attempt to place himself in the shoes of the author at the time when he had written the play, nor did he attempt to study closely the characters' moods. Garcia came from the generation of directors who rejected psychology and who constructed a production by reorganizing the elements of a text which they no longer considered a literary monument. He established his own universe on the stage and inserted Genet's play into it. Treated as a new material, the play acquired an unsuspected density. Genet approved the production.

It was probably with Roger Blin that Genet accepted most fully a collaboration of author and director, and still he balked when the question of rewriting a passage was brought up. After having produced *The Blacks* and played in *The Balcony,* Blin created *The Screens* in Paris. Genet participated in numerous rehearsals at the Théâtre de France. He agreed to cuts, supported Blin's quarrels with the actors over their resistance to their roles (or their roles' resistance to them), was angered by the absence of ideal technical conditions, and ended up by publishing, in homage to his director, the notes that he had sent him all during this time to guide him or to impose new difficulties. Often, in the course of the rehearsals, it was Genet who sensed the weak points, but he knew neither how to explain himself using the terms of the trade (I am not acquainted with your jargon!), nor how to help the actors find inside themselves the way to deal with the situation. It was Blin who served as a mediator. Having reached a certain point and especially with the revival of the play in the following season, Genet felt that he could no longer help the play to progress, and he left.

Genet also went to Essen where Blin restaged *The Screens.* He seconded the technical demands, appreciated the violence of the German actors, admired the handsome Sergeant, and disappeared without even waiting for the dress-rehearsal.

Peter Brook, who directed *The Balcony* in Paris and *The Screens* in London, admires Genet very much, although he considers his plays impossible to perform. Brook, who is always in search of a renewed mode of expression, came up against Genet's work, as against a stumbling block, a challenge. Just as we in France are attempting to escape from the routine of the classics, yet without having discovered any durable contemporary authors, Brook is attempting to escape from Shakespeare, or, at least, to renew the interpretation of him. Thus, in order to break in his actors, he leads them through several detours before bringing them back to Shakespeare. His detours pass through Beckett, Artaud, Brecht, Genet, (African and Hindu rites), among others. When he confronts Genet, Brook knows that he will never reach the dimension dreamed of by the author, because he does not have the actors necessary. He created work groups and broke them in by a non-realistic training, in vain. He could measure the distance between what he was able to obtain from them and the scenic demands of Genet. Brook is perhaps one of Genet's most lucid directors, glimpsing the best that the poetic act might be, the intense deflagration of the author's dream, instead of a series of repetitions of a text, where one recites the words and nothing happens between the actors and the spectators. With Brook, something happened during the twelfth tableau of *The Screens,* something electrified the room when the hatred of the Arabs broke out in painting on the screens. Brook has captured the theatrical material proposed by Genet, the idea, and has realized it to the greatest degree. With Garcia, it was the director who proposed the idea, the image, the theatrical spring, on which the text was superimposed, thereby gaining a new vitality.

Some directors wanted to accentuate the theme of homosexuality. At the Living Theatre, Judith Malina staged *The Maids* with three men, as Genet had suggested in the beginning; in Paris, Jean-Marie Patte also brought together a male cast; in Saint-Etienne, Roland Monod cast two women and a man. In Munich, Hans Lietzau had two of the characters of *The Screens* (the Vamp and the Son Harold) played by actors of the opposite sex. J.-L. Barrault had toyed with the idea of playing the old woman Ommou. This supplementary ambiguity is unnecessary and Garcia was probably right in his refusal to cast a man only in the role of Madame in *The Maids.* Whatever Genet may think of the androgyny of the actor, the actors themselves are ill at ease if they must act as members of the opposite sex (except in the case of broad farce or if they have a penchant for that sort of thing); as for the audience, instead of being ill at ease or taken aback, it quickly accustoms itself to the situation, sneers at it, and the inversion is no longer effective. Who can say that Genet's theatre would resist if one were to decide on a unisex action with a mixed cast? We have seen, however, that the reduction of the distinction colonizer-colonized under Lietzau's direction was not successful. We will, however, not the most outstanding attempts.

If Genet calls an asshole an asshole and if in his novels he describes in detail bodies and their pleasures, in his theatre he has never written a pornographic or even an audacious scene. Thus, the young Arcady wanted to give a little more salt to a play staged in 1949 and practically never produced in Paris since that date: *Deathwatch*. He asked Bernard Rousselet (Green-Eyes) to strip naked in order to execute his dance before his cell companions. He must have thought that it was more in keeping with the tone of the theatre in 1970. *Hair* was not far away, peeling was becoming current on the stage... For all that, nudity was not, however, in keeping with the tone of the work.

With more integrity, Andre Steiger in his staging of *The Balcony* in Strasbourg wanted to base his production on Genet's writings. In "The strange word of..." ("L' étrange mot d'...") which appeared in *Tel Quel*, Genet suggests that in order to restore to the theatre a gravity that it has lost, plays should henceforth take place in cemeteries, so that, in the presence of the dead, one wouldn't come to participate in a frivolous amusement. Instead one would feel as if he were attending a ceremony similar to the sacred ceremonies of the past. Steiger applied this return to origins, this nostalgia reminiscent of Artaud, to a play written much earlier by Genet: *The Balcony*. He placed the scene of Irma's house of illusions in a cemetery, in all probability to distance the action and to deny the viewer the easy images of a brothel. In other words, at the same time he transgressed the stage directions of *The Blacony* and the half-serious half-mocking proposal to abandon the usual theatrical structure and to organize a black Mass/ happening. Through his scenery, deprived of everything "aesthetic" that Brook had succeeded in placing in his interpretation of the play, Steiger set up an austere universe with the ambition of arousing the viewer's reflection.

Here lies the exact point of friction between the dramaturgy of Genet and that of contemporary directors. All the critics recognize that his work exercises a sort of fascination, that it is poetic, gifted with an incantatory lyricism. Directors who have received Brecht's lesson of distance, of a non-illusionist theatre, of critical reflection, attempt to apply it to Genet's dramaturgy. Thus, Hans Lietzau or Leon Epp in Austria have tried to apply a freezing technique to *The Screens*. They tried to clarify, to explicate a text distinguished for its abundant, hybrid and disorderly character, a text which asked only for madness and immoderation *("demésure")*. They de-po-eticised Genet's language by reducing it to the proportions of ordinary prose, they clipped the wings of its lyric flight, they broke the spell.

There is another reason why they renounced the poetic leaps: Genet, some say, has written a political theatre. Now, Genet has always denied such an interpretation. In his prefaces, his interviews, his letters, he has energetically opposed this hypothesis. He forbade anyone to transform his works into political pamphlets committed to a cause. Very well, one may answer, if he defends himself so strongly against this, it is because it is true. The sociologist Lucien Goldmann has seen in Genet's works a critical analysis of European society and the revolutionary movements of the twentieth century. This is a somewhat personal "reading." Certain directors, anxious to present their audiences with a work that possessed political overtones, wanted to make *The Screens* into an anticolonial satire. Once the Algerian war was over, the play could be applied to Vietnam or to any other colony. A viewer is always free to distance himself from the primary action and at the same time to reflect on an historical situation broader than the anecdote represented. But the actor who plays the anecdote is dependent, whether one likes it or not, on the text imposed upon him. If a text exists.

Genet's writing is a corset. One cannot escape from it. Each word bristles up, said Maria Casares. One must enter the mold. In order to carry the text to the viewer, one must supply it with a breath that originates in the depths of one's being. No distantiation holds up. The joy of the Word and the bestiality of the body must be rediscovered. Let the actors transform themselves into animals, clamors Genet. If political satire exists, let it emerge by itself, outside of the way the play is performed. It should sprout up in addition, in the margins, making the microcosm of the play the reflection of a greater world, referring indirectly to society as it is, and as it should know itself.

Genet and Actors

He gives them a holy fright. In 1947 at the Athénée, he must have been considered a rather unseemly individual, an habitual criminal who had wandered into a place where he did not know what to do, and who forced the actresses to pronounce dirty words in *The Maids.* Jouvet strove to blur the situations and to emphasize the text's lyricism, the musical character of its phrases. It was rehearsed (repeated) note by note.

For the Griots, the young black troupe that created *The Blacks* with Roger Blin, the play was a marvelous opportunity for them to express their negritude; that did not come about without raising problems. Some were afraid of being marked by the fact that they had played a white author — which might prevent them from being able to play in the theatre once back in Africa. However, they perservered. They felt the accuracy of the alienation evoked and immediately entered into the simulacrum, the parodic play, the contestation of white society. Their greatest difficulties were to be found in delivery, in the arduous task of breaking up Genet's syntax. In addition, the coarseness of the vocabulary shocked them.

The Balcony's brothel did not bother anyone, the play of the roles was felt as naturally theatrical. *The Balcony* attracted at least one actress in each of the theatres considered — the one who would play the role of Irma. Consciously or not, the actresses had all been seduced, not by the play, but by the role (an actress who plays a queen). Rotten luck! It only seems to be a good role. For the women, it is Carmen who leads the situation, in spite of appearances.[1] The actors have often suffered from the superficiality of the stage-setting and have found themselves on the edge of a cliff, not knowing any longer if they were an appearance or a reality, an actor or the reflection of an actor.

The actors in the troupe of the Théâtre de France flatly refused to play in *The Screens.* The play seemed base to them. They did not want to compromise themselves in what the English would have called a "dirty" or a "kitchen sink play." The German actors in Essen easily accepted the filth and the universe of Evil. On the other

---

[1]Cf. Genet: "Who directs — the house and the play? Carmen or Irma?" ("How to Play *The Balcony*").

hand, they were surprised by the Arab characters. They said that they had never seen any. They showed themselves to be incapable of rendering the local color that Blin desired, their square shoulders refused to sag, their vitality was a hundred miles from the fatalism and oriental nonchalance of the play. However, not having been conditioned by the loss of colonies or by a vague complex of collective guilt, they acted the satire of the colonizers very effectively.

Using approximate translations, all foreign actors were deprived of the support of the original language. Only the Spanish actresses of *The Maids* benefitted from sounds that reinforced the text's expressivity. In France, the actors of *The Screens* had to fight with the complexity of the original, unmutilated text. Behind the scenes they enjoyed calling it a Claudelian text, as if using Claudel as surety might compensate for the reticence provoked by the scabrous aspects of the play and justify the owner's audacity in introducing this unhealthy charge of dynamite into the repertoire of the Company. But, whether the text was Claudelian or not, there was no question of letting them take cover behind the simple recitation of a text. "Above all, none of your Comédie-Française!" Genet would repeat. "Why does he say that to me?" queried an astonished actor, "I was never a part of that troupe." Genet abhors above all falsely traditional tone, uninspired, conventional style, academic training stamped with prettiness, delivery characterized by urbanity, and classical bearing. The actor's entire being must be engaged in a theatrical creation, and not in a routine.

The actors whom Genet and Blin made work the longest and who came the closest to what was demanded of them were outside of the permanent troupe of the Théâtre de France. Broken in on a more eclectic repertoire, and perhaps having greater curiosity for new experiences, they brought to their search greater suppleness. Above all, they were conscious of the fact that it was necessary to search and not to be content to bring to this author a trade acquired once and for all. "Make all of these actors work," Genet would say about the others, "I have the impression that they know how to do everything." Their illusion was quickly dissipated. Genet takes pleasure in putting others—especially actors—ill at ease. Far from helping them or encouraging them, he takes away their assurance, proves to them that they are not in a position to execute without a moment's warning apparently the simplest act, and bears down on them as soon as he senses their confusion. He provokes them with increasing difficulties, defies them, and always demands more. For *The Balcony,* he thought of perching his actors on pattens fifty centimeters high. "How will they be able to walk with that without breaking their mugs, without catching their paws in the trains and the lace of their skirts? They must learn." For *The Screens,* he refused to unburden the soldiers of a metal drinking cup that they found constricting.

Does the actor think that he has a voice admirably situated to the medium, as is common in the conventional theatre? Genet could not care less. "Invent for me a voice that you have never used." Does the actor take great care of his inflexions? Genet asks him to misapply them. The least conventionality irritates him; nothing should be mechanical. "When I would say: 'under the moon,'" Maria Casarès recalls, "I had to think of it." And he knew when she was not thinking of it. At the beginning of the rehearsals, he forbade the actors to make the smallest movement. Then they had to establish the conscious movements that they would make and hold to them. On one hand, Genet wanted thus to avoid every movement that would naturally help to "speak" the text; he preferred those that would be in opposition to it and that would emanate neither from everyday life nor from a lawless spontaneity. On the other hand, he does not want movements "endured" by a reflective actor, but a corporal score based on the out-of-the-ordinary: "to show and to make heard what usually passes unnoticed." This effect of strangeness has nothing to do with Brecht's intention of distantiation and critical perspective, but proceeds from the wish for a scenic "find," from the joyous invention of a new expression.

When you least expect it, he asks you why at that precise moment you are in a resting position when you should be participating in the action in progress. When the actors are not speaking he would like to compel them to dream of "the death of their son or of their well-loved mother, or of being mugged by a hooligan, or of being seen naked by the audience." They must discover the desired movements "near the confines of death." Genet not only leads the actors along, engaging them in his universe where "the aesthetics of the stage replace morality," and corrupting them by the costumes in which he clothes them, but he also demands of them a poetic sense and inner life. An approach to the sacred. Consciousness of celebrating a solemn ceremony.

That is why Genet attacks without pity the ethics of the French actor, relatively unsuited for the hieratic, for transposition, for silence, for meditation. Those who read the Letter to Pauvert, published in the 1954 re-issue of *The Maids*, received a sharp reprimand. Genet criticizes the haughty stupidity of actors and theatre people, their triviality, their lack of culture, their silliness, their exhibitionism, their search for stardom, identification with a fictional character, and interpretations where everything takes place in the visible world. He judges Western actors incapable of expressing major themes and deep symbols, of being signs charged with signs. He is of the opinion that those who attempt to draw inspiration from oriental techniques "do it in the way that women of high society practice yoga." In his directives for *The Screens*, he renews his attempts. After having performed one of Genet's plays, the actors might be transformed. "They must not revert—according to the sense you want to give to the expression." He would be inclined to use a strong hand in order to make himself understood. "Arsenic or blows," he quips. The least of his remarks at rehearsals is a subtle caustic. He puts one on guard. He wants interpreters as hard as he is. Without useless modesty. Without a trace of a good education. Without pity for themselves. Without pity for their character. Intelligent animals who transform an animal cry into an artistic spark. In the gestation and in the execution of the performance, outer life no longer exists, the theatre absorbs everything. Genet thrashes those who claim to separate themselves from the action in progress by watching the television in the artists' center, rather than remaining in the universe of *The Screens*.

In love with rigor, or a greater sacred monster than the actors themselves, Genet places himself on stage in the first person: "I go to the theatre in order to see myself, on the stage (reproduced in a single character or with the help of a multiple character and in the form of a story) such as I could not—or would not dare—see or dream myself, and such as I, nevertheless, know myself to be." Thus, he writes in the 1963 Preface to *The Maids*, the actors' function consists in "putting on the movements and the garb that will permit them to show me naked, in solitude and its happiness." That is enough to say that the interpretation of the work should reflect the portrait of the author and espouse his reactions. The actor penetrates the inverted universe of Genet, turns himself inside out like a glove and plays as if he as well were an adept of Evil, moving with ease in a milieu where hate and crime reign supreme. The actor does not so much owe it to himself to study the play or his character as to study the character of Genet in his life and in all of his works. Once he has been permeated with this reverse morality, and keeping well in mind the postulate: Bad = Good, the actor must raise himself towards poetic expression by the oblique path of transposition.

Language helps him first. All of Genet's characters express themselves like Genet—even the maids: elegant syntax, surprising images, lyric breath. The dialogue never lowers itself to the everyday. Then, everyone is placed on a pedestal. Lifted up on his pride, having become an Image, an Effigy, sometimes concretely elevated on stilts, he walks higher than the common mortal. In an absolute with neither complaisance nor concession, the theatrical creation must provoke Beauty without affectation, without a false poetic. Of the man-woman duality of the actor, it is the most virile half which must intervene.

Scenic Space and Dramatic
Illusion in *The Balcony*

Michèle Piemme

Genet has been greatly concerned by the manner in which his plays could be read and produced; he is a meticulous and exacting dramatist who, in the case of *The Balcony,* has done everything possible for the producers to avoid reductive readings. "Another point," he writes, "do not produce this play as if it were a satire of this or that. It is—and will thus be staged as—the glorification of the Image and of Reflection. Its signification—satiric or not—will appear only in this case."[1] It is not a coincidence that *The Balcony,* this hymn to reflection, to facticity, was written for the theatre. Fulfilling itself in and by representation, every work of dramatic literature, independently of its content, is first of all an imitation, an image, an appearance. That the issue in Genet is in large part defined by this coincidence of form and content will be made clear by a quite thorough study of the scenic and dramaturgic spaces in *The Balcony.* The scenic spaces are those that one sees on stage, while the spaces that one hears named and that can be quite different from the former are called "dramaturgic spaces." Starting with this fundamental distinction, several ramifications are possible. In *The Blacks,* for example, scenic space is divided in two: at the beginning of the play, the spectator finds himself before a stage on which is enacted a scene before a law-court. But the scenic spaces can be multiplied, especially if they follow one another. As for the dramaturgic

"Scenic Space and Dramatic Illusion in *The Balcony*" by Michèle Piemme, translated from the French by Kathyrn Kinczewski. From *Obliques 2: Genet,* pp. 23-31. Reprinted by permission of *Obliques.*

[1]Jean Genet, "How to stage *The Balcony,*" in *Le Balcon* (Lyon: Barbezat, L' arbalète, 1970).

spaces, their number is still less limited, since during a single play an infinite number of different spaces can be evoked by means of words.

In *The Balcony*, however, there is only one dramaturgic space: the place of which the characters speak and which will never be seen by the spectators is that of the city in which true generals, real judges, and authentic bishops hold the power. It is the place of the Queen and the Royal Palace, it is the place of reality. The scenic spaces, on the contrary, follow upon one another, different at each scene, which is no doubt what prompted Geneviève Serreau to remark that "Genet did not worry much about connecting various episodes of the play with each other: he only wanted to stage some magnificent rites and their degradation, in an obsessional universe where sexuality and power counterbalance and devour one another."[2] It appears to us that this commentary is erroneous insofar as all these spaces, no matter how numerous they might be, in fact never designate anything but a single universe: that of appearance. The unity of the play, then, is this very disparity which causes various different spaces to act upon one another, each comprising a well-defined action but all reducible, at least schematically, to the interaction of appearance and reality. We will see, in the course of the analysis, how the notion of "reality" in *The Balcony* is subtly transformed since, contrary to what many critics—notably Leonard Pronko—have to say, the revolutionaries who appear in the sixth scene themselves exist in a world of appearance, images, and roles. In Pronko's words, "At the revolutionary headquarters, we see a picture of reality which contrasts strongly with the illusion of Madame Irma's Balcony,"[3] the term "picture" is in flagrant contradiction with the quote from Genet that the same critic refers to elsewhere. "In the theatre everything happens in the visible world and nowhere else."[4] In other words, if Genet gives us on stage an image of reality, he is not recreating reality. Genet manipulates theatrical convention for his own purposes: unable to show us life in the theatre, he consciously offers us reproductions of it. Theatre and life are not to be confused. In-

---

[2]Geneviève Serreau, *Histoire du "Nouveau Théâtre"* (Paris: Gallimard, coll. "Idées"), p. 125.

[3]Leonard C. Pronko, *Avant-Garde: The Experimental Theater in France* (Berkeley and Los Angeles: Univ. of California Press, 1963), p. 148.

[4]*Ibid.*, p. 140.

deed, this exigency impregnates the whole of the *Letters to Roger Blin*. Witness this particularly clear passage: "In the same way, don't let the Arab worker light a cigarette: the match flame not being able to be imitated on stage; a lighted match in the audience or elsewhere is the same as on stage. To be avoided."[5] This imperative governs the whole of Genet's theatre which toys with what is usually called dramatic illusion.[6] At no time does Genet try to deceive: on stage he never presents life, but exclusively its image. This is not to say, however, that Genet's theatre is an "alienated" one such as Brecht's can be, for example. It is from a critical standpoint that Brecht presents images, "tableaux" as such. He refuses identification, he prevents participation so that the spectator's critical sense and intelligence remain intact. As he himself says: "From now on, it is no longer permitted for the spectator to be satisfied with entering into the characters, with abandoning himself to emotional reactions, without exercising his critical sense and without drawing practical lessons from his reactions." Representation submits the subject and the *mythos* of the works to a process of alienation. It is this alienation which allows one to understand: "as soon as something 'goes without saying,' does one not simply refuse the slightest attempt at understanding?"[7] Genet's position on political theatre has been sufficiently clarified by himself as well as by the critics,[8] so that we need not return to it. It allows us to understand immediately that the goal of our playwright is not at all the same as Brecht's, and that his conception of theatre is very different as well.

Genet's intent does not concern politics, but rather the theatre itself, its rites and ceremonies, which has led certain critics to compare him to Antonin Artaud. Yet this comparison is applicable only superficially, and Bernard Dort, who has analyzed it, concludes: "Genet's theatre is the exact opposite of that of Antonin Artaud. While the lat-

---

[5]Jean Genet, *Letters to Roger Blin* tr. by Richard Seaver (New York: Grove Press, 1969), p. 47.

[6]We understand this word in a very precise sense: there is dramatic illusion when the spectator has the possibility of believing in the characters represented on stage. This illusion is obviously never total, but nevertheless occurs in traditional theatre when the characters with a very limited psychology permit the audience to believe in the authenticity of their deportment.

[7]Bertold Brecht, *Ecrits sur le theatre* (Paris: L'Arche, 1966), p. 112.

[8]See Bernard Dort, "Genet: The Struggle with Theater," in this volume.

ter challenges representation insofar as it is repetitious, belittling, and travestied, Genet makes of this the very object of his theatre, he puts it on the stage, he exalts it. His theatre is, in the proper sense, a theatre of representation; not only theatre within the theatre, but theatre on the theatre. A theatre doubly theatrical. But let us add that such a technique is not possible without putting back into question this theatre of representation itself. Genet celebrates it the better to destroy it. Thus, by means of a remarkable chronological reversal, Artaud could be said to begin where Genet leaves off."[9] If every theatrical manifestation presupposes an audience, the dramatic work of Genet, more than any other, since it "exalts representation," demands a receptive presence; and this is why Genet includes the spectator in his play. The space called "the house" in a theatre is part of the scenic space where Genet's universe is unfolded. The spectators' participation is not active, they do not have any part in the action, but they do give meaning to the play since, as we have already said, in *The Balcony*—as in other plays by Genet[10]—the signification is born of the interplay between the various spaces, including the one attributed to the audience.

Whereas there is only a single dramaturgic space in *The Balcony* —the city, that is to say the exterior where the seething revolution and the authentic pillars of power are in their element—there are several scenic spaces. Genet introduces us successively to the interior of the Grand Balcony: its drawing-rooms, then, the bedroom of Madame Irma; next, the Balcony where the figures appear is seen from the exterior; and finally, the last scene divides the scenic space in two since the spectator sees Irma and her acolytes looking at the scenario that Roger enacts in the interior of the mausoleum. But in addition, during the entire length of the play, there is inevitably the house which, in the course of the first three scenes, is supposed to be situated in the interior of the Balcony: "On the wall to the right, a mirror—whose frame is gilded and carved—reflects an unmade bed which, if the room were logically arranged, would be in the house, in the first rows of the orchestra."[11] Hence, by a play of mirrors, the house as well is supposed to be part of the house of illusions.

[9]Bernard Dort, "Genet: The Struggle with Theater".

[10]For an analysis of spaces in *The Blacks*, cf. Michèle Piemme, in *Marche Romane* (Etudes théâtrales), xx, 3, 1970, pp. 39-52.

[11]Jean Genet, "How to stage *The Balcony*," p. 11.

Where Appearance Copies Reality

The first four scenes present four analogous but nevertheless differentiated spaces. The global arrangement of the four spaces is identical, but variable elements modify their signification each time. Whereas the chandelier, the invariable element, "will remain the same in each scene," certain elements of decoration change as well as the color of the folding-screens which, in the fourth scene, will be replaced by mirrors. Moreover, this scene is distinct from the others because it is much shorter and because it does not dovetail with the scenes it follows, as Genet had specified for the two preceeding set changes. In addition, the first three scenes each present a part of the scenario. These three scenes taken together form a complete scenario inscribed within an inverted chronology. The third scene introduces the beginning of the scenario, the second the middle and the first its end. The fourth scene might appear redundant since it takes up the beginning of the scenario again. In fact, that is not at all the case: rather, it completes the first three scenes. The latter exalted the figures of power, the former exalts the figure upon which this power is exerted.

But, in both cases, during the entire first part of the play, the dialectic of appearance and reality appears clearly: men are coming to the Grand Balcony to play their roles with partners, themselves disguised prostitutes. Thus, in the course of the first four scenes, Madame Irma's drawing-rooms appear as the spaces wherein acting copies life, and, in effect, the figures are supposed to resemble as much as possible those holding the real power in life: "Contrary to what has been done in Paris, the Three Figures (Bishop, Judge, General) will be dressed in uniforms, or in the attire in use in the region where the play is being staged," requests the playwright, thereby indicating his refusal of abstraction.

This copy of reality is not only very exact and very precise (the bishop demands, for example, that the sins have really been committed), it is also very complete. In the Grand Balcony, the real is reproduced in all its aspects: not only is the figure imitated, but also its function. For this reason, each scenario comprises at least two characters. The figure requires a partner well-prepared for the ritual without which it would not be able to play its part: whence the difficulties that the Judge encounters with the Thief who, recently arrived at Madame Irma's, is unfamiliar with the rules of the game and confesses too quickly. This scene explicitly reveals the necessary condition without which the relationship between dominator and victim could not be lived as authentic: "The Judge: Look here: you're got to be a model thief if I'm to be a model judge. If you're a fake thief, I become a fake judge. Is that clear? (...) Thus far everything has gone off well. My executioner has hit hard...for he too has his function. We are bound together: you, he, and I. For example, if he didn't hit, how could I stop him from hitting? Therefore, he must strike so that I can intervene and demonstrate my authority. And you must deny your guilt so that he can beat you."

"Arm, side of beef, without you I'd be nothing. ... (To the Thief) And without you too, my child. You're my two perfect complements. Ah, what a fine trio we make! (To the Thief) But you, you have a priviledge that he hasn't, nor I either, that of priority. My being a judge is an emanation of your being a thief. You need only refuse... but you'd better not!...need only refuse to be who you are—what you are, therefore, who you are—for me to cease to be...to vanish, evaporated."

But the figures are not content with reproducing reality as it exists. Their imitation must achieve perfection, which reality and its viscissitudes never allow. That is why "the brothel where they act in this way (...) can justifiably be called by its proprietress, Madame Irma, a house of illusions. It is the place where the being of our society can fully realize itself in irreality, that of *clean hands.*"[12]

This grandeur of the irreal is scenically expressed by the imposing silhouette of the actors mounted on tragedian's cothurni and whose costumes are padded at the shoulders: it is thus not possible for the spectator to imagine that he is in front of a real bishop or an authentic general. But this is also signified by the speeches of the characters themselves. Thus the Bishop wants to be a bishop "in solitude, for appearance alone," and he explains himself:

"Never, I affirm before God Who sees me, I never desired the episcopal throne. To become bishop, to work my way up—by means of virtues or vices—would have been to turn away from the ultimate dignity of bishop. I shall explain: in order to become a bishop, I

---

[12]Bernard Dort, "Genet's game." in *Théâtre Public* (Paris: Seuil, 1967), p. 137.

would have had to make a zealous effort not to be one, but to do what would have resulted in my being one. Having become a bishop, in order to be one, I should have had—in order to be one for myself, of course!—I should have had to be constantly aware of being one so as to perform my function." Only appearance which permits direct access to Being posseses the purity of that which did not have to pass by a Doing in order "to become." Figures tend towards a perfection which can exist only in an absolute Being, detached from all contingencies, immobile, hieratic, and definitive. Madame Irma's brothel does not satisfy banal or vulgar aspirations. There the rite and the ceremony are solemn affairs; their ultimate though never attained finality is the immutability of death. Perhaps that is what explains Genet's requirements concerning the dress and the bearing of Madame Irma.

The yearning after death is more particularly illustrated by the scenario of the General who comes to the Grand Balcony to rehearse relentlessly his glorious death. If his death is, by himself, exalted to such an extent, it is because death alone can confer on the function of the pure image the perfect appearance which they all seek. Thus the General says: "Man of war and in full regalia, behold me in my pure appearance. Nothing, no contingent trails behind. If I went through wars without dying, went through miseries without dying, if I was promoted, without dying, it was all for this minute close to death (...) close to death...where I shall be nothing, though reflected *ad infinitum* in these mirrors, nothing but my image (...). For I'm about to die. It is indeed a descent to the grave... (...) but a formal and picturesque descent, by unexpected stairways. ..."

The Girl: "You're a dead general, but an eloquent one."

The General: "Because I'm dead, prating horse. What is now speaking, and so beautifully, is Example. I'm now only the image of my former self. Lower your head and hide your eyes, for I want to be a general in solitude. Not even for myself, but for my image, and my image for its image, and so on." This long quote could apply to other characters and also prefigures the yearning after death of the Chief of Police who will find his consecration in the mausoleum where, at the close of the play, he will shut himself up alive to perpetuate in person the image destroyed by Roger. The first four scenes thus illustrate in a supposedly closed bedroom various aspects of the play's main action, the one that concerns the accession of the Chief of Police into appearance and that will take place at the same time in the drawing-room and in Madame Irma's bedroom.

Reality in Appearance

The fifth scene introduces us for the first time to Irma's bedroom: "Very elegant. This is the very bedroom we saw reflected in the mirrors during the first three scenes." The perspective offered to the spectator has changed as if the house had been transported onto the stage. From Madame Irma's bedroom, everything that is going on in the drawing-rooms can be seen thanks to a "curious piece of furniture at the left, a kind of switchboard with a viewfinder and earphones." This setting is no longer where the acting takes place, but that from which the person who organizes, who "directs," looks on. And the two women who are now evolving under our very eyes no longer copy reality, they do not imitate real characters, they are supposed to be real ones. Only supposedly, though, for dramatic illusion does not occur. Irma's mourning dress prevents the spectator from automatically identifying her as a real madam of a brothel and an element of the decor upsets the reality of the setting. Indeed, it is "the same chandelier" illuminating Irma's bedroom as the one that is in the drawingrooms. This is a subtle reminder which seems to indicate that this bedroom, even if it is not the place where reality is copied, is nevertheless not so very different from the other drawing-rooms. And of course, even the diction of the actress must distance us from her character: Genet demands that the actress who plays Irma adopt "a narrative tone that is always equivocal, always not quite right."

Irma settles her account with Carmen, an activity which belongs to the domain of the most tangible and the most material reality. But, whereas the Bishop and the General perform other functions in life once they are out of the Grand Balcony, Irma and Carmen, however, never go out; Carmen even likens the Grand Balcony to a convent: "Entering a brothel means rejecting the world. Here I am and here I'll stay. Your mirrors and orders and the passions are my reality." While the figures are able to distinguish between make-believe and life, the two women are not: they live by the game, they thus live within the game and do not possess any other reality. In the fifth

scene, the cards get mixed-up for, here, appearance does without
concrete reference. Irma and Carmen do not imitate "a madam and
her favorite," that is what they are. And yet they present their functions as scenarios which would imitate the general, abstract relationship that traditionally exists between the madam of a brothel and
one of her employees. Thus Irma's friendship for Carmen does not
appear as real but as "part of the role." Furthermore, as far as Carmen is concerned, to settle accounts is to go through a scenario, like
confessing her sins or admitting her thefts except that the accounts are
settled behind the scenes, so to speak. But that is pure chance, for
Carmen has been in the drawing-rooms, she used to play the Im-
maculate Conception for an employee of the Bank of Lyon and when
she lost this part, Irma, as compensation, added her on to the books,
thus creating for the spectator an equivalence between the functions
that are performed in the drawing-rooms and those performed in
the bedroom.

"Come come, Carmen," Irma asks, "when you mounted the snow-
covered rock with the yellow paper rose-bush — by the way, I'm going
to have to put that away in the cellar — and when the miraculously-
healed leper swooned at the sight of you, you didn't take yourself
seriously, did you, Carmen?" It is a purely rhetorical question. Irma already knows the answer: For Carmen, real life does not exist.
Her reality, she herself said, consists of the mirrors of the Grand
Balcony and its passions, that is to say the successive roles that she
plays. Without a role, she lacks life. Even her relationship with her
daughter (but then does she really have a daughter?) is theatrical.
"You're the fairy godmother," Irma tells her, "who comes to see her
with toys and perfumes. She pictures you in heaven."

Carmen's only reality are her roles; Irma's only reality is the manner in which she plays her character of the "madam." The dialectic
of appearance and reality, as it is lived by the two women, thus differs from that which the figures of the beginning live. In the first
four scenes, appearance copies reality by making it purer and more
essential; in the fifth, appearance is the sole reality. Advice given
by Genet for the play's interpretation quite clearly establishes that
the figures, on the one hand, and the two women, on the other,
should not signify the inauthenticity of their characters in the same
fashion: "In the four scenes at the beginning almost everything is
overdone, still there are some passages where the tone must be more
natural and thus permit the exaggeration to appear even more out

of proportion. In short, nothing equivocal, but two opposing tones. On the contrary, however, from the scene between Madame Irma and Carmen up until the end, it is a question of coming up with a narrative tone that is *always* equivocal, always suspect."

Nevertheless, even though this place is where "the ceremony maintains its purity," the Grand Balcony is not as isolated as Irma would like. From the start, machine-gun fire is heard, people speak of the seething revolt on the outside, in the dramaturgic space of that which, at that very moment of the play, the spectator believes to be that of true reality. The ceremony, in the Grand Balcony, does not have a chance to unfold as it should since everyone is preoccupied with events on the outside. Interference between the Balcony and life becomes concrete at the end of the fifth scene by the violent death of Arthur, killed by a bullet from the outside. To the eyes of those within the Grand Balcony, Arthur is really dead. This death constitutes a profound violation of order and ritual practised in the Grand Balcony since the physical death of Arthur fixes him definitively within reality, preventing him from ever again playing roles in appearance. Indeed, in order to attain its maximum of credibility, appearance must copy the real as exactly as possible, while including a fake detail by which it designates its imposture.

The Appearance of Reality

This reality, which can thus upset the pomp of the Grand Balcony, will be shown to us by Genet. He is going to transfer it from the dramaturgic space to the scenic space. For the audience, it will thus become a spectacle as are the scenarios of the figures, and the roles of Madame Irma and Carmen. Entering into the scenic space, reality itself becomes appearance, so to speak. Genet suggests this to us in several ways. First, he places the revolt doubly under the sign of the Balcony since "in the background, at some distance, we perceive the façade of the Grand Balcony"; especially since the rebels have chosen Chantal as symbol, a prostitute who has long worked for Madame Irma. Then he suggests that the rebels wear masks, thus signifying that this function is an accessory one for them and hardly impinges on their being: "It is necessary to invent the revolutionary type and then paint it and model it on a mask, for I don't see anyone, even among the Protestants of Lyon, who would have a face long enough, sad enough, and fierce enough to play this role. The fixity of the masks would do fine." It is thus evident once again that the audience is not able to abandon itself to dramatic illusion, it must believe, on the contrary, in an image of a rebel invented, perhaps, by a long bourgeois tradition both in literature and in film. In addition, it is worthwhile to note that the revolutionaries are related to the other figures to the extent that they have achieved the fixity towards which the latter were striving. Furthermore, at the close of the play, Irma will speak of "rebels who allow the revolt to congeal."

But it is not to the first four scenes that this scene corresponds, but rather to the fifth. After having shown reality in appearance, Genet now shows appearance in reality. The rebels, indeed, are playing roles and do not have any true life in themselves. They aspire to it, however, and in this their procedure is the inverse of that of the figures. It is for this reason, no doubt, that it is destined to fail. When Roger will want to enter into appearance, it will be too late. He will only manage to castrate himself and not to render powerless the image of the police. But in the sixth scene, Roger believes that having abducted Chantal from the brothel, from the "grave" as he says, would suffice to bring her back to reality. In point of fact, since he no longer possesses the pomp, the decor, and the ceremonial of the Grand Balcony, Roger is not able to make love to her: being nothing but an appearance, he cannot take action in reality. As for the rebels, they are not any better armed than Roger for real life since they do not know how to conduct a revolution other than by repeating the practises of the Grand Balcony; indeed, they ask Chantal to do, in life, what she used to do in the brothel: act out a scenario. They ask her to incarnate the character of an enticer of men in order to become the symbol of the revolution, an image, just as the judge's partner was supposed to become the image of a model thief.

The dramaturgic space of the revolution becomes irreal in becoming scenic. Believing at last to see reality, the spectator only once again sees people playing roles. Dramatic illusion is again refused to him. The move from the Grand Balcony to the revolt does not transform Chantal's life. Like Carmen, she only exists through her roles.

For Goldmann, "the struggle of the rebels against the Balcony constitutes a struggle between life and death; between the order in the inside of which values exist only in the imagination and in ritual, and the attempt to create a new order in which these values would penetrate life itself and in which the flight into the imaginary would no longer be necessary because life would have become authentic."[13] But it is this authentic life which the rebels do not possess. On the contrary, they are confined within roles, which will lead them to their destruction. When Irma plays the role of a madam, there is an adequation between the character she plays and the one she wants to play. But the case of the revolutionaries is totally different: they try to construct a reality by using elements borrowed from ritual and from the imaginary. The apparition of figures will put an end to this revolution which has involuntarily refused the mutability of the real in order to attempt to fix itself in the scenario, thus leading itself to the organized scenario of the figures of the Balcony for whom it is enough to kill Chantal (the image of the revolution) to annihilate the revolution itself.

Appearance Copies Reality and Takes Precedence

The scene of the revolutionaries provides a closure, in a certain manner, to the first part of the play. The three scenic spaces which were successively presented to us have defined three types of relations between appearance and reality: in the drawing-rooms a game is being played which copies the real; in Irma's bedroom the reality of appearance is played out; and, finally, on the public square there are rebels acting out appearance in reality. In the seventh scene, appearance again copies the real, but this time Irma's status will be profoundly modified. From "director," which she was in the closed world of the Grand Balcony, she will become an actress by the same token as the other figures, in a scenario imagined by a character coming from the outside: the Court Envoy; and their roles are going to have an effect on the outside world. It is not indifferent that Genet should choose to show us the preparation of this scenario in the drawing-room, that is to say in a place where appearance copies reality. For, indeed, Irma and her acolytes are now going to represent the real power that exists — or has existed — outside of the Grand Balcony. The signification of this scenario, nevertheless, is quite different from that which was conveyed by the first scenes. This time, it is no longer a question of playing for oneself, in solitude, it is no longer a question of an infinite reflection of images in mirrors of the uni-

[13]See Lucien Goldmann, "The Theater of Genet: A Sociological Study," in this volume.

verse closed in on itself. On the contrary, it is a question of carrying the images toward the outside world, in order to have an effect on the real and to thus replace real power in its repressive function. The relationship between appearance and reality has changed, not only in the finality of the game, but equally so in the very nature of the real that is copied. The latter, indeed, shows itself to be evanescent, difficult to grasp and to describe. The Envoy's words, "irreal to the point of being able to mingle with the figures of the Balcony,"[14] are incomprehensible: it is impossible to know exactly what the Queen is doing. Is she still living? Did she die crushed? One is not certain whether or not the explosion affected the Royal Palace. One does not know the fate that is reserved for those who hold the real power. What one does know is that they are no longer capable of performing their functions. Whereas Genet was pointing out, in the sixth scene, a reality destined to failure because fixed as appearance, he now shows us an evanescent reality, and an appearance that is fluid to the point of departing from its ritual so as to replace the reality of power and to master that of the rebels. It is enough that these figures appear on the balcony and kill Chantal for the revolution to be vanquished.

However, certain details of the scene in which victory is achieved prevent us from considering *The Balcony* as a traditional play on revolution. On the one hand, the figures appear accompanied by the beggar—a character also belonging to the nomenclature of the brothel—on the other hand, Genet does not foresee any walk-ons to represent the people. The realistic illusion of the theatre is thus refused to us since the spectator has before his eyes the entire population of the brothel. But this scarcely realistic apparition has consequences that are realistic since the spectator is indeed obliged, by virtue of the traditional convention of dramatic illusion, to believe that Chantal is really dead. This scene is thus the setting for a fundamental contradiction which forces the spectator to believe and not to believe in the elements that the theatre puts before him. The nonrealistic apparition of the figures tells him: "You are at the theatre and not in real life." But, on the other hand, theatrical convention forces him to believe in the death of Chantal; that is, in the power of the figures as the "dramaturgic" people. At once a satire of power— and especially—a satire of the western theatre of illusion, this scene

[14]Bernard Dort, *art. cit.,* p. 138.

is characteristic of Genet's dramaturgy which plays with a normal deck of cards, but which does not obey the rules of the game. In other words, Genet's theatre is a veritable discourse on theatre—and on theatre within the theatre as well—which forces the spectator to believe in the power of characters whom he knows to be even more fake than those he usually confronts in the dramatic repertory. Thus, at the same time as the "dramaturgic" people, those spoken of in the ninth scene, it is also the real audience who ought to recognize the power of the figures and who will undergo the victory of appearance.

Victory of Appearance

The ninth and final scene concludes the play with the victory of appearance: the world of disguises, of figures, has checkmated the revolution of the fixed rebels. In slaughtering Chantal, the fake—true—power has overthrown the symbol of the revolution, thus its force. Because of this defeat, the Balcony is enriched by a new scenario and the scenic space is doubled under our very eyes. Soon the dream of the Chief of Police will be realized, he is going to enter into the nomenclature of the brothel. The audience will be able at the same time to see Roger acting out the scenario and Madame Irma watching him with the other figures and the Chief of Police. This means that in the Grand Balcony it is possible, presently, to represent reality in an even more complete manner: not only will they play at dominator and victim, but also at repression as well.

The three figures, however, would like to use the newly acquired power to transform their appearance into reality: so long as the Chief of Police is not represented in the brothel, the three figures retain the possibility of seizing power for themselves. But that is merely an ephemeral temptation, for they fear that the execution of an action would mar the perfection of their appearance. Besides, Roger's entrance irremediably puts an end to what had only been a whim since he introduces repression into the nomenclature (giving to the Chief of Police—or to his image—supreme authority within the Grand Balcony) and thus into the heart of appearance which now holds sway over reality.

That it should be the chief of the revolt who has the Chief of Police entered into the nomenclature is not a mere dramatic coincidence. With Roger, the action of the rebels which has failed in reality tries, in a last ditch effort, to attain the appearance which conquered it. Goldmann, who does not explain why Roger enters the brothel, considers his castration to be an act of auto-aggressivity provoked by despair: "But Roger will very quickly realize that it is a question of an imaginary game, a ritual. Now, his very being as a revolutionary was precisely constituted by the attempt to create a reality which would no longer have need of the imaginary or of ritual. In extreme despair—Nothing! Nothing remains to me.—he will castrate himself, thus reconciling the imaginary with the reality of the defeated revolt."[15] Our analysis has shown, on the contrary, that Roger's reality was quite unreliable, because it was already ritualized, precisely. Consequently, he is in a better position to fight on the grounds of the imaginary. Roger's despair does not arise from the fact that he is disappointed in finding appearance in the Grand Balcony—he was already familiar with the ceremonies of the place since he had met Chantal there. His "Nothing remains to me" comes after his final attempt to introduce reality into the world of appearance by speaking of Chantal to Carmen. But the latter, terrified, refused to answer him and thus foiled this attempt. Action on the grounds of the real having become completely and definitively impossible, there only remains for Roger to assault the image of the Chief of Police. He attempts to devirilize him by castrating himself, hoping to render impotent the image of repression. But Roger only succeeds in diminishing himself, without the slightest benefit for the cause he is defending, for the Chief of Police is there, in person, to play his own role and to perpetuate his own intact image. With reality abolished, he is able to enter definitively and completely into the appearance which possesses the true power: "The Chief of Police: Well played. He thought he had me. *(He put his hand on his fly, very visibly feels his balls, and, reassured, heaves a sigh.)* Mine are here. So which of us is washed up? He or I? Though my image be castrated in every brothel in the world, I remain intact. Intact, gentlemen." Since "that plumber didn't know how to handle his role," he will replace him personally and will play his own role.

The spectators, who have almost without knowing it played their part during the entire play, are then directly taken aside by Madame

[15] Reference is made to another version of Goldmann's essay.

Irma who turns out all the lights of the Balcony, thus of the theatre, while saying to the audience: "You must go now. You'll leave by the right, through the alley." She addresses herself to us in the very same terms by which she addressed the characters who would come to play the dominators. She thus creates an equivalence between the situation of the audience who comes to participate in the ceremony of the theatre and the anonymous beings who have accomplished their own rituals during the first four scenes. The audience can almost be said to have played the role of traveller in an ultimate scenario imagined by Genet. But, just as the revolt upset the figures, in similar fashion the constant reminder of the facticity of the theatre upset the mode of participation in which the western theatre of illusion traditionally contains the spectator.

This is what founds the value of Genet's theatre and its power. The play is not "a satire of this or that," which would merely situate its power at the level of content. It denounces at the same time its own means of production as well as the product it engenders. It is a satire, intrinsically, even at the level of the signifier.

Profane and Sacred Reality in
Jean Genet's Theatre

Jean Gitenet

Genet's two approaches to what çan be called profane reality are: one, *explicit* (direct reference in discourse to tangible and explicable realities), the other *implicit* (the affirmation of a fact or a truth in sacred reality throwing the corresponding profane reality in relief). In other words, "the world of Genet" (a sacralized world) takes root in the profane world that it rejects. "Sacred institutions" in Genet's plays are positive projections of institutions of identical but negative structures in the profane world. Prison, for example, is, in the profane world, an institution which eliminates the individual who has transgressed the law. This individual thus finds himself in the situation of a being rejected by the positive system of profane reality and his behavior (like all "transgressive behavior") can lead to three possible outcomes:

1.   an immanent attitude of acceptance of his situation without any attempt at sublimation, at opening up to what constitutes Genet's world,

2.   a magical attitude (in the Sartrian sense of the word), neurotic or suicidal, or

3.   a transcending attitude, that is, the construction of a sacred universe, valorized, around the notion of crime and lending positive value to that to which Society (the profane world) lends a negative one.

The criminal's valorization of the reverse of profane reality may simply be an attitude of resentment and merely lead to cheating

"Profane and Sacred Reality in Jean Genet's Theatre" by Jean Gitenet, translated from the French by Janie Vanpée. From *Obliques 2: Genet,* pp. 70-73. Reprinted by permission of *Obliques.*

behavior in the sacred order of Evil, like Lefranc's behavior in *Deathwatch,* but most of the heroes in Genet's theatre and in any case those who evolve in abjection (sacred reality) live a reversal of the values of profane reality, precisely because these values are contrary to those espoused by the Society in which they are, after all, involved.

The opposition between the sacred and the profane worlds is significant, not only as a basic structure of Genet's mythology, but also as a structure of *discourse, (play) acting* and *stage set.* For example, in *The Maids* two series of terms and expressions can be analyzed and grouped into those emanating from the profane world and opposing ones emanating from the sacred. This opposition, found on the level of discourse (of language) is as valid on the phonological level (cf. "…I was preparing Madame's *tilleul* [she pronounces it *tillol*]"), that is, in the manner of pronouncing words and sentences, as it is on the rhetorical level (cf. Solange's and Claire's curt answers when speaking to Madame, as well as their lyricism, their inspired gab when celebrating the "rite") and on the lexical level.

Moreover the structure of the (play) acting depends on the same opposition: in *The Maids,* the characters' acting changes according to whether it is set up as ceremonial (the actresses play at playing with the mirror, the dresses, etc.) or whether it makes reference to the profane world (the actresses, once again "maids," put things away, dust, etc.).

Finally, this same opposition is found again in Genet's conception of scenic space; the plans of the superimposed stage set in *The Screens,* the well in scene 9 of *The Balcony,* and even the cothurni that Genet has the "Figures" wear in the first three scenes of this same play.

Thus, we have on one hand a hyperbolic movement leading towards solitude where ecstasy and illusion reign; and on the other, a parabolic movement which respects the natural ties between profane realities and organizes them in realistic language (play)acting and stage set. And, just as hyperboles are grafted onto reality in order to transfigure it while going beyond it, that is, by denying it in a certain way, Genet's sacred world, with its hymns, its liturgy, and its sacred places, demands the presence of the profane world in order simply to be able to be.

But if this antithetical structure, because it commands a whole

series of motives on different levels, is the first one sensed in a reading of Genet's theatrical work, it is only the matrix of a dramatic
dialectic situated in a cathartic scheme as much on the level of discourse as on the level of (play)acting and on the level of stage set.

In other words, one could say that the antithetical structure of
profane world/sacred world is an exterior signifying *form,* decom-
posable into simple elements, and that inside this form there is a
signified structure, a *content* which no longer includes the forms of
the drama at all levels of composition, but includes the different
levels of statement *(énoncé),* or more precisely of that which is represented, recognizing, of course, that the (play)acting as well as the
stage set are, no less than the text, statements. Thus, we find zones
variously laden and variously graded, evolving within the framework of the structure generating theatrical action.

In *The Blacks* there are, at the level of discourse, at least three
zones of statement: that of the Figures, that of the Blacks, and that of
the victim. These three zones correspond to the zone of play acting
and stage set. The statement of the Figures takes place *above,* in
The Blacks, where the Figures are found on a gallery, as well as in
The Balcony, where the Figures are perched up on cothurni or else
appear on the balcony. Thus, the structure of the set corresponds to
the statement of the Figures, and it could be shown that the structure
of scene-play corresponds to this same structure of stage set and to
this same statement.

In short, the relationships between these different statements give
us (incompletely, of course) the most general, most organized statement in the dramatist's symbolic system; a system arranged in motifs
whose structure of sacred world/ profane world is the organizing
principle. The whole impetus of drama for Genet, that is, the intent
of the ambiguity of the language, the discontinuity of the staging,
and of the hieratic vulgarity of the acting, is the privileged moment
(all the others are merely preparation or amplification) of the supreme celebration through which the totality of the profane world's
values themselves come to found, that is, create, the veracity of the
values of Genet's sacred world.

Consequently, we believe that Genet's theatre is not a presentation of the sacred world, a kind of discovery of a presupposed universe, contrary to the profane world; it is truly a *sacralization* (the
sacred in action).

Although most of them belong to it, the characters in Genet's plays do not proceed immediately into the domain of the sacred, but rather penetrate into it. Every play then becomes a *quest* (or conquest of the others and the self) for the sacred dimension. Every character marked by the sacredness of Evil passes through the following double movement: first a movement of *disillusion* (tearing himself away from profane reality by emptying himself—cf. Lefranc, in *Deathwatch* who "empties" himself of his crime), then a movement of *illusion* (projecting himself into sacred reality, because it is empty). What happens next to dramatic action? It becomes the "performance of *emptiness,*" the purifying and regenerating catharsis, the leap into another world, which no longer has a bottom or a foundation other than the one left behind.

As Genet writes in *L'etrange mot d'...* (Gallimard, *Oeuvres complètes,* t. IV, page 13):

> What of drama? If it has, in the author, its brilliant origin, it is up to him to capture the lightning and to organize, from the flash that lights up the emptiness, a verbal architecture—that is, a grammatical and ·ceremonial structure—artfully indicating that an appearance which shows up emptiness is torn from emptiness.

It appears that the characters in Genet's plays are conscious that sacred reality is a void (cf. the Blacks' remarks about their play-acting, Irma's light attitude when the Queen is enthroned, Said's reluctance to embrace the sacredness of abjection...). Genet knows very well, as do his heroes, that nature abhors a vacuum, but they also know that one can be drawn to emptiness, simply to experience that feeling of horror and vertigo that it offers. One can then ask whether Genet likes sacred reality (whose primary sentimental and psychical motor is *hatred* of profane reality) because it is sacred or because it is empty?

In any case, Genet's characters, when they officiate, when they play at the game of the sanctifying sacrilege, do not have any hold on profane reality which remains intact. The sacred attitude does not operate on the level of *facts,* but only on the level of *fiction.* Hence, Genet's characters can and must act out failure in relation to profane reality if they want to achieve *sovereignty* in the order of the sacred (cf. Claire's camouflaged suicide, Roger's castration, Said's and Leila's fake death). For Genet's heroes, profane failure is the *sine qua non* condition for sacred success.

To return to the primary truth of Genet's theatre, his theatrical space, it must be said that everything in his theatre, is profane *and* sacred. The characters, consequently, are all double, either explicitly (each has its double in the opposite world), or implicitly (doubling of personality).

This space situated between the profane and sacred worlds, precisely the leap into the void that constitutes Genet's theatre, can be called the ABSURD. Indeed, whether one goes in one direction to the edge of the real or in the other direction to the edge of the unreal (or surreal or transcendental) one finds oneself in the region of the Absurd, where the void, simultaneously EVERYTHING AND NOTHING, is the only possible "form," that is, lack of form, lack of utterance *(énonciation)*, lack of statement *(énoncé)*. The Absurd thus appears as the epitome of reality, profane or sacred, the scene of language, (play)acting, and staging where everything cancels out in a profusion of words, gestures, and objects, all of which derive their reality exclusively from the reality of metaphors, mimes, and reflections (or simulacrums)—cf. *L'étrange mot d'...*

In Genet's theatre nothing happens, and nothing is said. Reversing this proposition one can also affirm that everything is said and everything happens. For this theatre is at once creation and destruction in action. It is a geometric scene, situated in space and time at the cleavage point between two realities, a scene where illusions and disillusions in action ally themselves according to particular structures.

Therefore, this cleavage point, this leap into the void, which is the center of Genet's theatre and sacred intention, is not to be found in the antithetical categories of sacred/ profane world, illusion/ disillusion or destruction/ creation. It is rather to be found in a dimension which at once affirms and denies both terms of these pairs, and this dimension is DEATH.

DEATH is the only notion which, for the profane world just as for the sacred, *is not operative,* precisely because it is only a notion and it is not backed up by experience. Genet's true theatrical universe is therefore not a dreamt universe, a negative double of the profane world, in which everything would be, *a priori,* the opposite of what society does. It is, one could say, a perspective from which the dramatist's intention is to project, in profane reality as well as in sacred reality, that which reveals authenticity: *humor.* The dramatist, in Genet's own words, "is capable of true audacity in an effort to mediate, that is, of internal laughter." *(L'etrange mot d'...).*

Therefore DEATH, guarantee of the sacred and negation of the profane, seems to be for Genet, the supreme point, pivot of the absurd, from which all objectification of dramatic character (dialogues, acting, and staging) takes on sense *and* non-sense. Sense, because, it enables the dramatist to structure a reality into words, gestures and staging: non-sense because all that is nothing but fiction, mime, at best clowning (precisely Genet's definition of *The Blacks*).

Speaking of theatrical language, Genet writes this:

> For the grand parade before the burial of the cadaver, the funereal mime, if he wants to make the dead relive and redie, will have to discover and dare to speak out those dialectophagous words which, in front of the public, will devour the life and the death of the dead.

What Genet says of words, can be said of gestures and staging as well. The theatrical performance of Genet then becomes, and here we reach the apogee of his theatre (in scene 4 of *The Balcony*, for example) a play of mirrors in a tomb.

I Allow Myself to Revolt

Jean Genet interviewed by Hubert Fichte

HUBERT FICHTE: Monsieur Genet, until recently you had no permanent address. You lived in small hotels...

JEAN GENET: That's right. I happen to have my passport with me. Here is my address. Read it!

FICHTE: 5, rue Sébastien-Bottin. The address of Gallimard.*

GENET: That is my official address.

FICHTE: Isn't it difficult not having one's own apartment? One can't invite friends. One can't do one's own cooking.

GENET: So what? Of course, there are problems. But it also makes irresponsibility possible. I am not responsible for anything, socially. And it makes possible an immediate *"engagement,"* decisions on the spot.

FICHTE: Are you afraid to be trapped by certain bourgeois luxuries which you could now afford because of your success?

GENET: No. I don't think so. I have no admiration whatever for bourgeois luxuries. Unless they had the qualities of a Renaissance castle. My income doesn't allow me to keep a princely household like a Borgia. Splendid architecture that is habitable hasn't existed since the Renaissance.

FICHTE: Why do you admire Strindberg's *Miss Julie* and reject Brecht's *Galileo Galilei?*

"I Allow Myself to Revolt—Jean Genet interviewed by Hubert Fichte," translated from the German by Christa Dove. From *Die Zeit,* 13 February, 1976. Reprinted with permission of Hubert Fichte.

*Genet's publishers.

GENET: Brecht has uttered mere rubbish. Galileo quotes stuff that's obvious—but the Strindberg of *Miss Julie* does not. With Brecht I always know what's coming. Nothing of what Strindberg says can be expressed otherwise than poetically. Everything that Brecht says can be said in prose and has been said in prose.

FICHTE: That's the way he meant it to be. He called it "epic theater." But Strindberg before him and especially in his introduction to *Miss Julie* actually already introduces the estrangement effect and the Brechtian type of cigar-smoking audience.

GENET: By adopting the stance of a cigar-smoker one adopts an attitude of unceremoniousness toward the work of art which it does not allow for. I don't know the Rothschilds, but I could imagine that with the Rothschilds one talks about art while smoking cigars.

FICHTE: You take the Brechtian gesture to be a bourgeois, capitalist stance?

GENET: That's the way it looks to me.

FICHTE: At least before works of art—since you are at the moment smoking a cigarillo.

GENET: I believe the attitude in front of a work of art is contemplation. I lose more and more the feeling of being myself, the sensation of the Ego. It takes such a tremendous effort before a work of art that in a museum I can only look at two or three pictures and in a concert can only listen to two or three pieces. I am too tired...

FICHTE: And when you are reading?

GENET: It's the same thing. It took me two months to read *The Brothers Karamazov*. I stayed in bed. I was in Italy at the time. I read a page... And I had to think about it for two hours. And then the same thing all over again. That is monstrous. It really does you in. When I, with my modest capacities, don't compose Monteverdi's Mass of the Beata Vergine while listening to it, I hear nothing. When I don't write *The Brothers Karamazov* while reading the book, nothing happens.

FICHTE: In your own work there is admiration for beautiful, elegant brutality.

GENET: You know, I was thirty years old when I wrote my books. Today I am sixty-five.

FICHTE: Has this admiration for murderers, for Hitler, for concentration camps become empty?

GENET: Yes and no. It has become empty. But the space has not been filled by anything new. A void has remained. That is rather strange for one who is alive. I no longer have this... What did this fascination with killers, murderers, Hitler mean? (More drily) I must remind you that I have neither father nor mother. I grew up on public welfare. I learned when I was very young that I am not a Frenchman, that I don't belong to the village. I grew up in the Massif Central. I learned it in a very stupid, ridiculous manner: the teacher told us to write a short composition. Every pupil was supposed to describe his home. The teacher thought that mine was the prettiest description. He read it out loud, and they all made fun of me. They said: But that's not his home. He is a foundling. And at that moment such a void appeared. I immediately felt totally a stranger. Oh, the word "hating" France is not strong enough, it is nothing, there should be more than "hating," "spewing out France"... The fact that the French army, the most renowned one in the world thirty years ago, capitulated before the troops of an Austrian corporal, made me absolutely ecstatic. I could only adore the man who had brought about the downfall of France. Subsequently I could only join all those suppressed colored peoples who revolted against the whites. Against all whites. Perhaps I am a black man who happens to have white or pink skin. I don't know my family.

FICHTE: You have said that the Black Panthers are making an artistic, a poetic revolution. Artistic, poetic revolutions rarely coincide with economic, social revolutions.

GENET: Political revolutions are never supplemented by artistic revolutions. When political revolutionaries have brought about a complete transformation of society, they are confronted with the following problem: They have to give expression to their revolution in the most adequate way possible. It seems to me that all revolutionaries make use of the most academic means of expression, means of expression of the very society which they have destroyed or which they want to destroy. As if the revolutionaries said to themselves, let's prove to the regime we have destroyed that we are just as good as they were. And then they imitate the academicisms, official painting, official architecture, official music.

Very much later they plan a cultural revolution and then they no longer make appeal to academicism but to tradition, and search for new forms to express the tradition. What do we owe the Revolution of 1848? Baudelaire, so they say, went on the barricades. But Baudelaire had already written, before that time, the most beautiful poems of *Les Fleurs du Mal.* To the Revolution of 1848 we owe *Sentimental Education,* written by Flaubert who was not at all in favor of the revolution.

Toward the end of the First World War it seemed as if a new way of feeling would find its equivalent in the Russian revolution. I am talking about surrealism, which however did not take place in the Soviet Union. And finally the surrealists very quickly broke off all ties with the Soviet Union—at that time Aragon wrote "Moscou la Gâteuse" ["Moscow the Senile"].

FICHTE: Did you ever travel in the Soviet Union?

GENET: No.

FICHTE: Why not?

GENET: I was afraid I would be bored stiff.

FICHTE: You were invited to go to Cuba and refused to go there, too.

GENET: When the cultural functionary in charge invited me, I said: All right, I would like to come to Cuba. Under one condition. I pay for the trip myself. I pay for my stay there, and I go where-ever I want, I live where I want. I would like to come to Cuba if there is a revolution taking place there as I imagine one. Which means, if there are no flags there any more, for a flag as a sign of recognition, as an emblem around which one congregates, has a theatricality which castrates, which kills. And if they no longer have a national anthem.

He answered: You are out of luck. The national anthem of Cuba was written by a black.

FICHTE: Did May 1968 bring a revolution as you imagine it?

GENET: No, no. A lot has been written about May '68. It has been called a "Mimodrama" and to me that seems pretty close to the truth. Some of the most courageous students occupied the Theatre de l'Odéon. I was twice in the Théâtre de l'Odéon when it was occupied. The first time there was a kind of incantatory violence there. When I came the second time, this violence had disappeared.

The words spoken on the stage—they were partly directives—were taken up by the audience and thrown back to the stage, like an echo, from the stage to the audience, from the audience to the stage, every time weaker...

The students thus occupied a theater.

What is a theater?

First of all: what is power?

It seems as if power could never get along without theatricality. Power protects itself by means of theatricality. And that is the case in China, in the USA, in England, in France, everywhere.

There is one place in the whole world, where theatricality does not conceal power—in the theater. It is wholly undangerous.

In May '68 the students occupied a theater, which is to say a place wholly deprived of all power, where only theatricality remains.

If at least they had occupied the Palais de Justice—it would first of all have been more difficult, the Palais de Justice is much better guarded than the Théâtre de l'Odéon. They would have been forced to hand down judgments, to throw people into prison. It would have been the beginning of a revolution. They didn't do it.

FICHTE: Could you tell me what your revolution would look like?

GENET: No. Because, to be honest, I don't really want a revolution to take place. The situation at this moment, the present regime, allow me to revolt. The revolution would probably not allow me my individual revolt. Now I can be against it. If a real revolution were to take place, I couldn't be against it. I would become a follower of this revolution. But a man like myself is never a follower of anything. I am a man of revolt. My standpoint is very egoistical. I don't want the world to change in order to permit myself to be against the world.

FICHTE: As I understand what you call "poetic revolution," I see the following components: erotics, play, provocation.

GENET: Yes, indeed. I don't know whether I would agree with the sequence. But the components are correct. Yet at the same time: the will to side with those most powerless against every established power.

FICHTE: When you say, in May '68 the students should have thrown people into prison, this appears to me a very harsh judgment, especially from your own point of view.

GENET: Or do away with prisons altogether. In any case, make a judgment, take a definite position.

FICHTE: Can't one ask for something more progressive than a death sentence?

GENET: Oh yes! The Chinese did it in the case of the old Manchu Emperor. They made him into a gardener.

FICHTE: And to you that seems more progressive than the death sentence against Louis XVI?

GENET: No, more ironic. In both cases the question was how to destroy the sovereignty of one man. Louis XVI was very skillful with his hands. He made locks. If the French Revolution had turned him into a good or mediocre locksmith, it would have been just as beautiful as cutting off his head. But the balance of power in the years 1791/92, the Reign of Terror, was such that it was only possible to condemn him to death or to exile. And to exile him would have been very dangerous.

FICHTE: You find it admirable, when someone deprived of his rights commits a murder?

GENET: One mustn't confuse the categories. There are literary categories and categories of experience. The idea of a murder can be very beautiful. An actual murder is something else.

Shortly after the liberation I saw an Algerian murder a Frenchman. They were playing cards. I stood next to them. The Algerian was twenty-four years old. He had no money left. He had let the Frenchman completely get the better of him. He asked to be lent some money in order to try his luck once again. He was refused. He drew his knife and killed and I watched the guy die. It was very beautiful. Why? This murder was the apogee of a revolt which the young Algerian had harbored within himself for a long time. It was the revolt that was beautiful, not so much the murder itself. The danger he was in gave him strength, conviction. The murderer had to flee and was never caught. To kill without risk, like a policeman, no, I don't find that very admirable.

FICHTE: Why haven't you ever committed a murder?

GENET: Probably because I was writing my books.

FICHTE: Were you ever obsessed by the idea of committing a murder?

GENET: Yes. But a murder without a victim. It's an effort for me to believe someone's life or death is unimportant, just because death necessarily comes in the end, whether I am its instrument, or a heart attack, or an automobile accident. It shouldn't be important for me, and yet it is.

You now could ask me whether I have ever caused someone's death.

FICHTE: Yes.

GENET: And I wouldn't answer you.

FICHTE: Unintentionally?

GENET: No. Intentionally. The question is: Have you ever intentionally caused someone's death?

FICHTE: Yes.

GENET: I am not answering.

FICHTE: What does violence mean to you?

GENET: Oh! I would have to talk about something I don't know anything about. I would probably have to talk about "Potlatch." Of destructive drunkenness. A destructive drunkenness that overcomes even the most circumspect and most intelligent people. Remember Lenin who promised golden pissoirs to the Soviet people. In all revolutions there is an element of panic drunkenness. It came to light in France, in Europe as a whole, before the French Revolution, in the *Jacqueries* and it appears—in ritual and ritualized form—during the carnival.

In certain periods whole nations want to liberate themselves. They want to abandon themselves to the phenomenon of "potlatch," to complete destruction, complete exhaustion.

FICHTE: Shortly before he was murdered, Pasolini* said that the violence of the proletariat had fundamentally changed, that it was only aimed at consumer goods, that it must be punished just like neo-fascist violence. Hasn't murder become something completely banal, unritualized? One kills whomever, whenever, for

---

*Italian film director Pier Paolo Pasolini was murdered near Rome in 1975. His killer, seventeen-year-old Giuseppe Pelosi, told the police that Pasolini had made homosexual advances to him.

a dollar or not even that much—it is a violence which is very different from the one you have described.

GENET: But you are saying the opposite of Pasolini. Isn't it above all a matter of expressing oneself violently and to find a cover for this violence? Thus one says: it was done for a dollar for a piece of clothing. When in point of fact violence itself was at stake.

FICHTE: Does that mean that for you the violence of your *Querelle* is the same as the violence of Pino Pelosi who murdered Pasolini?

GENET: As far as this baker's apprentice is concerned, I don't know. Perhaps he only wanted money. Perhaps he was upset that Pasolini wanted to hold his ass. It is possible that this young baker is sitting in his prison cell, and, encouraged by his lawyer, tells himself: After all, I killed a multi-millionnaire who was estranged from the people. My cause is just.

FICHTE: When you are writing, are you addressing anybody?

GENET: Never! What I am telling you now is not a joke, I probably haven't attained my goal, either: I wanted to shape the French language as beautifully as possible. Everything else was indifferent to me.

FICHTE: The language which you know best, or the French language?

GENET: The language which I knew best. But the French language too, because I was condemned in French. The courts which condemned me passed their sentence in French.

FICHTE: And you wanted to counter them on a higher level?

GENET: Precisely!

FICHTE: When did you begin this poetic endeavour?

GENET: You are forcing me into a difficult retrospect. I don't have many points of reference. I think I was twenty-nine or thirty years old. I was in prison, around 1939. I was alone in my cell. Up to then I had never written anything but letters to male and female friends. And I think those letters were very conventional. Preformulated phrases, nothing felt. And then I wrote a Christmas card to a [female] German friend who lived in Czechoslovakia. I had bought the card in prison, and the reverse of it, meant to be written on, felt rough. The roughness of this card touched me deeply. And instead of talking about Christmas, I talked about the roughness of the postcard and about snow and what it conjured up, and from that moment on I was writing. That was the decisive click.

FICHTE: Which books had left an impression on you up to that time?

GENET: Popular novels. Books that were available in prison. Except that when I was fifteen I had gotten hold of Ronsard's poetry, in the reform school of Mettray. And I was enchanted.

FICHTE: And Marcel Proust?

GENET: I read *Within A Budding Grove* in prison. The first volume. We were in the prison courtyard and exchanged books secretly. It was during the war. And since I wasn't paying much attention my turn came towards the end and somebody said: Here. You take this. And I see: Marcel Proust. And I say to myself: That must be boring as hell! And then...
Please, believe me. Even if I am not always honest, now I am. I read the first sentence of *Within A Budding Grove*. The sentence is very long. When I had read it I closed the book and said: Now I can have peace, I know I will fall from one enchantment into the next. That first sentence is so dense, so beautiful. That beginning was a great flame announcing a blazing fire. And I needed almost all day to recover.

FICHTE: Had you already written one of your books?

GENET: No. Or I was in the process of writing *Our Lady of the Flowers*.

FICHTE: Did other works of literature affect you as much as Proust did?

GENET: Yes. Even more deeply. *The Brothers Karamazov*.

FICHTE: How do you yourself experience time?

GENET: You are forcing me to give a very difficult answer. Because for the last twenty, twenty-five years I have been taking Nembutal —a narcotic which puts me to sleep almost immediately. But it has side effects. It's not enough to drink coffee in the morning. The nembutal itself must stop affecting the brain. During the whole time I am under its influence, I don't take time into account at all. If it's a question of carrying out strictly delineated tasks, I call them, to be brief, "profane," like going shopping, I do those very precisely, in a precisely limited period of time. I don't get confused.

But if I want to write I need unlimited time. The other day at Gallimard's I got rather angry. I had asked for a rather large amount of money and Claude Gallimard wanted to pay me in monthly installments. Comfortable installments. But I said: No! I want all the money at once. Today. I want to be completely free for a whole year. Sleep when I want to. Go where I want to. Otherwise I'm not going to write anything. I must be able to write two, three days uninterruptedly, stay in bed night and day or just for an hour.

FICHTE: And he didn't want to?

GENET: Oh yes. I felt somewhat bothered during our first talk because I had all my pockets full of banknotes.

FICHTE: How much would one monthly installment have come to?

GENET: I don't know how much money other authors make. I have never asked for details. I am not ashamed of money and I am not ashamed to say how much I earn. I can't say "earn." When one writes, it's a little painful and a little pleasant—it's not work. In 1975 I "earned" 20 million old francs,* from my books, if you will. And then there is still my theater...

FICHTE: Do you like banknotes and coins?

GENET: Yes. Especially when they come in large denominations. I like that.

FICHTE: Does money for you mean gaining time or gaining sensuousness?

GENET: Time. Not sensuousness. I don't earn much but it's enough. I can allow myself to dress badly, go unwashed. I have my peace. I don't need to get haircuts. It's a shitty feeling to get a haircut.

FICHTE: Some time ago you were on one side of the ditch. Now you stand on the other. What sort of a feeling do you have when nowadays you encounter social outcasts?

GENET: I have no guilt feelings. If I am asked for money, and even if I am not asked, I give very easily, really very easily. There is injustice in the world—but not because my author's royalties are relatively high.

FICHTE: You yourself have described how you robbed homosexuals

---

*Approximately $40,000.

who expected caresses from you. Did young men ever attempt to rob you?

GENET: Yes. That has happened very very very often. In Hamburg, for instance. There was nothing for me to do but to give all the money I had on me to those two guys.

FICHTE: And that doesn't upset you?

GENET: Not at all! Not at all! Not at all! It only bothers me when it's a large sum. I get furious because then I have to go back to Gallimard.

FICHTE: When did you discover your preference for men?

GENET: Very early on. I was perhaps eight, at the most ten years old. At any rate in the country. And in the reform school of Mettray, where homosexuality was suppressed. But since there weren't any girls around, the boys had only one way out, either temporary or permanent homosexuality. I could say that in reform school I was truly happy.

FICHTE: And were you aware at the time that you were happy?

GENET: Yes. Yes. Yes. Yes. Despite all punishments. Despite the insults. Despite the beatings. Despite the terrible conditions, the work, the wooden shoes—we all wore wooden shoes—despite all that I was happy.

At that period of my life I very rarely asked myself questions about others. For a long time my attitude remained narcissistic. What counted was my happiness. Everything turned around my happiness.

FICHTE: Were you isolated?

GENET: My revolt against that authority, the prison authorities—my revolt was much stronger, much wilder than that of the most hardened ones there. I think I very quickly began to expose the absurdity of the attempts at our resocialization, the absurdity of the prayer periods, of the gym classes.

Today you are asking me questions about myself. Well, I have reached a point in my life where my own person is no longer very important. I don't think I am trying to hide something—but you are asking me about my personal problems, and my personal problems no longer exist.

FICHTE: You have projected your obsessions, accidents, resentments onto the world and have influenced the attitude of a whole generation...

GENET: Yes, but you are talking about matters 35 or 40 years past and which have been more or less erased by old age, by drugs that wipe out anything unpleasant and leave only what is pleasant. You remind me of the jungle which for all I know still exists but where I no longer live in the same way. I have pruned the thickest branches. I have created a clearing. And when you say: There, where you are living, used to be ferns, lianas—when you are saying that I know it is true, but I no longer remember what they were like, and I am no longer interested. All that has faded.

FICHTE: In certain initiation rites of secret sects in Africa one often finds a similar ensemble: flagellation, betrayal, murder of relatives, urine, excrements, animal skins, iron etc. In your novel *The Miracle of the Rose* the same components appear, perhaps not quite so closely related. Do you believe that in your experiences you have attained a quasi-ritual ground, an archaic ground?

GENET: Yes. I don't know anything about anthropology, but what you have just described are rites of transition. The point is to betray the tribe in order to be reintegrated into it in actuality; to drink urine so as not to drink it any longer in actuality. It is possible that in *The Miracle of the Rose* I have attempted all by myself, and of course unconsciously, to discover rites of transition. This idea occurs to me for the first time. But that could explain why, after my release from prison, I haven't written any more books, except *The Thief's Journal*. I had no more books to write. The transition had been brought about.

FICHTE: What is your theory of homosexuality?

GENET: I don't have one. I have several. Several theories have been developed. None is satisfying. Whether it's the Freudian theory, the Oedipus complex, or the theory of the geneticists, or the theory of Sartre, which he developed with reference to me in one of his books—that I was reacting in a certain way, but freely, to my social conditions: None of this I find satisfying. I note that I am a homosexual. How and why are questions merely to pass the time. It's somewhat similar to wanting to know why the pigment of my eyes is green.

FICHTE: In any case you don't consider homosexuality as a neurosis?

GENET: No. I even ask myself whether I haven't experienced homosexuality as a way out of neurosis, whether my neurosis didn't
exist prior to my homosexuality.

FICHTE: Do you believe that this interview gives a fairly accurate
idea of your present thinking?

GENET: Truth is only possible when I am completely alone. Truth
has nothing to do with confession. Truth has nothing to do with a
dialogue. I am speaking about my own truth. I have tried to answer your questions as precisely as possible. Actually I was very
imprecise. I cannot tell anything to anybody. I can only lie.

FICHTE: Lies express a two-fold truth.

GENET: Yes, discover the truth in them. Discover what I wanted to
hide.

Selected Bibliography

Jean Genet's plays and novels have all appeared in English. Between 1949 and 1969, *Deathwatch, The Maids, The Balcony, The Blacks, The Screens, Our Lady of the Flowers, Miracle of the Rose,* and *Funeral Rites* were all translated for Grove Press by Bernard Frechtman, who also translated *The Thief's Journal. Querelle* has been translated by Anselm Hollo.

Abel, Lionel. *Methatheater: A View of Dramatic Form.* New York: Hill and Wang, 1963.

Aslan, Odette. *Jean Genet,* "Theatre de tous les temps," no. 24. Edited by Pierre Seghers, 1974.

Bataille, Georges. *Literature and Evil.* Translated by Alastair Hamilton. London: Calder and Boyars, 1973.

Bonnefoy, Claude. *Jean Genet,* "Classiques du XXe siecle." Editions Universitaires. Paris, 1965.

Brooks, Peter. "The Passion of Our Lady." *Partisan Review,* no. 3, (Summer, 1964), pp. 443-46.

Brustein, Robert. *The Theater of Revolt.* London: Methuen and Co., Ltd., 1965, pp. 361-411.

Coe, Richard N. *The Vision of Jean Genet.* London: Peter Owen; New York: Grove Press, Inc., 1968.

————. "Jean Genet: A checklist of his works in French, English and German." *Australian Journal of French Studies,* Melbourne, January-April, 1969, pp. 113-30.

Coe, Richard N., ed. *The Theater of Jean Genet: A Casebook.* New York: Grove Press, 1970.

Cruikshank, John. "Jean Genet: The Aesthetics of Crime." *The Critical Quarterly,* 6, no. 3 (Autumn, 1964), 202-10.

Deguy, Michel. "Théâtre et réalisme: le cas des paravents." *Critique,* 17e annee, no. 233 (October, 1966), pp. 787-93.

Derrida, Jacques. *Glas.* Paris: Editions Galilée, 1975.

Driver, Tom F. *Jean Genet.* Columbia Essays on Modern Writers, no. 20. New York and London: Columbia University Press, 1966.

Ehrmann, Jacques. "Genet's Dramatic Metamorphosis: From Appearance to Freedom." *Yale French Studies,* no. 28 (Summer, 1962), pp. 33-42.

Esslin, Martin. *The Theater of the Absurd.* New York: Doubleday, 1961.

Grossvogel, David J. *Four Playwrights and a Postcript: Brecht, Ionesco, Beckett, Genet.* Ithaca: Cornell University Press, 1962.

Jacobsen, Josephine, and William R. Mueller. *Ionesco and Genet: Playwrights of Silence.* New York: Hill and Wang, 1968.

Knapp, Bettina. *Jean Genet.* New York: Twayne Publishers, 1968.

Magnan, Jean-Marie, *Essai sur Jean Genet,* "Poètes d'aujourd'hui," Edited by Pierre Seghers, Paris, 1966.

McMahon, Joseph H. *The Imagination of Jean Genet.* New Haven: Yale University Press, 1963.

Morris, Kelly, ed. *Genet / Ionesco: The Theatre of the Double.* New York: Bantam Books, Inc. 1969.

Obliques, no 2 (1972), "Genet."

Pronko, Lenard C. *Avant-Garde: The Experimental Theatre in France.* Berkley and Los Angeles: University of California Press, 1963.

Sartre, Jean-Paul. *Saint Genet, Actor and Martyr.* Translated by Bernard Frechtman. New York: George Braziller, Inc., 1963.

Thody, Philip. *Jean Genet: A Study of his Plays and Novels.* London: Hamish Hamilton, 1968.

Chronology

1910   Born December 19, the illegitimate son of Gabrielle Genet. Abandoned by his mother and brought up by the state.

1917   Placed as a foster child with a peasant family in Le Morvan.

1926   Sent to the reformatory at Mettray for three years. For the next fifteen years he is in and out of jail as he wanders over Europe as a beggar, smuggler, thief, and male prostitute. May have joined the army and deserted.

1942   In Fresnes prison, he writes his first poem, "Le Condamné à mort," and *Our Lady of the Flowers.*

1943   Cocteau writes a letter to the Court on Genet's behalf.

1944   Meets Sartre.

1946   Publishes *Miracle of The Rose* and his ballet, *'Adame Miroir,* is danced to Milhaud's music.

1947   Publishes *Funeral Rites* and *Querelle of Brest.* First production of *The Maids.*

1948   Granted a pardon for his crimes as the result of an appeal by Sartre, Cocteau, Mauriac, and others.

1949   First production of *Deathwatch.* Publishes *The Thief's Journal.*

1952   Sartre's *Saint Genet* appears, as volume 1 of Genet's *Complete Works.*

1957   First production of *The Balcony,* in London.

1959   First production of *The Blacks.*

1961   First production of *The Screens,* in Berlin.

1966   *The Screens,* performed for the first time in Paris, causes violent incidents, bomb threats, and a riot.

1970   Tours the United States, speaking on behalf of the Black Panthers. Travels widely, writing articles, and preparing material for a work of political import, and for a film.

Notes on the Editors and Contributors

PETER BROOKS, Professor of French and Comparative Literature at Yale University, is the author of *The Novel of Worldliness* and *The Melodramatic Imagination* and editor of *The Child's Part.*

JOSEPH HALPERN teaches French at Yale University. He has published *Critical Fictions: The Literary Criticism of Jean-Paul Sartre,* and articles in a number of periodicals.

ODETTE ASLAN is a member of the Groupe de Recherches Théâtrales of the Centre National de la Recherche Scientifique in France. She has worked in theatrical productions at the Théâtre des Nations in Paris, and published poems, essays, and *L'Art du théâtre.*

BRIGID BROPHY is an English novelist who has also written extensively about art, music, and literature. Her novels include *Hackenfeller's Ape, In Transit, The Burglar, The Adventures of God in His Search for the Black Girl.* Many of her critical essays and book reviews are collected in *Don't Never Forget.*

RICHARD N. COE is Professor of French at the University of Warwick, England. He has written extensively on contemporary French drama (Ionesco, Beckett, Genet), and other French authors.

BERNARD DORT is one of France's leading drama critics. He has edited the theater of Marivaux, written a study of Corneille, and published collections of his drama reviews and essays.

FRANÇOISE D'EAUBONNE has published novels, literary biographies, poems, and her memoirs, as well as essays in literary criticism and issues of feminism.

RAYMOND FEDERMAN, Professor of French at the State University of New York at Buffalo, has had a dual career as critic and novelist, carried on in both French and English. He has published critical studies of Beckett, Jean-Luc Godard, and various contemporary novelists.

JEAN GITENET, a Belgian theater critic, is associated with the Centre d'Etudes Théâtrales at Louvain.

LUCIEN GOLDMANN was until his death in 1970 an outstanding critic of Marxist persuasion, concerned with problems of literary sociology. His best-known books are *The Hidden God: A Study of Tragic Vision in the "Pensées" of Pascal and the Tragedies of Racine and Pour une Sociologie du roman.*

JACQUES GUICHARNAUD, currently Professor of Romance Languages at Harvard University, is the author of *Molière: une aventure théâtrale* and *Modern French Drama* (with June Guicharnaud), as well as many essays on the contemporary theater.

MICHÈLE PIEMME-FABIEN, who has written on Marivaux and Ghelderode as well as Genet, teaches at the University of Liège, in Belgium, and is active in the productions of the Ensemble Théâtral Mobile in Brussels.

JEAN-PAUL SARTRE has been a shaping force in modern thought through his philosophical writings (especially *Being and Nothingness*), novels *(The Paths of Freedom)*, plays *(No Exit, The Flies)*, and critical essays, of which the book-length study of Jean Genet is perhaps the most remarkable.

PHILIP THODY is Professor of French Literature at the University of Leeds, England, and author of critical studies of Albert Camus, Jean-Paul Sartre, Jean Anouilh, as well as Jean Genet.